The Social Work Interview

Alfred Kadushin

THE
SOCIAL
WORK
INTERVIEW

Columbia University Press

New York

Alfred Kadushin is Professor of Social Work
at the University of Wisconsin.

Library of Congress Cataloging in Publication Data

Kadushin, Alfred.
    The social work interview.

    Bibliography: p.
      1. Interviewing.   2. Social service.
I. Title.
HV43.K26   361.3'2   70-190192
ISBN 0 231 03290 0

TO MY FAMILY, IN APPRECIATION.

Contents

~.~

The Social Work Interview

Introduction

$\sim\!\cdot\!\sim\!\cdot\!\sim\!\cdot\!\sim\!\cdot\!\sim\!\cdot\!\sim\!\cdot\!\sim\!\cdot\!\sim\!\cdot\!\sim\!\cdot\!\sim\!\cdot\!\sim\!\cdot\!\sim\!\cdot\!\sim\!\cdot\!\sim\!\cdot\!\sim\!\cdot\!\sim\!\cdot\!\sim\!\cdot\!\sim$

Many people, representing many different professions, conduct interviews. Social workers are only one such group.* But for the social worker, interviewing is a very important activity. He spends a great deal of his time interviewing, and much of what he is responsible for doing depends on interviewing. Although social work interviews are, in many respects, like all others, they differ in some crucial ways, reflecting what is unique about social work. This book describes the general art of interviewing as adapted and enacted by social workers in a social work setting. The image of the reader that most frequently came to me in writing was of a relatively inexperienced social worker struggling on the job with all of the recurrent problems of interviewing, and seeking some specific guidelines and answers. In addition, I believe that experienced practitioners may profit from an explicit examination of their interviews and I hope this book may stimulate such self-assessment.

Because interviewing is the most consistently and frequently em-

---

* The English language has a bias toward use of masculine pronouns for undefined persons ("the reader . . . he") that is especially ill-suited to social work, in which many practitioners and clients are women. Except in discussions of case material where the sex of a person is specified, masculine and feminine pronouns have been used interchangeably and at random.

ployed social work technique, because it is so much a part of all that social workers do, a book focused on interviewing faces a special problem. It is difficult to single out interviewing and discuss it as a separate skill, but I have aimed at a discussion of interviewing rather than of casework or integrated methods.

A major part of the book is concerned with the techniques of social work interviewing. *Technique* has a bad sound—cold, mechanical, inhuman, manipulative—applicable to things but not to people. It carries considerable negative freight. The word deserves to be rescued, its image refurbished. Techniques are devices whose application enables us to accomplish our purposes, to carry out our professional responsibilities. They are clear formulations of what we should do in a given situation to offer our service effectively and efficiently. They need not be learned by rote, mechanically or inflexibly. They are, in fact, learned best when the student understands the theoretical basis for their use; they are applied best when the interviewer chooses among them with discrimination.

The interviewer should, of course, be the master of the techniques rather than their obedient servant, bound by rules. Technical skill is not antithetical to spontaneity. In fact, it permits a higher form of spontaneity; the skilled interviewer can deliberately violate the techniques as the occasion demands. Technical skill frees the interviewer in responding as a fellow human being to the interviewee. Errors in relation to technique lie with rigid, and therefore inappropriate, application. A good knowledge of techniques makes the interviewer aware of a greater variety of alternatives. Awareness and command of technical knowledge also has another advantage. To know is to be prepared; to be prepared is to experience reduced anxiety; to reduce anxiety is to increase the interviewer's freedom to be fully responsive to the interviewee.

A mastery of technology is a necessary prerequisite to competent artistry. The French say that "it is necessary to know geometry to build a cathedral; building a cathedral is, however, an act of faith" —and, I would add, an artistic creation. But neither the act of faith nor the artistic creation would have been possible without the knowledge of geometry.

But all of this is, in part, an aspect of an old controversy—the conflict between an analytical and an intuitive approach to people and their problems; between general, monothetic knowledge and unique, individual, idiographic knowledge. Technique requires generalization. It places the emphasis on the elements that are common to different interviews, making feasible a common response. An approach that rejects the emphasis on techniques focuses on what is unique about each interview encounter. While every man is different from all other men in some respects, all men are alike in other respects. To the extent that each man is like others, there are regularities that one can anticipate as one moves from one interviewee to another—regularities that legitimize techniques appropriate to all interviews.

One objection to concern with technique derives from yet another attitude prevalent among social workers. The opinion is that technique is unimportant, a poor, secondary consideration to the feeling the worker has for the client. If this feeling is right, then everything will be right; if it is wrong, then no technical expertise can rescue the interview from failure. The viewpoint is expressed well in the Chinese maxim, "When the right man uses the wrong means, the wrong means work in the right way; when the wrong man uses the right means, the right means work in the wrong way." But what then is the power of the right man using the right means in the right way? Surely he accomplishes more, more efficiently, than the right man using the wrong means even if they do work, for him, in the right way.

Many might say that if they had to choose between feeling and technique they would choose feeling as the more important prerequisite. Perhaps so, but if one has to make a choice between these qualifications, an injustice has already been done to the client. It should be possible to offer the client an interviewer who is both attitudinally correct and technically proficient. The better interviewer is one who combines the appropriate feeling and attitude with skilled interviewing techniques.

My opinion is that in balancing the requirements of attitude and technique we have exaggerated the importance of feeling and attitude and underestimated the importance of knowledge and technique. The proper attitude does not have the exclusive priority we have assumed; technique is not as secondary as we have supposed. Social work has generally given emphasis to the act of faith—our values, our philosophy, our general attitudinal stance that stresses our desire to be helpful and our confidence in our helpfulness. It is time we emphasized "geometry," the necessary technical knowledge that gives substance to our faith and enables us to implement our good will.

The greater measure of truth lies, as is so often the case, not with "either-or" but "both." If technique without feeling is ineffectual, feeling without technique is inefficient. If technical competence without compassion is sterile, compassion without competence is an exercise in futility.

A good relationship is a necessary but not sufficient condition for good interviewing. Good technique permits optimum utilization of a relationship. A good technician working in the context of a modest relationship is apt to achieve better outcomes than a technically inept interviewer in an excellent relationship. The emotional response of the interviewer may be unfailingly correct. Yet feeling does not automatically translate into effective interview behavior. And the fact of the matter is that clients are more responsive to behavior than to feelings. Only as feelings are manifested in behavior —verbal, non-verbal, open, or covert—do they have an impact on the client. Educating toward good interviewing is guiding the student to learn how to manifest, behaviorally, the appropriate feelings by applying the correct techniques, because correct techniques are the behavioral translation of the helpful attitude.

Even if it is conceded that social work interviewing techniques should be taught, can they be taught through a text? Of course not. Ultimately, interviewing is learned only through doing. But even though *to know* is a far cry from *to do*, it is still an advance over not even knowing what action would be desirable. A book on interviewing is like a manual on courtship. No manual can tell the lover how to achieve his aims. But such books "can suggest some of the issues and tactics which are worth thinking about, consideration of which can make victory somewhat more likely" (64, p. 24).

Some people feel that competence in interviewing inevitably grows out of the repeated interaction with the client and that this is the way the skill should be acquired. It is true that if the student is forced to interview, he will interview and learn by doing. It is not true, however, that practice makes perfect. Perfect practice makes perfect, but imperfect practice merely makes imperfect interviewing habitual. There has to be some prior knowledge of what differentiates technically good interviewing from poor interviewing.

There is no doubt that one can know all about the techniques of interviewing and yet be unable to apply them effectively. It is also true that some gifted practitioners perform brilliantly without being able to say what they do or how they do it, often achieving success while breaking all of the technical prescriptions. There is, further, some measure of truth in the contention that good interviewers are born, not made. Some intuitively gifted people seem to have a natural competence for the art of good personal relationships, of which interviewing is only a special example. But those with a natural aptitude for this sort of thing and those who interview well without knowing exactly what it is they are doing can both profit from a conscious examination of their art. Whatever the limits of our natural capacities, learning may extend them.

One must recognize in the objections the desire to protect the existential magic of the good interview. There is a fear that dispassionate, didactic analysis of what goes on in the interview will destroy the creative spontaneity of the intuitively gifted clinician in the encounter. Yet the fact that we support schools of social work and conduct in-service training courses and institutes is confirmation of our confidence that interviewing can be taught. The problems in interviewing that confuse and frustrate the student-worker have been encountered by those who preceded him on the job. Some solutions have evolved and are part of practice wisdom and the professional knowledge base. There is no reason why the beginning interviewer should not be provided with the cumulative experience of others as a basis for his own practice. What is attempted here is a description and codification of some of the helpful responses that have been developed by the field in answer to recurrent situations and difficulties encountered in social work interviewing.

The book developed out of my twenty-year experience in teaching interviewing as a unit in courses on casework and integrated methods in schools of social work in the United States and abroad. I have led institutes on interviewing for staffs of voluntary and public welfare agencies and have been a consultant on social work interviewing to public agencies. The raw material for the book was provided by almost continuous engagement in social work research over two decades, much of which involved interviewing social agency clients or observing interviews. Many of these interviews were tape-recorded and transcribed. Additional recordings and transcriptions were provided by students as part of assignments for courses on casework and integrated methods. As a consequence I had available some seven thousand pages of transcribed interviews from a wide variety of social work settings. Extracts from these transcriptions provide the illustrative vignettes presented here.

I am grateful to the social agency clients who participated, as interviewees, in all these interviews. But I owe a greater debt to all the students who shared the courses and institutes with me. Sometimes students, sometimes partners, sometimes colleagues, sometimes the teacher's teacher, they helped me learn what I needed to know in order to teach. And I owe them further thanks for making available the interview typescripts.

Because interviewing anywhere, conducted by professionals of all disciplines, has much to teach us that might be useful in social work, I am indebted to the general body of literature on interviewing. I have drawn freely on the insights available without always being aware of their specific sources. The references and citations, which I have tried to keep to a minimum, are a confirmation of this debt to accumulated wisdom. They also serve as bibliographical leads for the reader interested in some particular aspect of content which he would like to pursue in greater detail on his own. This resource relieves me of feeling apologetic about the need to cover so much that only a little could be said about many different things.

Chapter I

~~~~~~

The Interview
in Social Work

Although social work involves a great deal more than interviewing, social workers spend more time in interviewing than in any other single activity. It is the most important, most frequently employed, social work skill. This observation is most clearly true for the activity of the direct-service caseworker. But the group worker, community organizer, and social actionist also frequently participate in interviewing.

Although the interview is very much a part of social work, it does not belong to social work alone. The aim of this chapter is to delineate the way in which the social work interview is different from interviews in any other discipline. It is first necessary to define the interview and to make a distinction between it and another activity with which it is frequently confused, conversation.

Distinguishing the Interview
from a Conversation

The simplest definition of an interview is a conversation with a deliberate purpose, a purpose mutually accepted by the participants. An interview resembles a conversation in many ways. Both involve verbal and nonverbal communication between people during which ideas, attitudes, and feelings are exchanged. Both are usually face-to-face interactions, aside from the telephone interview or conversation. As in a conversation, participants in the interview reciprocally influence each other. A good interview, like a good conversation, gives pleasure to both participants.

The crucial characteristic which distinguishes an interview from a conversation is that the interaction is designed to achieve a consciously selected purpose. The purpose may be to establish a purpose for the interview, e.g., the protective service worker, visiting a family on the agency's initiative, may be exploring with the mother how the agency can be of help. The purpose may be to resolve differences in perception of the purpose of the contact between agency and client. The adolescent on probation may see his contact with the correctional social worker as purely a formality in meeting agency requirements. The social worker perceives it as an opportunity to help the client with some specific problem. Given such disparity in expectations, the purpose of the interview may be to find some *mutually* acceptable purpose. In another interview the worker may encourage the client to define the reason for the contact. But this too is a purpose. If the interaction has no purpose, it may be conversation but it is not yet an interview.

From this critical characteristic of the interview flows a series of consequences for the way participants relate to each other in the interview, as distinguished from a conversation, and for the way the interaction is structured.

1. Since the interview has a definite purpose, its content is chosen to facilitate achievement of the purpose. Any content, however interesting, that will not contribute to the purpose of the interview

is excluded. On the other hand, the agenda of a conversation may include unrelated and diffuse content. Where there are no boundaries, nothing is extraneous. The orientation of the conversation is associational, and there is no central theme. Because the interview has a purpose, the content is likely to have unity, a progression, and thematic continuity.

2. If the purpose is to be achieved, somebody has to take responsibility for directing the interaction so that it moves toward the goal. Thus there has to be a differential allocation of tasks between the interview participants. One person is designated as interviewer and charged with responsibility for the process, and someone else is designated interviewee. The role relationships are structured. There are no comparable terms to indicate status positions and selected role behavior in a conversation.

We will discuss the task of the interviewer in greater detail below. It might suffice, at this point, in making clear this distinctive aspect of the interview, to note that at the very minimum anybody who accepts the title of interviewer needs to know something about the process of interviewing to keep the interview moving toward the objective. He or she needs to know enough about the content to be able to recognize what is extraneous material and what is pertinent.

3. That one participant is interviewer and another the interviewee implies a nonreciprocal relationship. In an interview between a professional and a client, one person asks questions and another person answers them. This relationship is partly a result of the fact that someone has to take leadership, that one person does know how to conduct an interview and has more expert knowledge of the subject matter. But this nonreciprocal relationship also derives from the fact that the structure of the encounter is designed to serve principally the interests of the client. This is why the client comes and why the professional practices. The profession of the interviewer entails an obligation to perform clearly defined services for the client.

The interviewer acts in a manner that encourages the interviewee to reveal a great deal about himself while she herself reveals little. The interviewee reveals a wide segment of his life; the interviewer only her professional self. If the interviewer asks, "How is your wife?" it is not expected that the interviewee will at some point reciprocate by asking, "And how is your husband?" Such reciprocation, the expected form in a conversation, is not helpful in resolving the client's problem in the interview.

4. Although the behavior of all parties to a conversation may be spontaneous and unplanned, the actions of the interviewer must be planned, deliberate, and consciously selected to further the purpose of the interview; this is part of the prescribed role behavior. Thus, the pattern of behavior is predetermined by the positions people occupy in the interview, by the formal structure of reciprocal roles and expectations.

5. No one is obliged to initiate a conversation. The professional is, however, obliged to accept the request of the client for an interview, whatever his expectations are about how it might go. And since the contact is initiated for the purpose of meeting the needs of the client, the interviewer has an obligation to maintain contact until the purpose is achieved or until it is clear that the purpose cannot be achieved.

Whatever his own feelings about the interview, the interviewer cannot terminate it for personal reasons without being justifiably open to a charge of dereliction of responsibility. There is less compunction or guilt associated with withdrawal from a conversation if it is boring.

An interview requires exclusive attention to the interaction. The commitment on the part of the interviewer to participation in the interview is recognized as more intense. A conversation, however, can be peripheral to other activities. The commitment to participation is more lightly held.

6. Because it has a purpose, the interview is usually a formally arranged meeting. A definite time, place, and duration are established for the interview, unlike a conversation.

7. Because an interview has a purpose other than amusement, unpleasant facts and feelings are not avoided. In fact there is a specific obligation to stimulate introduction of unpleasant facts and feelings if this will be of help. In a conversation the usual implicit agreement is to avoid the unpleasant.

These characteristics, rather than any formal setting, define the interview and distinguish it from a conversation. An interview can, and does, take place on the street if a client, in a crisis, unexpectedly meets her caseworker. Interviews take place in tenement hallways, in supermarkets, and on buses as a worker accompanies a client to the hospital, employment office, or day-care center. What starts as a conversation may suddenly turn into an interview.

In summary, then, the interview differs from a conversation in that it involves interpersonal interaction for a conscious, mutually accepted purpose. Following from this premise, the interview, as contrasted with a conversation, involves a more formal structure, a clearly defined allocation of roles, and a different set of norms regulating the process of interaction.

Distinguishing the
Social Work Interview

The characteristics and attributes which distinguish an interview from a conversation hold for interviews in any setting. What distinguishes the social work interview from other kinds of interviews?

Social work interviews are concerned with social work content, are scheduled to achieve social work purposes, and take place in social work settings. To say this is to recognize immediately the difficulty in making such distinctions. If social work as a profession were designated by society as having clear and exclusive concern with definable, unique areas of activity, the statement would have unambiguous meaning. As it is, one must concede that the content area of social work concern overlaps those of psychiatry, psychology, educational and vocational counseling, the ministry, and others. Despite the overlap, despite the blurred boundaries between related disciplines, social work does have an area of principal concern which is distinctive—its concern with people in the enactment of their social roles and in their relation to social institutions. All of the attempts at defining social work point to the relationship between people and their social environment as the focus of the worker's activity.

Social service is defined by the United Nations as an "organized activity that aims at helping to achieve a mutual adjustment of *individuals and their social environment*" (300, p. 105) (italics added in this group of quotations). A comprehensive study of the social work curriculum defines the focus of social workers' activity as "that aspect of man's functioning only which lies in the realm of *social* relationships and *social* role performance" (27, p. 54). A federal task force defines social welfare as "the organized system of functions and services that support and enhance individual and *social* well being and that promote community conditions essential to the harmonious interaction of persons and their *social* environment" (301, p. 7). The Model Statute Social Workers Licensing Act defines social work as "the professional activity of helping individuals, groups, or communities enhance or restore their capacity for *social functioning* and creating societal conditions favorable to this goal" (212, p. 7).

More specifically, however, different agencies perform different functions relating to different social problems. The psychiatric social work agencies are concerned with the social antecedents, concomitants, and consequences of mental disabilities; the medical social worker is concerned with the social antecedents, concomitants, and consequences of physical illness; the family and child welfare agencies are concerned with the social aspects of marital disruption and parent-child relationship difficulties; the correctional social worker is concerned with the social aspects of a disordered relationship to the legal institutions of society; the income-maintenance agencies are concerned with the social aspects of a disordered relationship to the economic institutions of society.

Each agency, then, by focusing on some particular aspect of social functioning, some recurrent significant social problem area, defines for itself the content most relevant for interviews.

At whatever level in the process the social worker intervenes, whether at the community level in trying to effect change in the social system or at the casework level in trying to effect change in the individual situation, the concern is, again, primarily with *social* phenomena. The function and focus of the profession thus determine, in a general way, the distinctive contents of social work interviews, distinguishing them from all other interviews. Purpose and content of the interview follow from the distinctive responsibilities of the social agency and the profession.

The social worker in private practice indicates, by her professional designation, that there is a specific kind of content about which she has particular concern, a specific kind of problem situation for which she has a special competence. The content and the problems of concern to the social worker in private practice are, or should be, the same as those of concern to the social worker practicing in an agency setting, if the practitioner is not to belie her designation. Wherever social workers conduct interviews might be regarded as a social work setting even though the interviews might not take place in a social work agency.

Some further characteristic aspects of social work interviews should be noted. The concern of the social work interview is with the unique entity—the unique individual, the unique group, the unique community. Casework means "the individual instance" and is not a term indigenous to social work. The use of the term "case book" in law or in business management illustrates the generality of the word "case." But the concern with the unique instance gives the social work interview a character that distinguishes it from the public opinion interview, for instance. The public opinion interviewer's approach to the respondent is as one of a number of comparable entities. The interest is not in the response of this particular person per se but in the particular person as a member of an aggregate. Hence the effort to standardize the public opinion interview, to see that one is as much like another as possible, and to do everything possible to discourage the development of anything unusual, or special, in any particular interview. Participation is controlled and is confined as far as possible to the set series of questions raised by the interviewer.

The antithesis is true of most social work interviews. Effort is made to maximize clients' participation, to encourage the development of the interview so that it follows the clients' preferences, to minimize standardization and maximize individualization of content. The social worker has no set interview schedule and attempts to keep her control of the interview at the lowest possible level. This statement must be qualified, for some social work interviews do require the worker to cover some uniform content, even though this requirement might not be spelled out on a specific form. A mental-hospital social study requires coverage of psychosocial development, school history, marital history, work history, symptoms of developmental difficulties, etc. An adoptive interview typically requires coverage of motivation, reaction to infertility, child preference, experience with children, and marital interaction. A public-assistance eligibility interview has to cover family composition, need, resources, and the situation precipitating the application.

The social work interview generally takes place with troubled people or people in trouble. What is discussed is private and highly emotional. Social work interviews are characterized by a great concern with personal interaction, with considerable emphasis on feelings and attitudes and with less concern for objective factual data.

Social work interviews are also apt to be diffuse and concerned with a wide segment of the client's life. Although there is some demarcation between the areas covered by different agencies, agency functions tend to be rather broadly stated. The tendency is for the worker to feel that he needs to know much about the client that, in a strict sense, might be regarded as extraneous to agency function. The more the worker explores the client's personal world with him, the greater the likelihood of affective interaction and of emotional involvement.

The diffuseness of conceivably relevant content derives also from the imprecision of technical procedures for helping. The more precise a profession's technology, the more definite its solutions, the more likely that it will be limited and circumscribed in its area for exploration and its area of intervention. If we could specify what we needed to know in order to do precise things for and with the client in effecting change, our interview would be less diffuse.

In recapitulation, compared with many other kinds of interviews the social work interview is apt to be diffuse, unstandardized, nonscheduled, interviewee-controlled, focused on affective material, and concerned with interpersonal interaction of participants. As a consequence the social work interviewer has a difficult assignment. Much of what he generally has to do in the interview cannot be determined in advance but must be a response to the situation as it develops. The interviewer has to have considerable discretion to do almost anything he thinks might be advisable, under highly individualized circumstances, to achieve the purpose of the interview. The content, the sequence in which it is introduced and how it is introduced, the interpersonal context in which it is explored —all these matters of strategy and tactics in interview management need to be the prerogative and responsibility of the interviewer.

Purposes of Social Work Interviews

The purposes of the social work interview follow from the functions of social work. The general purposes of most social work interviews can be described as informational (to make a social study), diagnostic (to arrive at an appraisal), and therapeutic (to effect change). These are discrete categories only for the purpose of analysis; the same interview can, and often does, serve more than one purpose.

The psychiatric social worker in a child guidance clinic may interview a father to obtain more detailed information about a child referred for service and, at the same time, seek therapeutically to support the father in the disturbed parent-child relationship. The child welfare worker in an adoptive-application interview may have, as one objective, to obtain the information necessary for a reliable and valid decision and, as a secondary therapeutic purpose, to help the applicants adjust to the idea of adoption as a way of completing a family. The delinquent explaining to the probation officer for a court report what precipitated his illegal actions is, at the same time, also clarifying the situation for himself.

Consideration of questions raised to obtain information forces many clients to review those questions more explicitly than they have previously, making them more aware of their own feelings about these aspects of their lives. The reverse can also be true, of course. An interview whose primary purpose is therapeutic may bring the revelation of information previously withheld. Instead of achieving clarification as a result of an interview whose purpose is social study, you sometimes receive social study information from an interview whose primary purpose is the therapeutic one of clarification.

Differences in primary purposes of interviews are reflected in the ways they are structured and conducted. An interview focused on social study is distinguishable from an interview conducted for assessment, both being further distinguishable from an interview whose purpose is primarily therapeutic. Consequently, despite overlap, there is value in reviewing separately the major purposes of social work interviews.

INFORMATIONAL OR SOCIAL STUDY INTERVIEWS

The purpose of informational interviews is to obtain a focused account of the individual, or group, or community, in terms of social functioning. The point of departure and the center of interest for such exploration is the socially stressful situation for which agency help is or might be requested.

The informational–social study interview is a selective gathering of life-history material related to social functioning. The information enables the worker to understand the client in relation to the social problem situation. *Knowledge* about the client and her situation is a necessary prerequisite to an *understanding* of the client in her situation. And understanding is a necessary prerequisite for effectively intervening to bring about change. Hence the parameters of selectivity in information gathering include both information relevant to understanding and information relevant to the kind of help the agency can provide. We do not seek to learn all there is to know about the client but only what we need to know in order to understand so that we can help effectively. The information we seek includes both objective facts and subjective feelings and attitudes.

In a series of contacts with the client such information gathering is cumulative; in every interview some new, previously unshared information is obtained. Early interviews are likely to be devoted more exclusively and explicitly to obtaining information, for social study is often their principal purpose. In later interviews, social study information is typically incidental to the achievement of some other purpose.

In some instances, a social study interview is the specific charge to the interviewer. The probation-parole office is asked to do a social study of offenders in order to guide the court in dealing with the delinquent. The psychiatric social worker in a guidance clinic or mental hospital is sometimes asked to do a social study for presentation at a staff conference to determine the next step for the patient. A worker in a neighborhood service center may be asked to interview people in the community to determine what social problems cause them the most concern.

DIAGNOSTIC–DECISION-MAKING INTERVIEWS

Another type of interview is geared towards appraisal and determination of eligibility for a service. These interviews facilitate definite administrative decisions. The child welfare worker, for example, interviews the foster-care or adoptive applicant in order to determine if the agency will place a child with her. The public assistance worker interviews the applicant in order to determine his eligibility for a grant. The protective service worker interviews a family to determine whether a petition of neglect should be filed. Although such interviews are highly individualized, they are conducted so as to permit the worker to assess some particular characteristics of the interviewee. The characteristics are those deemed essential in an interviewee for eligibility for a particular service. Some capacity to establish a relationship and some ability to verbalize are required for acceptance of a child to a child guidance clinic; some willingness to work with the agency is required of foster-parent applicants; some motivation to change is necessary for marital counseling in a family service agency; some ability to observe group norms and contribute to group interaction is required of a client at group meetings. The adoptive applicants need to have resolved their marital problems if a child is to be placed in their home; an abusive parent must be assessed as very likely to repeat the assault to justify removing his child from the home.

Whatever the social policy criteria which affect the decision—

whether the agency offers services at a preventive rather than a re-
habilitative level, whether it works with the very disabled who can
make limited use of help but who need it most or with those
slightly disabled who need it less but make most effective use of
service, whether it plans to focus on changing the system in social
institutions or changing symptoms in individual clients—whatever
the orientation of the agency with regard to these and other central policy issues, an assessment interview of some kind will be
necessary for the agency to make decisions regarding applicants.
Because requirements for eligibility have been defined prior to the
interview, an outline of the kinds of content which might be covered in such interviews is generally available to the interviewer.

The purpose of the appraisal interview is to obtain selective information needed to make some necessary decision. The decision
itself involves a diagnostic process in the mind of the worker—a
process of applying theoretical generalization to the data obtained
and organizing and interpreting the data for valid inferences. The
assessment process leads to an evaluative product—a decision on
what the agency will do.

Studies of social work decision-making suggest that social workers do look for definite, limited kinds of information in assessment
interviews and that the decisions made are frequently associated
with such information (104, 254).

THERAPEUTIC INTERVIEWS

The purpose of the therapeutic interview is to effect change in
the client, in her social situation, or in both. The goal is more
effective social functioning on the part of the client as a consequence of the therapeutic changes. Such interviews involve the use
of special remedial measures to effect changes in feelings, attitudes,
and behavior on the part of the client in response to the social situation. They can also involve efforts to change the social situation
so as to reduce or ameliorate social pressures impinging on the
client. Because therapeutic interviews are the most highly individualized and idiosyncratic, it is more difficult to develop outlines for
them in advance.

The interview might itself be the instrument through which

change is effected. The interviewee then is the person with, and for whom, the change in feeling, attitude, and behavior is attempted. The interview is psychotherapeutic, that is, the interviewer employs psychological principles and procedures in an effort to exercise a deliberate, controlled influence on the psychic functioning of the interviewee, with her consent and on her behalf, for the purpose of effecting changes in her feelings, attitudes, and behavior. The purpose of such interviews is helping and healing through communication in a therapeutic relationship.

The school social worker interviews a child to help him adjust to the classroom setting. The family service worker interviews a wife to help her deal with some of the inevitable dissatisfactions in marriage. The medical social worker interviews a convalescent mother to improve her attitude toward the homemaker assigned to the family; the gerontological social worker interviews an aged client to intensify his motivation to use golden-age club facilities in the community.

Interviews may have a therapeutic purpose but the person for whom the therapeutic change is sought may not be present. These include interviews with persons important in the client's life, where the social worker acts as a broker or advocate in the client's behalf. The social worker engaged in brokerage or advocacy may interview people in strategic positions in an attempt to influence them on behalf of the client. The purpose of the interview is to change the balance of forces in the social environment in the client's favor. The school social worker may interview a teacher in order to influence her to show more accepting understanding of a child. The social worker at the neighborhood service center may interview a worker at the housing authority or at the local department of public welfare in order to obtain for his client full entitlement to housing rights or to assistance. Or a social worker may accompany an inarticulate client to an employment interview in an effort to influence the decision in the client's favor. In each instance the scheduled interview has a definite, and in these cases, therapeutic purpose in behalf of the client.

In this book the focus is on social work interviews conducted with agency clients as the interviewees. Social workers often engage in supervisory and consultative interviews where another professional is the interviewee. And they conduct interviews with clients and non-clients for specialized purposes of their own, as in research interviews. Yet even in these interviews the primary purposes can sensibly be subsumed under the headings used above. The interviewer as supervisor or consultant or researcher is trying to find out about something (informational, social study), make some decision (diagnosis, data assessment), or effect change in some situation (treatment).

There are, then, many different kinds of interviews for many different purposes. The diversity of interview types is compounded by the fact that each kind can be conducted in different ways—as a dyad (interviewer-interviewee), as a group interview (one interviewer–multiple interviewees), as a board interview (one interviewee–multiple interviewers). And further, interviews for the same purpose may be conducted in different ways according to the orientation of the interviewer. Thus a therapeutic interview would be conducted differently by a Freudian, a Rogerian, or a behaviorist.

It might be appropriate, at this point, to comment on the behavioral-modification interview since behavioral-modification approaches are assuming progressively greater significance among social workers.

Even though a social worker may be oriented toward standardized behavioral-modification procedures in helping the client, the interview still retains significance for him. As Kanfer notes, "Conditioning provides a methodological approach for the *process* of treatment. It has few guidelines for selecting the *content* of treatment" (155, p. 174). The behaviorist social worker needs the interview for the purpose of collecting life-history data to determine the focus for conditioning procedures. The worker also needs life-history data obtained through the interview to determine which of the available procedures may be most congruent with the preferences and predispositions of the client.

The interview also serves to instruct the interviewee about the procedure, to motivate him to participate, to help him develop confidence and, perhaps, faith in the behavioral-modification approach and, most important, to determine from information shared by the interviewee exactly what specific behavior needs changing.

As is true for every interviewer, the focus of the behavioral-modification interviewer derives from the presuppositions of the theory which guides his approach. The focus follows from his beliefs as to how people develop psychosocial difficulties and how they can be helped to change. Consequently, the interviewer's line of questioning and the content which engages his attention revolve around trying to determine, as clearly as possible, the stimulus which initiated the dysfunctional behavior and the current stimulus conditions, internal and external, that reinforce and sustain it. The objective of his communications with the interviewee is to inform him of the relationship between the stimulus conditions and the dysfunctional response so that the interviewee can understand the situation.

However, because behavioral-modification treatment approaches depend on concern with the interviewee's overt behavior, the interview as a therapeutic device takes a secondary position for the behavioral-modification interviewer. There is no great discussion of feelings. There *is* a response to overt behavior. The child is given a candy or a coin for a display of acceptable behavior, or he may be ignored or placed in a separate room ("time out") for engaging in unacceptable behavior. The adult may be exposed gradually to the thing he fears (night, a closed space, snakes) or given an electric shock if, for instance, as a homosexual, he responds positively to a picture of a naked man.

Since the therapy is behavioral rather than verbal, there is less reliance on interview interaction as the medium for change. The psychoanalytically oriented interviewer seeks to change attitudes through verbal communication and assumes that a change in attitude will lead to a change in behavior. The behavioral-modification oriented interviewer, on the other hand, seeks to change behavior through action and assumes that a change in behavior will lead to a change in attitude. For the behavioral modificationist the interview is an adjunctive therapeutic procedure rather than *the* therapeutic procedure.

Alternatives and Limitations

The interview is the principal technique through which social work purposes are achieved. It is not, however, the sole technique for achieving them. As a participant observer in the activities of a street-corner gang, the group worker obtains a great deal of social study data. A family therapist poses a problem for family decision, such as having to decide on a family vacation, and learns much about the family from watching its members in action. Information for understanding the client might also be obtained from documents, from records of previous agency contacts, or from medical examinations and psychological tests.

Although the interview is the most frequently employed social work procedure for learning about, understanding, and helping the client, it has limitations. A series of studies has compared information on family functioning obtained through interviews with information obtained through direct observation (56, 178, 280, 322). Other studies have compared information about child development obtained retrospectively, through interviews, with the records compiled on the same child while he was actually growing up (120, 195, 241, 323, 337). In each instance there were discrepancies between the interview data and the observed or documentary material. There was typically less discrepancy regarding factual data and more discrepancy regarding attitudinal data. The studies establish some of the general limitations of the interview as a technique for obtaining information of concern to social work on child development and family functioning. Other studies in related fields have established the limitations of the interview as a source of valid and reliable data (194, 299).

The interview is nevertheless the most versatile procedure for access to a wide variety of insights about the client in his social situation. Through words, which are vicarious actions, the worker can experience with the client various situations in the past, present and future. The interview is bound by neither time nor space. Furthermore, through the interview the worker has access to the client's feelings and attitudes, the subjective meaning of the objective situation.

Observation presents the worker with a sample of behavior; he still has to infer its meaning. The worker observes a mother, for example, who has come to the day-care center at the end of the day to pick up her child. She shouts at her child for his slowness in putting on his boots and overcoat. Is her action displaced hostility toward her boss, with whom she has had an argument earlier in the day? Is it anxiety at the possibility of getting home late and risking another argument with her husband in a shaky marriage? Is it shame that her child is not as capable as other children? Is it an expression of generalized hostility toward the child, who is seen as a sibling rival for her husband's affection? Is it impatience because of physical fatigue? Does the child's slowness reactivate anxiety that as a working mother she is failing her child? The same unit of observed behavior—many possible meanings. An interview with the mother can help the worker understand which of the possible interpretations best explains her outbursts. Observation without interviewing yields doubtful inferences. That the same can be said about inferences derived from interviews alone indicates that, despite advantages, interviewing has its definite shortcomings, deficiencies which have been discussed at length in the literature and supported by empirical research.

Summary

An interview and a conversation were distinguished in terms of purpose, structure, role, and functions. A further distinction was made between social work interviews and other kinds of interviews in terms of the fact that social work interviews are concerned with problems people have in dealing with their social environment. Three principal purposes of the social work interview were delineated and discussed—the social study interview, the diagnostic-appraisal interview, and the therapeutic interview.

Chapter 2

~~~~~~

Communication
and Relationship

Communication

An interview is a specialized form of communication. A communication interchange in the interview involves two people, each of whom possesses a receiving system, a processing system, and a transmitting system. The receiving system consists of the five senses, the receptors. Communication in the interview involves primarily the use of two sense receptors—the eyes and the ears. Having received the incoming signal, one processes it; this involves making sense of the received message, giving it meaning. The processing activity consists of recalling stored information, relating relevant information to the message, thinking about the message, evaluating the message, translating it so that the message is coherent with the receiver's frame of reference. As receivers, we select certain items from the incoming message, ignore others, and rearrange what we hear into interpretable patterns. We then typically formulate a message in response. Selected words and nonverbal gestures are transmitted by "effector organs"—the voice, the mouth, the hands, the eyes, etc.—so that they can be received by the other participant in the interview who, in turn, processes the message as a basis for formulating his response.

While receiving, processing, and responding to messages which originate externally, the participant in the interview is also receiving, processing, and responding to messages which originate internally. We are constantly engaged in checking how we feel inside, physically and emotionally. The brain acts as a communication center processing all the messages, interpreting them, and formulating an appropriate response.

Let us follow the details of the process of communication, noting the more frequent problems encountered at significant points in the process.

THE MESSAGE TRANSMITTED

The message to be communicated originates as a thought in the mind of one of the participants in an interview. Events and experiences cannot be communicated as such. They have to be translated into words which "carry" a symbolic representation of the experience. When received, the experience has to be reconstructed from the words.

The message, as transmitted, is the thought or idea encoded into the overt behavior of words and gestures. (There are multiple channels available for communication, but for the sake of simplicity I shall, at this point, discuss only the verbal channel of communication, leaving for chapter 8 a discussion of nonverbal communication.)

Even before the thought is put into words for transmission, it must pass through a series of internal screens. A thought which, if encoded and transmitted, is likely to lead to our being rejected or derogated by the person receiving the message will not be spoken. A thought which, if spoken, would make us more aware of that which we are ashamed of, leading to a risk of self-rejection, will not be encoded. These screens of psychological resistance and psychic repression block communication of emotionally unutterable, anxiety-provoking thoughts. Resistance is conscious suppression of thoughts that seek expression. Repression indicates that barriers to the expression of some thoughts exist below the level of conscious awareness. The thoughts themselves are screened out without the person's recognizing that they exist or are being censored.

The client may be willing and ready but unable to communicate some of the necessary information, attitudes, and feelings about his situation. Some facts and feelings have been forgotten and are difficult to recall for retelling; some have been repressed so that they are beyond recall. Freudian slips are, of course, examples of thoughts that have eluded the screens and filters and achieved expression.

Other filters inhibit the encoding of thoughts that violate the etiquette of the communication situation. Four-letter curse words and openly hostile remarks get blocked out at this point. Interviewing regarding behavior and attitudes about which there are strong and unambiguous social expectations encounters the screen of social desirability. Self-censorship—suppression of socially and personally unacceptable comments—is illustrated from a postinterview interview with a client.

A woman, 46, white, has discussed a problem of residential care for her mother with a medical social worker.

When I first came, I thought I would say how I felt my mother was very difficult to live with, and I want an old-age home for her for my own comfort as well as because it might be good for her. But how can you say that, that you really don't like your mother when she is old? How can you tell that and not think people will feel you're lousy? Even when I say it to myself—that my mother annoys me, that she can be a pain—I think, "What kind of a daughter am I?"

Readiness to share and the location of the boundaries between public and private information vary among individuals and among groups. Individuals are more or less reticent; different groups in the community regard sexual life, financial situation, and marital interaction as more or less private.

Readiness to share, willingness to communicate, is a function of hope and confidence that such involvement will result in some benefit for us. We accept the doctor's request to undress because we feel some assurance that if we do so he can help us with our pain. But if we lacked such motivation, would we be willing to undress? Why should we share our secrets if nothing useful for us will be achieved in exchange for such self-disclosure? We only entitle the interviewer to access to as much of ourselves as he needs to know in order to help, and do so only because we feel some assurance that, as a result, he is willing, ready, and able to assist us.

A barrier arises from a feeling of social distance between client and worker. Clients have sometimes felt it hopeless to expect the worker to understand them. In the clients' perception, the parties to the interview live in two different worlds. Rather than attempt to communicate what is felt to be uncommunicable, the client screens out the message.

Male, 18, white, probation interview.

> So then they sent me to the school counselor, but he never took speed or acid—he never even tried pot—so I figured how can you talk to him? He wouldn't know how it was, and I didn't know how to tell him. I couldn't rap with him.

Discretion in the face of power is a barrier to free communication. Frequently the interviewer controls access to some service or resource which the client wants and needs—medical care, adoptive children, money, or institutional placement. Frequently the interviewer also can apply punishing legal sanctions—in probation and parole, in protective service, in public assistance. The client has to censor his communication so that he increases the possibility of getting what he wants and needs and prevents the application of negative sanctions.

There are filters that determine what is appropriate in a given context. What is appropriate in a conversation may be inappropriate in an interview, and a comment that is appropriate in an interview in a child guidance clinic may not be appropriate in a public-assistance district office.

Generally any thought or feeling that is considered for expression is part of a series of interchanges. The decision as to whether the thought is advisable, permissible, and appropriate for transmission is conditioned to a very considerable extent by the communications received from the other participant(s) in the interview. Thus communication is not only the product of what each person brings to the interview but also a consequence of what he experiences during it.

A thought which succeeds in satisfying the demands of the various criteria still needs to be encoded for understandable transmission. Having decided that a thought is permissible and appropriate to the situation and to the role in which she is engaged at the moment, the interviewer still must find the words to express the message for undistorted reception. The worker needs a vocabulary rich enough to convey the meaning of her thought, and varied enough to adapt to the vocabulary of different clients.

Worker and client may nominally speak the same language but actually not understand one another. The language community of the worker is not necessarily the language community of the client. There is no equivalence of meaning to many of the words they use in common. "Eligibility" sounds one way and has one meaning to the worker; it sounds quite different to and evokes a different set of responses in the client. We say "home study" and "court record" and "therapy" without knowing how these unfamiliar words sound to the client.

Middle-class language is different from lower-class language, black vocabulary and syntax are different from white vocabulary and syntax, professional language is different from lay language. Komarovsky notes differences in word connotation between blue-collar respondents and college-educated interviewers in a study of blue-collar marriages.

The word "quarrel" carried the connotations of such a major and violent conflict that we had to use "spat," "disagreement," and other terms to convey a variety of marital clashes. To "confide" often meant to seek advice rather than share for its own sake. "Talk" to a few implied a long discussion (telling each other news isn't talking). "Intelligent" and "smart" were the terms used, not "bright"; "unfair," not "unjust." What kinds of things make you pleased or satisfied with yourself, we asked.

"When I get my work done," "When I get a bargain," and similar responses were given by some. But to a large proportion of the men and women the phrase "pleased with yourself" implied the unfavorable connotations of being "stuck on yourself." These tended to answer the question in the manner of one confessing moral defects. (165, pp. 19–20)

As Kinsey points out, the lower socioeconomic interviewee "is never 'ill' or 'injured,' though he may be 'sick' or 'hurt.' He does not 'wish' to do a thing, though he 'wants' to do it. He does not 'perceive,' though he 'sees.' He is not 'acquainted with a person,' though he may 'know him'" (161, p. 52). Social workers rarely tell people anything—they "share information"; they do not explain agency service but "interpret" it; they may not make friends although they do "establish relationships."

A middle-aged man referred to a family service agency for marital counseling is talking about a problem he has in keeping appointments on time. The worker tries to determine whether tardiness is a general problem:

WORKER: Do you have other kinds of difficulties in this area?

CLIENT: No, not in this area, but I did have the same trouble when I lived in Cincinnati.

To ensure good reception of the communication, not only does the worker have to select the appropriate matching vocabulary, but he needs to consider the client's frame of reference as well. The communication will not be received unless the client can perceive it as relevant to his situation. The following indicates a failure in both choice of vocabulary and selection of content for effective communication:

Worker: male, 23, white.
Client: female, 67, black, Old Age Assistance application.

WORKER: People can be eligible for both Social Security and Old Age Assistance. If the budgeted amount is in excess of Social Security benefits, a public assistance grant can be authorized for the difference.

Instead the worker might have said:

> For instance, let's take your situation. You get forty-three dollars
> a month from Social Security. We have figured it out, and we
> know that is not enough to live on for a person like yourself. We
> figure that you need at least eighty-five dollars a month. So we
> might be able to give you the difference between what you get
> from Social Security—the forty-three dollars—and what we have
> figured somebody like yourself needs. If you are eligible, you
> would get forty-two dollars a month from us in addition to the
> forty-three dollars from Social Security.

Not only is word selection more appropriate, but the message is
apt to be perceived by the client as more relevant and applicable
to her situation. The client does not want a discussion on agency
policy and services in general. She wants to know only of those
services appropriate to her situation and those policies relevant to
her problems, communicated in a way which translates services
and policies in terms of these particular concerns.

Once the message is encoded and sent, the sender loses control
over it. What is done to it, how it is received or ignored or misin-
terpreted or distorted, is beyond his power to change. Just as the
receiver never actually knows the message as it was formulated for
sending, the sender never knows how his message was received.
The receiver only hears the words and sees the nonverbal cues
which stand for the message sent; the sender only sees and hears
the behavioral and verbal responses which stand for the message
received. He may try again, in response to feedback on how the
message is received, if he recognizes that he has been unsuccessful.
We are often tempted to say, "I know that you believe you understand what you think I said, but I am not sure you realize that
what you heard is not what I said."

We not only get feedback from others—in their nod of recognition, in their happy smiles or puzzled grimaces, in their responses
which indicate we have hit the desired target—but we also get
feedback from ourselves. We listen to the way we say what we
mean to say and evaluate the success with which we have said it.

If it sounds unclear to us, or muddled, or ambiguous, we pat it into shape with an explanatory phrase here or a clarifying sentence there. And since language is inexact, we make ourselves understood by a series of repetitive statements, a series of successive approximations to our meaning.

Having encoded the desired message in words that are most likely to ensure its undistorted reception, we still face the mechanical problem of transmission and reception. The setting for the interview might be very noisy. The message to be transmitted may have to compete with the rumble of traffic, cross-talk from other interviews, the hum from fans and air-conditioning motors, the sounds of radio or television. If the client has a speech defect or talks very rapidly or without sufficient volume, there is likely to be some failure in communication. The ear, fortunately, is highly selective and tries to screen out extraneous noises, but it does this at a cost of effort and loss of accuracy. It is surprising how few people articulate clearly with sufficient volume and how many talk through pipes clenched in their teeth, through cigarettes drooping from one side of the mouth, or from behind a hand. Clear transmission of a message in a quiet context, adequately protected from competing noises, is apt to be more the exception than the rule.

THE MESSAGE RECEIVED

Just as there are difficulties in speech transmission, there are possible problems in speech reception. The person to whom the message is directed may fail to hear it because he has a hearing loss, because of the high noise level, or because he is inattentive at the moment and has his receiver tuned to another internal or external message.

But let us suppose that his ears hear exactly what the speaker has said. Communication has not yet taken place. The message itself as sent is only one variable determining the message as received. The person to whom the message is directed has his own set of mental barriers, screens, and filters that guard against the reception of messages which make him feel anxious or uncomfortable or which threaten his favorable perception of himself, his psychic peace and quiet. He may hear what you said with his ears but never permit the message to reach his mind. The process of selective perception permits us to hear only what we allow ourselves to hear, in the way we allow ourselves to hear it. It has been noted that there is no "immaculate perception."

Each defense mechanism is a different kind of distortion of the message heard. In projection we hear the message not in terms of what was said but in terms of what we would have said in this situation; in displacement we attribute to one person the message from another; in repression we are deaf to the message being sent and block its reception; in reaction formation we hear the opposite of the message transmitted. These mental processes protect us from hearing what would be inconvenient, or hurtful, or frightening.

Our expectations increase the possibility that we will distort the communication we receive. Thus we hear not only what we choose to attend to but what we expect to hear—whether the person said it or not. Studies by Rosenthal (247) have established that the expectations of scientists in rigorous experimental situations tend to determine their observations of experimental results. If expectations are a contaminating factor in sharply controlled situations, one would expect them to operate more markedly in the more informal social work interview situations.

The interviewer's belief system comprises expectations that predispose her to "hear" certain responses. If the interviewer hears the interviewee say that he likes things neat and orderly, the psychoanalytically oriented interviewer, associating certain personality traits with the anal character, is all set to expect the interviewee to say things which suggest that he is also frugal and stubborn. We think in categories and expect a person to behave in some consistent manner, according to the pigeonhole to which we have assigned him. As a result we think we know more about the interviewee than we actually do. If a man is a policeman, we expect that he will behave as a policeman; if a girl is a "hippie," we expect that she will act like a hippie. We attribute to individuals the attributes of the groups with which we perceive them to be affiliated and we tend to hear what we expect them to say rather than what they did say.

But even if the person to whom the message is directed is psychologically free to receive it undistorted, communication has not yet taken place. The ear having received the message, psychological sentries having passed it, the mind now faces the responsibility of decoding it. As Whitehead once said, "Spoken language is merely a series of squeaks." The mind has to translate the squeaks so that they make sense. If the message is to be received with the same meaning that was intended when it was encoded, the words received have to be decoded by shared definitions. Few aspire to the extreme individualism of Humpty-Dumpty, who said to Alice, "When I use a word, it means what I choose it to mean—no more, no less." But shades of meanings we give to words differ for all of us because our experiences have been different. The word "ghetto" evokes very different images in the mind of a black militant in Chicago, a white matron in Greenwich, and a Hasidic Jew in Brooklyn. We need to be reminded often that there are about six hundred thousand words in the English language and that the five hundred most commonly used words have fourteen thousand dictionary definitions.

The message "It must have been hard for you" will be very differently received by people with different developmental histories and different reference groups. "It must have been hard for you" may reduce to tears a young girl who feels lonely, rejected, and misunderstood. It will be received with anger by a 25-year-old male who prides himself on his masculinity and his ability to cope with difficulties. The message is the same; the reaction is different because the perception of the meaning of the message is different.

Because the interests, needs, and previous experiences of the listener are crucial in determining the message which is actually received, no matter how it is sent, the interviewer must give active consideration to the listener's background and situation. This requirement is the source of one of the most frequently repeated aphorisms of social work practice wisdom, "Start where the client is." To ignore this precept is to risk ineffective communication.

Messages achieve part of their meaning from the context in which they are sent. The same question in different settings will evoke different aspects of the client's life situation. The question "How are things going?" in a public assistance setting relates to budget and finances; in a child guidance clinic setting, to the relationship with the child referred for service. In an interview in a medical social work setting, the question relates to an illness or disability; in the marital counseling agency, to the marriage.

All messages are received through intervening, mediating variables provided by the communication-processing center. The dictum "No communication without interpretation" implies that the message we ultimately receive is not the same as the message that was sent. We classify, catalog, and interpret the incoming messages by relating them to past experiences and learning. The material selectively received is organized in a search for meaning. We need to orient ourselves to whatever situation we find ourselves in and to do so we try to make sense out of any communication we receive. In imposing meaning on the communication, we bring to the communication itself the explanatory schemes we have learned through our education and life experiences. These include not only cognitive belief systems, but also affective schemes—our feelings about our relationship to the world and to people.

During an interview, the worker invests a considerable amount of energy in the processing of communications received. After the worker decodes what she has heard, but before she responds, she attempts to make sense out of the communication. This is the diagnostic process in microcosm. How does this particular item of communication fit into the series of messages previously received? What does the client mean? How am I to understand this? The process is illustrated in the following introspective comment by a worker in a public assistance agency:

Up until now we were discussing how hard it is to feed the kids adequately on the AFDC budget. The last remark was about the fact that she hadn't gotten a new dress in two years. What is she trying to tell me? That she, too, is deprived? That I should have some pity for her? That she is trying hard to be a good mother, putting the kids' needs first? That I ought to try to do something to help her and not only be concerned about the kids? That she missed, and wanted, some guy hanging around? What makes her say this at this point in the interview? I also tried to decide at this point how concerned she was with this, because I was not sure whether to shift the interview to focus directly at this point on her concern about a new dress or table it and bring it up later while I continued to focus on the problem of feeding the kids on the budget. I decided that she was upset, but not all that upset about it that it couldn't hold and, although I didn't clearly understand what prompted the remark at this point, I decided to acknowledge the remark, indicate we would come back to it later, but continue, for the time, to discuss the problem of feeding the kids.

The following interview and worker's introspective comments demonstrate the problem faced by the interviewer as she processes what she hears:

Client: female, 54, white, protective service.

MRS. L.: Yes he is, I'm telling you. He's very hard to understand. If I knew to this day . . . that he was mean to his first wife in —— here, he lived here . . . I'd've never married the man. (Pause.) His folks are . . . oh, *wonderful* people, they're . . . they love me, and they love the kids, but I never hear from them. Because they're real old. They're uh. . . . They uhm. . . . They stopped sending Christmas cards after uh . . . I was divorced from him. . . . They didn't send no more Christmas cards. . . . They, uh, ask about me, they ask about my stepson —they ask, they all ask *about* me, and that's all right. They ask about us, and I ask about *them.* We get, I get along with the two sons that I kept in touch with, even Sid came and seen me, and he was jealous of his own son come and visit me. His son come and stayed . . . when he was goin' away to Chicago, he came and visited me. . . . And just 'cause he stayed here till noon . . . to have dinner with me, he was very jealous. He thought I had intercourse with his own son. (Pause.) His imagination, you know, I mean sort of. . . . And then when I visited, we used to be down to his own father. . . . He thought I'd have intercourse with his own dad, imagine. . . . His imagination, that was all in his head. . . . Because he, that's all what *he* always wanted all the time I lived with him. Constantly. And that's what he wanted.

The worker comments:

This is the type of response which confused me most. I just did not and do not understand this "free association" of topics and lines of thought. Similarly, I do not understand what function this seemingly aimless talk played for Mrs. L. Was it to ward off questions or comments which she feared? Was it preferable to any silence? Was the tension of the interview bringing it about or does she always speak in such a manner? Was it a desperate attempt to show me she was "good" and worthy of my care, that it was everyone else who did "bad" things? Was she not even perceiving me or was she checking out my reactions while she talked? All these various alternatives were going through my mind and suggesting alternative modes of action. I did not know whether she was crying out for some external ordering from me or whether she feared that as of yet and needed to be accepted in her wandering, dissociated ways before she would be able to accept direction or direct herself.

We noted above the necessity for feedback by the encoder of the message in checking whether or not the communication he was sending was, in fact, being correctly received. Similarly the receiver of the message, the decoder, has the responsibility of seeking feedback in checking that the message he has received is the message which was sent. The fact that communication goes on at so many different levels, through so many different channels, and is so easily subject to distortion and misunderstanding argues for the necessity of such feedback. Often we do not realize that we do not understand. As Whyte says, "The great enemy of communication is the illusion of it." Achievement of good communication requires, then, a presumption of ignorance, the frequent acceptance of the fact that although we think we know what the interviewee said, we may, in fact, not really know. The corrective for presumptive ignorance is feedback. We check our understanding of the message by asking for confirmation.

Good communication exists when the thought is encoded and transmitted freely and with fidelity and where the message finally decoded in the mind of the hearer is a faithful reproduction of the message originally encoded. That communication is a serial process makes it a hazardous undertaking. Each step follows the preceding step in sequence, so that a difficulty at any point along the line of the process results in a fault in all subsequent steps in the series.

The difficulty of receiving the message exactly as transmitted is repeatedly confirmed by the parlor game of sending a whispered message around a circle of participants, each repeating to the next person the message he thinks he received. The message as stated by the last person in the chain invariably is substantially different from the message as sent on its way by the first person.

ADDITIONAL PROBLEMS IN COMMUNICATION

Communication involves not only an external dialogue between worker and client, but also a series of internal monologues—client with herself, worker with herself. They are talking and listening to themselves while talking and listening to each other. Both the external dialogue and the internal monologues go on at different levels of more or less explicit communications. There is the overt, manifest content and the latent, covert content. There are the words directly spoken and the less obvious, indirect meanings of what is said.

The following is a section of a social work interview with both manifest and latent content presented, the material having been obtained from the participants after the interview.

Interviewer: male, 32, white, social worker.
Interviewee: female, 30, black, lower middle class, family
services—homemaker unit.

Manifest Content	*Latent Content*
WORKER: Could you tell me something about what brings you to the agency?	Black. Hope she won't think we're racist if we refuse her request, whatever it is. Hope it's something simple we can handle.
CLIENT: The social worker at the hospital. . . . I have to go for an operation, and there is not going to be anybody to care for the kids because my husband works all day, and the kids have to have somebody look after them, and she said I might have a homemaker to look after the kids while I am away.	Honky, always a honky. Can't I ever get to talk to a black worker? Is he going to think I really need this, or is he going to give me all that "uh" "uh" and get my black ass out of here? What will the kids do then? I really got to sell this.
WORKER: What kind of an operation is it you're scheduled for? How long will you be in the hospital?	How necessary is this and for how long? We only have a few homemakers, and if we tie up one for a long time we will be in a bind.
CLIENT: I have this trouble with my gall bladder all the time, all the time. It gets worse, and the doctor said I need this operation. It will be worse for me and the kids the longer I put it off.	Does he believe me? Does he think I am making it worse than it really is? How the hell do I know how long it's going to take?
WORKER: Could you tell me who your doctor is and when we can contact him to discuss your situation?	You can't expect the patient to know the medical details. If we have to plan for this, we should find out the situation from the person who knows it best—the doctor.

CLIENT: Sure, sure. Dr. ——— is the one I see when I go to the clinic. He knows all about it. Why do you have to talk to him?

What does he want to know this for? Is he going to check what I tell him? I wonder if Dr. ——— will back me up on this. He gets sore if a lot of people ask him questions.

WORKER: That's a good question. It's not that we don't believe you or that we want to check up on you, but we find that the person asked to have the operation, in this case yourself, doesn't often know the medical details we need for planning. For instance, if we were going to put a homemaker in the home—and at this point we are just talking about it—we would have to know for how long and what you could do after you came home from the hospital on convalescence and how much the homemaker would have to do.

Suspicious? Worried about our talking to the doctor? Afraid he might tell us something she would not want us to know? Or is it that she really doesn't know what purpose would be served in contacting the doctor? Have to be careful about making it clear what we have in mind.

CLIENT: Well, I really need a homemaker if I am going for the operation. The kids can't care for themselves. They are too young.

Why do they always have to make it so complicated? He hasn't even asked me about how old the kids are and how many of them there are. Right away they want to speak to someone else. Speak to me. I know more about this than anybody else does.

Relationship

A further, and very significant, problem follows from the fact that all communication is interactive and interrelational. Each person in the communications network affects the other person and is, in turn, affected by him. The nature of the interpersonal relationship between participants in a communication system is, then, of considerable importance. Communication involves not only what is said and heard—the message encoded, transmitted, received, processed, and decoded—but also the interpersonal context in which the process takes place. The emotional interaction between parties in the communication transaction affects, positively or adversely, the pattern of communication. The emotional interaction between people is what we mean by the term "relationship" as used in social work.

If the relationship is positive, if there is good feeling—a relaxed, comfortable, trustful, respectful, harmonious, warm, psychologically safe feeling—between worker and client, they are more likely to be receptive to messages being sent.

If the relationship is negative, if there is bad feeling—hostile, defensive, uneasy, mistrustful, disrespectful, discordant, psychologically threatening—between worker and client, there is less desire and readiness to hear what is being said.

The relationship is the communication bridge between people. Messages pass over the bridge with greater or lesser difficulty, depending on the nature of the emotional interaction between people. Social and emotional screens and barriers are lowered or become more permeable in the context of a good relationship. The readiness to return to the agency and the willingness to participate in the interviews are heightened. It is easier to be an open person in such a facilitative, benign emotional climate of mutuality and nonpossessive warmth. A positive relationship acts as an anodyne, an anesthetic, to the sharing of painful material on the part of the client; it heightens the salience and credibility of the communication coming from the worker. It frees the client to reveal himself without defensiveness or distortion because a good relationship promises acceptance and understanding and freedom from punishing criticism, rejection, or reprisal. Such a relationship reduces the possibility that the interview will become a competitive struggle and increases the likelihood that it will become a collaborative endeavor.

In the interview the protective functions of the ego, which counsel concealment, are in conflict with the adaptive function of the ego, counseling revelation to obtain help. The conditions making for a good relationship favor those components of the ambivalence which favor revelation.

A good relationship has the effect of intensifying and amplifying the consequences of any interaction in the interview. It makes the worker's influence greater, her suggestions more appealing, any of her techniques more effective. The good relationship provides a favorable context for effective learning, for it predisposes the interviewee to accept the teaching communicated by the interviewer. Since the relationship mobilizes feelings and makes for a more emotionally fluid situation, it increases the possibility of effecting change. A good relationship makes the interviewer a more potent, more influential source of imitative behavior in accordance with which the interviewee can learn to model himself.

The interviewer, acting as a warm, accepting person, establishes an atmosphere which reduces anxiety and threat. As a consequence the relationship itself acts as a counterconditioning context. The interviewee may talk about problems and situations which normally provoke anxiety. However, in the context of a relationship which counters anxiety, the same material now evokes less anxiety. A positive relationship does the same work of counterconditioning as the behavioral-modification relaxation procedure which prepares the client for engagement in desensitization. When such a relationship has been achieved, there is a feeling of rapport between interviewer and interviewee. The word "rap," currently used to mean "to get together, to talk in an atmosphere of warm friendliness," derives from the word "rapport."

In and of itself, however, a good relationship accomplishes nothing. It offers the potential for use in communication, but it needs to be used toward this end. Rapport can be high, both participants may talk easily, spontaneously, and comfortably, but if there is no agreement on purpose and/or no one who takes responsibility for holding the participants to the accomplishment of the purpose, then there will be no productive interview. Both the interviewer and interviewee may share in a conspiracy to evade the painful interaction that may be required for a productive interview.

A good relationship is like the heat which makes bending of iron possible. But while the iron is hot, somebody has to make the horseshoe. Heating alone will not accomplish this. A good relationship is not invariably pleasant. What helps is not a relationship that is always nice, but one that is actively utilized to further the purpose of the interview, even if to do so is to risk challenge, conflict, and unpleasantness. The worker strives to be consistently useful rather than consistently popular.

This might require, on occasion, the use of confrontation in which the interviewer presents the interviewee with contradictions between his words and his behavior; it might require the use of authority, for example, to protect a child from abuse; it might require an unequivocal statement of the expectation the worker has that the client will implement whatever responsibilities he agreed he would accept. However painful for the client such necessary approaches may be, they meet with less resistance if they are advanced in the context of a good relationship.

A good relationship is desirable in any communication situation, but it is particularly necessary in social work where painful matters of personal concern are so often the content of communication. Even in a research study concerning intimate material, Kinsey noted this need.

One is not likely to win the sort of rapport which brings a full and frank confession from a human subject unless he can convince the subject that he is desperately anxious to comprehend what his experience has meant to him. Sexual histories often involve a record of things that have hurt, of frustrations, of pain, of unsatisfied longings, of disappointments, of desperately tragic situations, and of complete catastrophe. The subject feels that the investigator who asks merely routine questions has no right to know about such things in another's history. The interviewer who senses what these things can mean, who at least momentarily shares something

of the satisfaction, pain, or bewilderment which was the subject's, who
shares something of the subject's hope that things will somehow work
out right is more effective though he may not be altogether neutral.
(161, p. 42)

Because the relationship—the context in which communication
takes place—is such a crucial determinant of the success or failure
of communication, there has been considerable concern with attempts to define the attributes of a good relationship and the behavior of the worker-interviewer associated with the nurturing of
such a relationship.

It is at this point that a book is the least successful device for
teaching what needs to be taught. In talking about relationships
we are talking about emotional interaction. The nature of the technically correct feeling which the worker-interviewer needs to manifest might be described and, perhaps, clinically illustrated. One
can exhort the worker to feel what he should feel in order to develop a desirable relationship in the interview. But it is not possible to teach anybody to feel the necessary feelings through description or exhortation. For those who have achieved these attitudes,
the reminder is unnecessary; for those who have not, the reminder
is ineffective.

Recognizing the deficiencies of a book as an instructional medium
for teaching certain kinds of content, and recognizing the futility of
exhorting the worker-interviewer to be respectful and compassionate, accepting and understanding, gentle and noncritical, we will
only briefly and didactically review some of the essential attributes
generally recognized as components of a good relationship.

CLIENT SELF-DETERMINATION

In adhering to and encouraging clients' self-determination, the
worker-interviewer establishes an atmosphere of mutuality, encourages clients' participation in problem-solving efforts, and respects
clients' initiative. His behavior implements his belief that the client
has the right, and the capacity, to direct his own life; he works
with the client in problem solving; he communicates confidence in
the client's ability to achieve his own solutions and actively helps
the client to achieve his own solution in his own way. Self-determi-

nation guarantees the interviewer's support without domination.

There is wisdom in the adage that "a man convinced against his will is of the same opinion still." The clients see this in terms of the worker's behavior in the interview: "She acted as though we were co-workers on a common problem." "He made me feel that I didn't have to agree with him if I felt differently about something." "She tried to get me to make my own decisions." "He encouraged me to work on my problems in my own way." "He didn't seem to think it was necessary for me to accept his idea, opinions, advice, if I wanted him to like me." [*]

The case vignettes below are followed by a series of possible interviewer responses, some illustrating an attitude respecting self-determination and some illustrating an inappropriate violation of this approach.

Client: female, 27, white, lower class, public assistance.

CLIENT: So I don't know. I think I should try to put the kids in a day center or maybe even in a foster home and get a job and make some money so we can get back on our feet again—but that might not be so good for the kids.

APPROPRIATE RESPONSES:

1. You're puzzled about what to do.
2. It's hard to know what would be best.
3. Hard on the kids?

INAPPROPRIATE RESPONSES:

1. Well, if you got a job you would be off relief.
2. My own feeling is that it would be better to stay home.
3. It wouldn't be so bad for the kids.

Client: female, 55, middle class, medical social work agency.

CLIENT: I know I have to have this operation, but I would rather not talk about it.

[*] Some of the phrasing is adapted from G. T. Barrett-Lennard, "Dimensions of Therapist Response as Causal Factors in Therapeutic Change," *Psychological Monographs* 76, no. 562 (1962).

APPROPRIATE RESPONSES:

1. It's hard to talk about.
2. Thinking about it makes you anxious.
3. Okay, perhaps there is something else you would rather talk about.

INAPPROPRIATE RESPONSES:

1. But I was supposed to discuss this with you.
2. Not talking about it won't make the problem disappear.
3. Well, it has to be discussed sooner or later, so why not now?

Some of the problems and limitations around adherence to and encouragement of client self-determination have been discussed extensively in social work literature (18, 19, 21, 125, 172, 224, 294).

There is conflict between the desire to grant the client his own decision and a conviction about which decision is the more desirable one for the client to choose. The conflict is between honoring the promise of freedom for the client and meeting responsibility for client needs.

A medical social worker talks to a 32-year-old mother who is reluctant to schedule a needed operation because of concern about care for her three young children during the period of hospitalization. The worker has offered homemaker service, but the mother is rejecting the idea. The worker comments:

> I could understand her objections, but I also realized that unless she accepted the service she might delay scheduling the needed medical care. I wanted frankly to throw the weight of my influence in favor of inducing her to accept homemaker service, but I was deterred by the dislike for manipulating and denying her maximum freedom in determining her own decision. Despite everything, my bias in favor of getting her the necessary medical attention without undue delay got past my professional safeguards. The questions I asked in discussing this with Mrs. R. were formulated in a way to suggest answers in favor of homemaker service. Instead of neutral questions starting "What do you think . . . ," I tended to ask questions starting with "Don't you think that. . . ." My verbal skirts weren't long enough to keep my bias from showing.

INTEREST IN CLIENT

A high level of interest helps in establishing and maintaining a positive relationship. It is demonstrated by the worker showing concern about a client's needs, indicating readiness and willingness to help, communicating the feeling that she really cares what happens to the client, over and beyond her formal responsibility to the job.

Clients have testified to a high level of interest by the worker in such statements as the following: "She did everything she could to help me." "He could be trusted to do what he said he would do." "He was ready to do things to help me even if it meant some bother for him." "She cared about what happened to me." "She didn't rush to finish the interview." "He seemed to *want* to hear what I had to say."

We demonstrate interest by asking the interviewee for his story, his feelings, his reactions, his responses, by making replies that indicate how well we have been listening, how much we have remembered of the interviewee's statement, how carefully and attentively we have heard him. Examples below exhibit both appropriate and inappropriate worker responses.

Client: male, 22, black, lower class, probation agency.

CLIENT: I am not sure if I can explain how I got into this jam.

APPROPRIATE RESPONSES:
   1. Take your time.
   2. Tell it your own way and perhaps I can help if you get stuck.
   3. Uh-huh (expectant silence).

INAPPROPRIATE RESPONSES:
   1. Well, we have very limited time. . . .
   2. Well then, perhaps we can go on to something else.
   3. Well, it may not be so important.

The appropriate response indicates an interest in hearing what the client has to say, a receptiveness to and encouragement of communication. The inappropriate response indicates disinterest and readiness to hasten the end of the interview.

Client: female, 26, black, lower class, public assistance.

CLIENT: All those things you asked me to bring—some of them I have, some of them I can't find. I don't know how I can get them, where to go. I have the rent receipts and gasoline bills and for the electricity, but like the marriage certificate, and the birth certificates of the two boys—these I don't know about.

APPROPRIATE RESPONSES:

1. I'll be glad to show you how to get what you need.
2. Let's go over this and see what can be done.
3. Try again to find them. We'll help you get duplicates if you can't.

INAPPROPRIATE RESPONSES:

1. Well, I am afraid that until you bring these things we cannot make out a check for you.
2. Well, you'll just have to find them.
3. I thought it was clear that we needed this for your eligibility.

There is a thin line between interest and curiosity. Curiosity implies seeking access to information to which the interviewer is not entitled because it does not further the purpose of the interview. The focus of legitimate interest is selective and discriminating. Principled adherence to confidentiality would then suggest that we need to encourage and help the interviewee to be silent about anything which is none of our business.

RESPECT FOR CLIENT'S INDIVIDUALITY

Demonstration of respect for the client-interviewee's individuality helps to establish and maintain a positive relationship. This involves an attitude and behavior that tend to support or enhance the client's self-esteem. The atmosphere between interviewer and interviewee is one which suggests that, as people, they have equal value. The worker responds to the client as a unique individual rather than as one of a whole class of persons. The orientation toward the interviewee is not "as *a* human being but as *this* human being with his personal differences" (21, p. 25). It involves the personalization of any generalization and suspension of its application until there is clear evidence that it is applicable to this particular individual.

The client-interviewee perceives respect for individuality demonstrated by the worker-interviewer who behaves in the following manner during the interview: "He was friendly and had great regard for my feeling." "He was interested in me as a person." "She didn't talk down to me." "She never made me feel I was just another client." The vignette below is followed by appropriate and inappropriate worker responses.

Client: female, 19, white, lower middle class, child care agency.

CLIENT: Well, Catholics are against abortion, and here I am pregnant and all.

APPROPRIATE RESPONSES:

1. How do you yourself feel about abortion?
2. What are your ideas about what you want to do with the baby?
3. And you, what do you think?

INAPPROPRIATE RESPONSES:

1. Well I guess, as a Catholic, abortion is not a possibility for you.
2. Okay, so abortion is out then.
3. What is your thinking about adoption?

NONJUDGMENTAL ATTITUDE

An accepting, nonjudgmental attitude helps in establishing and maintaining a positive relationship.* The worker manifests acceptance by behaving so as to indicate her respect and concern for the client, regardless of behavior which the worker may reject; she is compassionate, gentle, sympathetic; the client is given the freedom to be herself, to express herself freely, in all her unlovely as well as

---

* We have phrased the conditions for a good relationship in terms that reflect social work usage. Other groups also vitally concerned with relationships have used somewhat different terms to designate essentially the same attitudes. Perhaps the best known comparable term for "acceptance" is the Rogerian "unconditional positive regard."

lovely aspects. The worker is not moralistic, cold, aloof, deroga-tory, or disapproving. She should be mindful of Samuel Johnson's statement that "God Himself does not presume to judge a man till the end of his days." The nonjudgmental attitude is one which sug-gests that the interviewer is not concerned with praise or blame but solely with understanding. The accepting worker seeks to de-termine what explains the individual's behavior rather than to de-termine the worth of such behavior. The "object of acceptance is not the good or the bad but the real; the individual as he actually is, not as we wish him to be or think he should be" (21, p. 70).

Although acceptance does not necessarily mean agreeing with the client's frame of reference, his point of view, and his concept of reality, it involves granting their validity. It implies interpreting others in terms of themselves. Perhaps it means being "human enough not to be alienated by some of the unpleasant manifesta-tions of being human."

The following poem expresses a client's conception of an accept-ing worker:

> This woman
> talks to me
> in a warm language
> between her feelings
> and mine.
> She has no whip
> in her talk,
> no snarling teeth;
> She does not need to
> see the color of my blood
> to know me.
> This woman,
> seeing the gap
> in my fence,
> walks through it
> knowingly; and I,
> I let her stand in my
> field,
> unharmed.   C. ANATOPOLSKY °

° Reprinted, with permission, from the *AAPSW Newsletter*, Winter, 1937.

The client feels accepted when the worker evokes the following kinds of responses in the client-interviewee: "He made me feel free to say whatever I was thinking." "I could be very critical of him or very appreciative of him without it changing his good feeling toward me." "I could talk about most anything in my interview without feeling embarrassed or ashamed." "I had the feeling that here is one person I can really trust." "I could talk about anything without being afraid she would think less of me as a person."

Client: male, 46, white, middle class, family service.

CLIENT: It's just that I can't keep my hands off the stuff. I run into the slightest trouble and I reach for the bottle.

APPROPRIATE RESPONSES:
1. There is trouble and you feel you need a drink.
2. You reach for the bottle.
3. How does reaching for the bottle help?

INAPPROPRIATE RESPONSES:
1. Well, drinking doesn't solve the problem, does it?
2. That's not so smart, is it?
3. You ought to have more will power than that.

Client: male, 75, lower class, Old Age Assistance.

CLIENT: All you social workers are alike, one God-damn question after the other. Why do I have to tell you so much just to get the help! You could see I need it if you only used your eyes more and your mouth less.

APPROPRIATE RESPONSES:
1. You think I talk too much?
2. We make it hard for you to get the help you feel you need.
3. You're sore because you feel much of this is none of my business.

INAPPROPRIATE RESPONSES:
1. I don't like having to ask them any more than you feel like answering them.
2. You're making my job harder to do.

3. Well, I am afraid you'll just have to let me get this information if you expect us to help you.

Being accepting and being nonjudgmental are different aspects of the same basic attitude—acceptance is an act of commission, being nonjudgmental an act of omission. The difficulties of implementing an accepting, nonjudgmental attitude are discussed extensively in social work literature (20, 21, 125, 213, 223, 294).

EMPATHIC UNDERSTANDING

In empathic understanding the worker is demonstrating response to the latent as well as the manifest content of a client's communication. She understands, sensitively and accurately, the nature of the client's experience and the meaning this has for him, and understands the client's world cognitively and empathically from the client's point of view. She understands with, as well as about, the client, and has the capacity to communicate her understanding to the client in words attuned to the client's feeling; she really hears what the client is saying, so her responses have an "I am with you" quality, fitting in with the client's meaning and mood. If she does not always understand, she is always sincerely striving to understand, to reach out and receive the client's communication.

The worker-interviewer feels *with* the client rather than for him. Feeling *for* the client would be a sympathetic rather than an empathic response. Somebody once said that if you have a capacity for empathy you feel squat when you see a squat vase and feel tall when you look at a tall vase. Empathy is entering imaginatively into the inner life of someone else. It is not enough simply to be empathically understanding; one needs to communicate to the client the fact that one accurately perceives and feels his situation.

The client perceives the worker acting in response to empathic understanding when, in the client's words, "He was able to see and feel things in exactly the same way I do." "Many of the things she said just seemed to hit the nail on the head." "He understood my words but also how I felt." "When I did not say what I meant at all clearly, she still understood me."

Client: female, 37, white, upper lower class, child guidance clinic.

CLIENT: I know I am supposed to love him, but how much can you put love in a kid without getting some back? You can't just go on feeling love without his showing you some love, too, in return.

APPROPRIATE RESPONSES:

1. It's very disappointing for you.
2. It must be hard to do what you have to do under such circumstances.
3. That must hurt.

INAPPROPRIATE RESPONSES:

1. Well, he is only a kid and he doesn't understand.
2. Still and all, you are his mother.
3. Many kids don't show their love for parents.

GENUINENESS AND AUTHENTICITY

The Rogerians, existential therapists, and others concerned with the interview, particularly the therapeutic interview, have identified genuineness, or authenticity, as an essential condition for a good relationship. The quality has received little attention from social workers, however.

Authenticity on the part of the interviewer requires that he or she be real and human in the interview. It implies responsiveness and spontaneity, the willingness and readiness to share with the interviewee one's own feelings and reactions about what is going on in the interview. The argument is made that the interviewer cannot expect openness and readiness to share on the part of the interviewee unless he himself sets an example of such openness. There is research support for the contention that disclosure by the interviewer of his own prejudices, difficulties, or deficiencies encourages a greater flow of such disclosures from the interviewee (145).

The social work literature generally counsels against the worker's emotional response in the interview, instead suggesting objectivity, detachment, and affective neutrality.

CONFIDENTIALITY

A strong assurance for the client-interviewee that, in revealing himself to the worker-interviewer, he is not making such information available to a wider public, reduces the level of ego threat and facilitates communication. Threat to self-esteem resulting from disclosure of unflattering material is limited if only the interviewer will know this potentially damaging material. Information about one's person is a private possession. In sharing it with the worker, the client is not giving permission that it be broadcast and used indiscriminately. The many problems regarding adherence to confidentiality are discussed in the literature (4).

These then are some of the necessary conditions of worker attitude, as reflected in appropriate worker behavior, which are prerequisites for establishing and maintaining a positive relationship.

A considerable body of literature validates the assertion that the conditions outlined above are correlated with a positive relationship (45, 243, 271, 298). Relationship is interaction, however, and interaction implies that more is required than the input of the worker-interviewer. The client-interviewee is an equally important factor in developing and maintaining a relationship. The worker may offer the necessary conditions for optimum relationship, but it may fail to develop because the client lacks the capacity or the desire to interact.

The worker's actions may not be the sole determinant of the client's response to her efforts. Interaction may be the result of transference as well as objective elements in the interaction. Transference means that the client reacts to the worker as though she were another person out of the past.

The more frequent situation, however, is that, having been met with interest, respect, understanding, and acceptance on the part of the interviewer, the client responds with reciprocal warm feelings of liking for the interviewer. The interaction then spirals in a positive direction, toward increased mutual attractiveness of the participants.

The importance of the interviewer-interviewee relationship is a factor common to all interviews conducted by social workers, whatever their approach to the client-interviewee. Both a worker employing behavioral-modification techniques and one who is psychoanalytically oriented need to give active consideration to the relationship (169, 332). Indeed, one may argue that these conditions are just a somewhat exaggerated delineation of what is required in any good human relationship. As Oldfield notes, "interviewing is a special branch of the general art of conducting human relations" (216, p. 139).

Expressive-Instrumental Satisfactions

In our concern for delineating the characteristics of the interview relationship we risk slighting the instrumental aspects of interviewing. It might be well at this point to discuss the balance between the client's expressive satisfactions and instrumental satisfactions in the interview. The expressive satisfactions are derived from the relationship established, the context in which help is offered. Instrumental satisfactions are derived from what the worker actually does to help the client deal with the problems he brings. Polansky (229), in postinterview interviews with social agency clients, confirmed the hypothesis that they received these two different kinds of satisfactions from the interview.

One important reward which motivates people to communicate in the interview situation is that, as a result of such communication, the pain, discomfort, and inconvenience stemming from a dysfunctional psychosocial situation will be reduced. The hope is that the interviewer will say or do something that helps solve the problem to some degree. This is the instrumental consequence of interview participation for the interviewee.

Another important reward is the pleasure, the ego gratification, which comes from contact with an interested, understanding, accepting person who appears willing to listen to your story with empathy, sympathy, and emotional support. This is the expressive consequence of participation for the interviewee. Such expressive rewards are most fully achieved as a result of the kind of relationship described in the preceding section.

The Vizier Ptah-Hotep, sometime between 2700 and 2200 B.C. gave advice to his son in recognition of these considerations.

If thou art one to whom petition is made, be calm as thou listenest to what the petitioner has to say. Do not rebuff him before he has swept out his body or before he has said that for which he came. The petitioner likes attention to his words better than the fulfilling of that for which he came. . . . It is not necessary that everything about which he has petitioned should come to pass, but a good hearing is soothing to the heart.

Some four thousand years later this statement is equally true, although social workers need to be more concerned with "the fulfilling of that for which he came" than was a grand vizier.

For many kinds of social work interview situations, the instrumental consequences are of overwhelming importance to the client. Without the public welfare grant, the client cannot pay the rent or clothe the children. The deserted mother about to be hospitalized needs to find foster homes for her children. The wife of the marginal-income worker needs to have her preschool child accepted at some low-cost day-care center if she is to accept the job she has just found.

While the clients, like all people everywhere, would like to be, and without question should be, interviewed with courtesy and respect, with concern for their autonomy and uniqueness, these expressive considerations are of secondary, or even tertiary, importance to some clients in situations of pressing need. Above all, they are concerned with what the interview can do to help them get money, find a suitable foster home, obtain admittance to a day-care center. What the interviewer does or can do is then of far more importance and significance to the client than the way he does it.

A study of the reactions of mothers to interviews with pediatricians, based on tape recordings of the interviews and postinterview interviews with the mothers, found that most of them expected technical competence and were not disappointed. The instrumental purposes of the interviews were, by and large, satisfactorily achieved (167). However, many mothers had expectations which transcended technical competence. They wanted the doctor to be

friendly, concerned, and sympathetic. It was with these aspects of
the interview, the expressive aspects, that most mothers were disappointed.

A similar careful study of social work interviews might find the
opposite to be true—considerable satisfaction with the worker's
handling of the expressive aspects of the interview, less satisfaction
with the instrumental problem-solving consequences of the interview. As a perceptive caseworker once said, "I feel like a Good
Humor man with an empty cart." We need to give greater consideration to our "utility value" to the client-interviewee, to what we
do as well as how we do it, to the instrumental purposes for which
the relationship is established, as well as to the nature of the relationship we establish.

Attitudes and Behavior

One more important consideration needs to be discussed regarding
the relationship we have attempted to describe above. The picture
which emerges of the good worker-interviewer may appear to be
that of God's perfect creature. It is, therefore, reassuring to note
that the interviewer's behavior rather than his attitude tends to be
of more critical importance. The client-interviewee reacts to the
overt behavior the worker-interviewer manifests, rather than to the
underlying attitudes. It would, of course, be most desirable for the
overt behavior and underlying attitude to be congruent. This
would reduce the possibility that the overt behavioral message
might be contradicted by the covert attitudinal message. It would
also reduce psychic stress on the worker who feels one way but is
constrained by his professional role to act in another way. But if
the two messages are contradictory, the message of behavior seems
to have clear priority, according to results of studies where both
worker and client were interviewed about their experiences after
their interview together (138). In some instances the worker confessed that, although he tried to act in an accepting manner, he did
not feel accepting, that although he acted as though he liked the
interviewee, he did not really like him. The interviewee's percep-

tion of the same interview rarely indicated any recognition that the worker's underlying attitude was negative. He perceived and reacted to the worker's positive verbal and nonverbal behavior toward him.

As Hyman notes, in reporting this study, "Feelings are one thing, overt conduct [is] another. It is purely an assumption based on little fact to conceive of the interviewer's feelings spewing forth in all directions" (138, p. 40). "Perhaps we have gone too far in thinking that the danger from the interviewer's strong feelings is that they might be *communicated* to the respondent and affect his replies" (138, p. 43).

A similar conclusion results from another careful study of interviewee-interviewer interaction in a health interview survey, based on reports of the same interview obtained independently from interviewer and interviewee. "The study started with the assumption that the attitude and feeling variables were the most important and significant factors determining interview interaction. The results of the study contradicted the hypothesis and indicated that the actual behavior of both interviewer and interviewee were the variables of greatest importance in determining the course of the interview" (44, p. 5).

This result should not be surprising to anybody who has engaged in interviewing, despite the fact that it contradicts a cherished social work myth—that the client (particularly a child) always "knows" what the worker is feeling. If the practiced professional feels it excruciatingly difficult to know what the client is feeling, as is often the case, why should it be easy for the client to be invariably so intuitively gifted?

The important implication of these findings for the student interviewer is that success in establishing good relationships is possible without his being godlike. It is not necessary, although most desirable, to feel invariably respectful and accepting. It is sufficient to *act* respectful and accepting. All one can ask of the interviewer is that he be capable of a disciplined subjectivity, not that he resolve all his prejudices, his human dislikes and antipathies. He is asked to control negative feelings in the interview so that they are not overt. If the research has validity, this control is likely to be sufficient for the establishment and maintenance of a good relationship that facilitates communication.

The fact of the matter is that many clients are so concerned with their own problems that they have little free psychic energy to devote to psyching out the interviewer. We often say exactly this about the interviewer, that concern with his own problem in the interview reduces his ability to empathize.

There is a further implication. It is true that if we feel the correct attitude we are likely to say the correct word. However, the reverse also tends to be true. If we keep saying the correct word, we are likely to begin to feel the correct attitude. Cognitive dissonance is a strain which is resolved by bringing behavior and attitude into congruence, this time by bringing the attitude closer to the word (125, pp. 55–56).*

One additional consideration of prime importance needs to be recognized and explicitly stated. Establishing a relationship as described requires considerable emotional energy. It is enervating and psychologically depleting. One cannot expect workers with large case loads, facing frequent emergencies and dealing with frustrating, intractable situations of considerable environmental stress, to establish such relationships with any frequency. Although knowing what is desirable, many workers, despite their commitment and dedication, may have to settle for less.

Summary

Some general principles and problems of communication, applicable to any kind of interview, were presented. The characteristics of the kind of relationship making for good communication were reviewed and illustrated. Included among the characteristics of the desirable approach are self-determination, interest in, and respect

---

* Dissonance theory posits a tendency toward psychological consistency. Inconsistency between behavior and feelings creates a psychological tension which is resolved by efforts to reduce the inconsistency. James Lange's theory of emotion also supports this; it suggests that although we act in response to our feelings, we also feel in response to our actions.

for, the client, acceptance, empathic understanding, confidentiality, and authenticity. It was noted that in addition to the expressive satisfactions in the interview which derived from the relationship, there were instrumental needs which the interviewer had to meet and that behavior, rather than attitude, was of prime importance.

Chapter 3

~~~~~~

Interviewer and Interviewee: Background, Characteristics, Tasks

Our concern in this chapter is with some further general material related to all social work interviews. We shall consider what each participant brings to the interview, attributes that are characteristic of the competent interviewer and interviewee, the general tasks each needs to perform in the interview, the problems encountered by interviewer and interviewee in performing these tasks. We are concerned with these considerations as related to the interviewee separately, to the interviewer separately, and to the interaction between these two.

Interviewee Background

The interviewee brings his reference group affiliations, his primary group affiliations, and his biopsychosocial history and current functioning. The client is a member of a sex grouping, and age, racial, occupational, class, religious, and ethnic groups. He is identified, for example, as male, young adult, white, bricklayer, lower middle class, Catholic, of Italian origin. Or as female, 45 years old, black, homemaker, lower class, Baptist, of American birth. Each of the identifying labels tells us something, within limits, of the likely behavior, feelings, and attitudes of the client. Affiliation with each of these different significant reference groups affects some aspect of the client's behavior in the interview.* But the client is more intimately a member of several primary groups—a family, a particular peer group on the job, a particular congregation, a friendship group.

All the primary-group contacts modify in some way the behavior, feelings, and attitudes dictated by membership in a particular reference group. It may be that lower-class adolescent males generally are likely to be struggling for emancipation from the family. It happens that the peer group of adolescents with whom John is most intimately associated are not as yet manifesting this kind of rebellion and alienation and seem comfortable in their dependent ties to their families.

John further has a particular body, a particular physiology. He is tall or short, fat or thin, active or lethargic, invariably healthy or somewhat ill. And he has had a particular psychosocial history. He grew up at a particular time, in a particular place, in a particular family, with a particular set of parents, and his life in growing up with these circumstances was unique and idiosyncratic—never before experienced in just this way by anybody, never again to be experienced in just this way by anyone else.

All of this background accompanies the client into the interview situation, shaping the way he will think and feel and behave. Not every role, not every group membership, has potency and relevance for determining the interviewee's reaction in the interview. Attitudes, beliefs, and behaviors associated with those roles which

---

* The reference group is that large identifiable social aggregate with whom the person identifies and is identified. The person's behavior is patterned in accord with its norms and perspectives. The primary group is the face-to-face group.

relate to the purpose of the interview will be of greatest influence. The middle-aged woman talking to the medical social worker will introduce into the interview those group and individual attitudes which are related to illness, to medical treatment, to temporary institutional living. The relevant social role is that of a patient in a hospital, and all the beliefs and feelings of her reference groups about being a patient, as well as those which derive from her own personal history, will be activated in the interview. Beliefs and feelings about her other significant social roles, as wife, mother, daughter, employee, etc., are less relevant to this interview situation.

Interviewer Background

The worker also brings to the interview a configuration of determinants. The worker also has reference group affiliations—male or female, young or old, of some color, ethnicity, and religion. But having been educated in graduate school, undergraduate school, or an in-service training program to enact a professional role, the social work interviewer does not allow these identities to determine her interview behavior. The whole point of such training is to replace the behavior generally anticipated from, let us say, a white, young, middle-class Protestant by the professional behavior expected of a social worker. If the interviewer consistently succeeds in doing this, we say she is acting professionally in the interview. She has developed a professional identity which reflects the ways of the occupational subculture. The principal reference-group affiliation which she brings to the interview is that of the profession. The picture she has of what is expected of a social work interviewer is the configuration to which she feels constrained to conform.

Professional affiliation will determine what areas will be explored in the interview and how the information obtained will be processed by the interviewer. It provides a particular orientation for the interviewer which guides his perception. A study of the response to the same social study data by interviewers who held different orientations toward human behavior concluded that they paid attention to different aspects of the situation. Each had a set of perceptions which determined what data she would unconsciously, or consciously, accept. The interviewers organized material presented to them in terms of these sets (48, 170). The way the profession teaches us to explain a situation determines the way we perceive the situation.

Although the profession generally dictates particular forms of behavior in the interview, these, too, are modified by primary group pressures. Here the principal primary group dictating the adaptation of professional behavior is the peer group of fellow social workers in an agency. For instance, the profession has declared allegiance to certain theoretical explanatory configurations. In general the concepts of ego psychology, with generous sociological modifications, are still the theoretical framework most consistently taught in schools of social work and through the literature of the field. Such a cosmology explains not only how social problems originate and develop, but also what can be done in the interview, or through it, to help people deal with such problems. This is the universe of discourse that is inculcated in students for explaining human behavior. But each agency is more, or less, ego psychological in its orientation, and some agencies have rejected this orientation altogether in preference for a Rogerian or a behavioral-modification orientation. Thus, whereas the general orientation of the profession may be ego psychological, working in a particular agency with a particular peer group may require that the social worker "speak" neo-Freudian, or Rogerian, or behavioral modification in the interviews.

Some agencies emphasize deficiencies in the social situation as the primary contributing factors in the client's problems; other agencies emphasize the client's personal deficiencies as contributing factors. The social workers in these agencies will therefore focus on different content in an interview and direct their interviews toward different solutions. Billingsly (22) found clear differences in the orientation of social workers in a family service agency as compared with a child protective agency. Both groups regarded themselves as social workers. But in both instances the agency, dealing with different groups of clients, dictated a different adaptation of the professional way of serving the client. Billingsly concluded that "the agencies exert a major and differential influence" (22, p. 187) on workers' role orientation and role performance.

Identification with the profession as a reference group not only implies adherence to certain interview techniques and utilization of a certain explanatory cosmology, but also calls for behavior in accordance with certain professional values and ethics. These values also undergo some modification in each particular agency. In any conflict between agency policy and standards of the profession, the worker tends to act in accordance with agency policy (22). The profession is a remote and ambiguous entity; the pressure and sanction of the agency are immediate and visible. The interviewer solicits agency peer group acceptance and the agency supervisor's approbation, and these needs determine her choices in interviewing behavior.

The agency may be only one of the primary groups to which the individual interviewer is responsive, particularly in a large social agency. The additional primary groups may be the unit to which she is assigned within the agency, or a friendship clique of fellow workers. The importance of such informal groups in determining workers' behavior has been noted by anthropologists who studied a large public welfare agency as participant observers.

We have noted that there exists within the welfare agency a subsystem, the clique group. It is this subsystem which exercises much greater control over the way in which public casework is administered. During our investigation we noted the opinion-molding aspect of the group was influential in areas of conceptions toward recipients, methods of casework, attitudes toward the official agency. (28, p. 77–79)

Within the same agency, social workers seek out colleagues whose orientation to the work is similar to their own (25). They support each other and reinforce their tendencies to handle their interviews in a particular manner. For many professionals the judgment of greatest concern is that of colleagues. The reputation a worker has in the agency is more frequently the result of how he relates to his colleagues, how he is perceived by them, than of the way he relates to and is perceived by the clients. The worker is under great pressure, therefore, to conform to the ways of the agency. Preserving an acceptable relationship with agency colleagues is likely to take precedence not only in any conflict between agency and profession but also in any conflict between the agency and the needs of the client.

The framework provided by the profession, as modified by the agency, is further adapted by the individual interviewer in terms of his idiosyncratic biopsychosocial preferences. The particular items within the framework that are emphasized, the particular interviewee responses that have high visibility, differ from interviewer to interviewer within a single agency. But again the professional requirement is that the worker make every effort to ensure that these considerations are excluded from the interview. Ideally the worker is aware of those needs which derive from his own psychosocial history and controls their manifestations.

The aim and hope of professional education and in-service training is to reduce the idiosyncratic component in the interviewer's behavior. Instead of responding as a middle-aged, middle-class, white female with a unique developmental history, the worker will respond as a professional in terms of some standardized, presumably technically correct, precepts. All social work interviewers following a uniform theory should, then, respond to the same interview situation in a similar manner.

That aim is only partially achieved. A study of tape-recorded interviews of experienced, professional social workers indicated that although there was some uniformity in their interview behavior, there was also considerable diversity (211). This result is to be expected even where a uniform theory, a set of clear explicit generalizations, is available to guide the worker in most situations encountered. The problem for the social worker is compounded by the fact that for many significant situations recurrently encountered in the interview, the field does not have an applicable generalization. The worker then has to fall back on responding in terms of his nonprofessional background and makeup.

Despite these qualifications, however, the process of socialization of the recruit has the goal of developing some uniformities in interviewer thinking, feeling, and behavior that reflect the profession's expectations for anyone occupying the status of social worker in a particular agency.

Interviewer-Interviewee Interaction

What happens in any one interview is the result of what the interviewee brings to the encounter, what the interviewer brings, and the interaction between the particular pair of participants at this point in time in the history of their contact with each other. The interaction is "reciprocally contingent," each person responding to the other's behavior, each a partial cause of the other's behavior. The interview is a system in which each participant is seeking, accepting, or resisting the other's efforts to influence him. The interviewer needs to ask himself, "What am I doing or saying that might help explain what the interviewee is doing and saying?"

All of this suggests a reevaluation of the relative importance of the various factors that feed into the interview. Despite the initial importance of background factors, reference and primary group affiliation, life history of individual participants, professional training and theoretical orientation, once the interview begins, one of the most potent factors determining the behavior of one participant is the behavior of the other. With the start of the interview a new set of variables is activated that is specific to this particular encounter.

Although interview interaction is one of reciprocal, mutual efforts by both participants to influence each other, the influence potential of the interviewer is greater than that of the interviewee because she has more power and greater varieties of power (60, 91). The interviewer has "reward" power in her control of access to special services the agency can make available. She has control of access to the "therapy" she dispenses, a therapy which the client very much wants if he has any confidence in its ability to make him feel less anxious, lessen his conflict, or help him to grow. The worker has "expert" power in the special knowledge she supposedly has available to help the client solve the problems which cause him anguish. She has "coercive" power in agencies which operate with legal sanctions, as in corrections or protective services. Once a relationship is established, she has "referent" power in the meaningfulness, to the client, of her expressions of approval or disapproval. Because the client wants her approval as a person of meaning in his life, the worker does exercise a measure of control over the client's behavior.

The interviewee has few sources of power at her command to give potency to her efforts to influence. She may, as in the case of the involuntary client, have the power that derives from her indifference. This is the power of the party of "least interest" in any transaction. The interviewee can refuse to cooperate with the interviewer; she can frustrate the accomplishment of the purpose of the interview; she can deny the interviewer the gratification of conducting a good interview; she can deny the interviewer the psychic compensations of expressions of appreciation and gratitude; she may refuse to make this an easy interview, offering limited or unproductive responses. The interviewee may deny the interviewer the satisfactions which come from a confirmation of her competence, or she may offer them selectively, in return for the interviewer's giving her what she wants.

Despite an apparent considerable differential of power in the interviewer's favor, the interviewee is not without influence. While it is clear, and expected, that the behavior of the interviewer exerts an effect on the behavior of the interviewee, available research indicates that the opposite is also the case (130, 135, 210, 303). Detailed studies of interviewer behavior indicate that although there is a core of reliability in the behavior of the same interviewer as she moves from interview to interview, there is some modification in response to the individuality of different interviewees (108, 109). One study showed that the interviewers tried to compensate for lower interviewee activity by increasing their own activity but that they decreased their own activity in contact with an active interviewee (173). Dependency in the interviewee evokes dominance and reassurance in the interviewer. Hostility or friendliness in the interviewee evokes a parallel response.

Although both interviewee and interviewer modify their characteristic patterns of interaction in response to each other's behavior, studies show that the interviewer tends to make a greater effort to accommodate than does the interviewee. This finding is to be expected since the interviewer has more of a professional responsibility to ensure the success of the encounter.

Nonetheless, the greater power of the interviewer gives him greater potential for influencing the content and direction of the interview. Numerous, well-validated studies indicate that the interviewer's responses determine what the client chooses to say (330, 331). By responding with interest every time the interviewee mentions his mother, one can "condition" him to talk at greater length about his mother. By responding with interest whenever the interviewee talks about his mother's overprotectiveness, but never when he talks about his mother's efforts to support his steps toward independence, one can condition the client to focus on the overprotective component of his mother's ambivalence and hear less about her concern for her son's autonomy.

In verbal conditioning, the interviewer conditions the interviewee by a deliberate, controlled use of words and vocalization. The rewards are words of praise, approval, and the sounds that indicate that the interviewer is paying close and interested attention. The punishments are the withholding of words of praise and vocal evidence of attention, or words actually used to discourage some statements: "No, that's not important." "Let's not discuss that now." Every interviewer, no matter how determinedly nondirective, conditions the client by some selective responses to what the client says or does.

We return now to take a further, separate look at the participants in the interview interaction—their personality characteristics, their tasks in the interview, the problems they face in implementing their roles.

The Competent Interviewer

Research which attempts to factor out the personality characteristics associated with competence in interviewing yields a rather confused picture. The confusion may result because interviews conducted for different purposes may, ideally, require different kinds of interviewing personalities.

The warm, accepting qualities necessary for interviews whose primary purpose is therapeutic are not those required for the interview whose primary purpose is assessment. The "therapeutic" interviewer in an assessment interview may fail to probe inconsistencies or may make compassionate allowance for interviewee reluctance to discuss essential but difficult areas. The interview whose primary purpose is reliable judgment–diagnostic assessment may require a reserved, extraceptively oriented person; the therapeutic interview may require a warmer, more spontaneous, intraceptively oriented person. The interviewer engaged in advocacy may need a more aggressive, directive, dominant approach to the interview.

Different interviewers may be more or less competent with different kinds of interviewees. For instance, some interviewers are uncomfortable unless the relative status vis-à-vis the interviewee is in their favor. Consequently, while they may be comfortable and competent in interviews with lower-class clients seeking agency help, they would be uncomfortable in interviews with the director of an agency whose influence they are trying to enlist in their client's behalf. In general, however, those interviewers who manifest the personal qualities associated with establishing a good relationship—warmth, patience, compassion, tolerance, sincerity—are likely to be among the more successful. These are the kinds of interviewers preferred by clients (6). The less anxious, less maladjusted the interviewer is, the greater the likelihood of competence (10, 38). Greater interview competence is associated with open-mindedness and low dogmatism in response to such instruments as the Rokeach dogmatism scale (2, 158, 252, 286).

Other studies of the characteristics of competent interviewers suggest that they have a rather reserved, controlled, low-level social orientation and retain a certain amount of objective, detached sensitivity to the interviewee (137). They are serious, persistent, reflective, and interested in observing and understanding their own behavior as well as the behavior of others, and they are tolerant and understanding of other people and human weakness (9). One recurrent finding is that a high degree of extroversion and sociability is not related to high interview competence. Greater interview competence tends to be associated with an interest in people that is scientific and objective rather than highly emotional or personal (138, pp. 292–294).

Studies show an association between intelligence and good interview performance, although intelligence is not a guarantee of good performance (272). It is generally agreed that it is desirable for the interviewer to have a variety of interests and a wide range of experiences. She then has the capacity to empathize with a greater range of people, since her own experience may parallel theirs. She also has a broader base for communication.

Some studies have attempted to determine the characteristics of the competent interviewer by more indirect methods. The assumption is that interviewers who establish the facilitative conditions for relationships that we have discussed must be competent. The research then seeks to find out what kind of people establish these conditions. Tape-recorded interviews are played to a group of judges who then decide the level at which the interviewer has established the facilitative conditions. After sorting out those who have done this very well, the study then goes on to determine their personality characteristics. As might be expected, the results tend to show that such interviewers are independent, self-actualizing, sensitive, and psychologically open (2, 92).

If the trait analysis of the competent interviewer still leads to ambiguous answers, the results of studying the behavior of experienced interviewers seem somewhat clearer. The supposition is that the more experienced interviewer is the more competent. Experienced interviewers are apt to manifest less control, to be less active, and to be less inclined to offer advice and suggestion than are inexperienced interviewers. Inexperienced interviewers are apt to talk more and to take more responsibility for the conduct of the interview. The difference may reflect the greater anxiety and insecurity of the beginning interviewer rather than his technical inexperience. The experienced interviewer is not passive, however. He tends to be more discriminating and modulates his activity. He says only what needs to be said, at the moment it needs to be said, so that he is more efficient, making every comment count.

Changes which result from training for psychotherapeutic interviewing may also suggest differences between experienced and inexperienced interviewers. As a result of such training, interviewers become more reluctant to initiate interaction, giving the interviewee greater opportunity for this, and become less inclined to assert themselves during the interview by interrupting the client (188).

In one study, interviewers were shown a film of an actual interview. The interview was stopped at various points and the interviewers participating in the research were asked what their response might have been at this time if they had been conducting the interview. Inexperienced interviewers tended to ask questions; experienced interviewers tended to make statements. Inexperienced interviewers tended to respond to discrete ideas, to specific words or phrases; experienced interviewers tended to respond to the gestalt of the client's presentation (218).

Experienced interviewers tend to make fewer directly manipulative responses and more communicative responses conveying a thought or feeling. For example, a client begins to pace the floor in an interview. The inexperienced therapist is more likely to make a statement designed to elicit a certain desired response (manipulative) such as: "If you don't sit down, I am afraid I won't be able to help you." A communicative response of the more experienced interviewer might be: "I have the feeling that you are trying to impress me with how upset you are" (219, p. 10).

The most judicious conclusion that might be drawn from the variety of studies available is that no clear pattern of personality traits clearly distinguishes the good from the poor interviewer. Good interviewing is the result of the complex interplay of the interviewer, the interviewee, the purpose of the interview, and the setting in which it is conducted. The general direction of the research findings tends to suggest that the more successful interviewer is likely to be warm, accepting, psychologically open, in flexible control of himself and the interview situation.

The Interviewer's Tasks

The task dimension of interviewer behavior relates to the function which the worker must perform if the interview is to accomplish its purpose. At this point we are concerned with outlining the general tasks required of the interviewer. In chapters 5 and 6 we will cover the detailed behavior associated with implementing these general tasks.

In general the interviewer has to keep the interview moving productively in the direction of its purpose and keep the interview system operating smoothly.

In accomplishing the first task, the interviewer has to do several things. She has to work collaboratively with the interviewee to establish a definition of the situation, a purpose for the interview, that is mutually understood and accepted. She must be skillful in the use of a variety of methods of intervention to keep the interview moving or get it started again. The interviewer acts as a dynamic force and catalyst. The interviewer helps the client select and articulate the information, feelings, and attitudes that have greatest salience for accomplishing the purpose of the interview. The interviewer has a great deal of mental work to do during the interview. The interviewer has to receive and process complex data, make complex decisions about how to respond, make the selected responses, and evaluate their effect.

The client's story is generally presented as pieces of a mosaic, disconnected, with significant items embedded in much irrelevant "noise." The interviewer has the task of assembling the items, organizing them in his mind, putting the pieces of the mosaic together so that they make a comprehensive picture. The interviewer has to listen actively as a data processor, not passively as a receptacle.

In implementing the second expressive task, that of keeping the system operating, the worker has to establish and maintain a good relationship with the interviewee, and stimulate the interviewee's motivation to participate productively in the interview.

In implementing the expressive tasks, the interviewer acts to re-

duce the interviewee's anxiety, embarrassment, irritation, and suspicion. She puts the interviewee at ease and gives her psychological support at difficult points in the interview. To do this, the
interviewer has to be sensitive to the changing emotional climate
of the system. Her responses offer gratification to the interviewee
for participation and reassure her of her adequacy as a person and
in the role of interviewee.

System-maintenance requirements operate as constraints on interviewer behavior. If the interviewee is present physically but has
withdrawn psychologically and emotionally from the interview,
nothing can be accomplished. However, if sole attention is devoted
to expressive needs and little attention is paid to the instrumental
reasons that brought interviewee and interviewer together, there
can be an interview system which operates smoothly and satisfy-
ingly but produces nothing of consequence to anybody.

At each meeting the social worker intervenes to guide and influence the natural development of the interactional process to ensure
that the purposes of the interview are achieved. Every response the
interviewer makes should be deliberately selected to further the
purposes of the interview. One might justly accuse the interviewer
of being manipulative. However, the entire process is manipulative, that is, it is designed to achieve certain results through selective interviewer inputs. The very attitudinal set manifested by the
interviewer—respect for and interest in the client, the concern
with self-determination and acceptance, etc.—is manipulative. The
attitudes are deliberately selected and communicated for the purposes of encouraging client communication, reducing anxiety, removing barriers to a confessional. The interviewee is presented
with a particular stimulus configuration to increase the probability
of responses regarded by the interviewer as helpful. We tend not
to use the word "manipulation" to describe this behavior. But in
the most accurate, most neutral, least pejorative sense, everything
the skilled interviewer does is manipulative.

The Interviewer's
Need for Knowledge

A thorough knowledge of the subject matter of the interview is a mark of the competent interviewer. The medical social work interviewer must have at her command a detailed, specialized knowledge of the social antecedents, concomitants, and consequences of physical illness; the psychiatric social worker, of mental and emotional illness; the gerontological social worker, of old age.

Unless the worker has detailed knowledge of the social problem area for which she is offering service, she will not know what questions to raise, what information is most significant, what items need to be pursued in greater detail. She needs to know the generalizations which the social and behavioral sciences have made regarding, for instance, delinquency, child placement, or school phobia, so that she has some concepts available to make sense out of what the interviewee is telling her. She needs to have sufficient grasp of the relevant generalizations regarding the particular social problem so that she can translate these into appropriate questions, comments, and probes during the interview. Chance favors a prepared mind. Some statements by the interviewee which have no meaning for an interviewer with scant knowledge will suggest a series of fruitful questions to the interviewer who knows what the remark implies.

Assessment interviews require a knowledge of normative expectations. If the child is toilet trained at 20 months, is it late or early? If he first started talking at 15 months, is this indicative of developmental lag or normal development? What parental behavior suggests "overprotection," and what kinds of separation behavior are normal for a hospitalized, school-age child? To know what is unusual, unexpected, or atypical, one needs to know the usual and typical.

The interviewer whose purpose is advocacy, and whose interview orientation is to persuade and convince, needs to have considerable knowledge about the rights and entitlements of his client;

he needs to have a good command of the regulations and procedure of the agency. Without such knowledge he cannot challenge,
with assurance, any decision denying aid or service. He must understand the agency's structure so that he can appeal, or threaten
to appeal, an adverse decision made at a lower level in the agency's administrative structure to somebody farther up the line.

Furthermore, knowledge about possible solutions, about available resources and therapeutic procedures, is also necessary, since
that guides the interviewer in determining which aspect of the client's situation might be most productively explored.

Knowledge increases security and lessens anxiety. If the worker
goes into the interview with an expert knowledge of what the literature and practice wisdom of the field make available, not only
with regard to the etiology of the problems but also regarding how
she might help, she is more apt to feel confident in her own ability
to conduct the interview successfully. This, in itself, increases the
probability that she will conduct a successful interview.

There are, then, two different clusters of expertness required and
expected of the interviewer. One is expert knowledge regarding the
conduct of the interview. The second is knowledge about the social
problem subject-matter—its nature, its origin, the approaches to its
possible amelioration. The social work interviewer is both a specialist in interviewing and a specialist in the social aspects of mental deficiency or old age or child neglect or marital conflict, the
stresses encountered by people facing such problems and the variety of ways people cope with such stresses.

The client is not competent to assess the knowledgeability of the
interviewer regarding interviewing, although a client knows in a
general way when an interview is competently or poorly conducted. The client is, however, very competent to assess the social
worker's knowledge about the subject matter since he is living the
problem. Senseless, irrelevant questions, or comments that clearly
betray that the social worker knows little about the situation, encourage disrespect for the worker and erode client confidence. A
thorough understanding of the subject area enhances the client's
confidence in the interviewer as someone who knows his job and
can therefore be counted on to help. A detailed knowledge of the

problem area reduces social distance. It indicates that both the interviewer and interviewee share some familiarity with the problem. If she perceives the interviewer as knowledgeable and realizes that any fanciful, deceptive responses are likely to be received with skepticism, the interviewee is more likely to be honest and straightforward with the interviewer.

Kinsey found knowledge of the subject matter to be an important component in rapport. "The background of knowledge which the interviewer has is of great importance in establishing rapport with his subjects. The importance of this cannot be over-emphasized. An [interviewee] is inevitably hesitant to discuss things which seem to be both outside of the experience of the interviewer and beyond his knowledge" (161, p. 60).

It is necessary to emphasize the imperative significance of knowledge, since among social workers an anti-intellectual derogation of the importance of knowledge is prevalent. The profession has emphasized "feeling and doing" rather than "knowing and thinking." Good interviewing is impossible, however, without a considerable amount of knowing and thinking. In public-opinion interviewing or in research interviewing, the public opinion staff or the research staff has thoroughly analyzed the relevant knowledge and has formulated a series of relevant questions and probes. The social work interviewer, however, has to be his own staff person, formulating his own appropriate, relevant questions and responses as he experiences the interview unfolding. He translates his hypothesis into an interview outline and into specific questions. Knowledge provides each interviewer with his own interview guide, a cognitive map of the area to be covered.

As I read typescripts of interviews, listen to tapes, and observe interviews, both role-played and real, I am impressed that frequently an interviewer fails for lack of knowledge rather than lack of the proper attitude. The proper attitude is frequently manifested —a basic decency, compassion, acceptance, respect. But the interviewer does not know enough about the particular subject matter which is the concern of the interview to ask the perceptive questions, to make sense of what he is hearing, to know what facets of the problem should be explored, to know the normative stresses the problem situation creates for people and the recurrent adaptations people have developed in responding to such stresses. Not only is there a lack of knowledge to permit helping the client productively explore his situation, but there is a lack of knowledge for feedback. The interviewer often does not know enough to answer the client's implicit or explicit request for helpful information or advice.

Interviewer Response Problems

The interview encounter evokes many kinds of feelings in the interviewer, some of which tend to create problems. It is useful and important to call attention to such feelings.

Every interviewer tends to dislike some kinds of interviewees. Sometimes the dislike is based on countertransference. Negative feelings are activated because the interviewer associates the client with some significant person in his own past. The interviewer may be aware that he experiences antagonism or anxiety in the presence of the client, but he may not be aware of the source of these feelings.

Sometimes the dislike is based on prejudice and suggests a denial of the client's individuality. It involves a preconceived judgment about a group and attribution of the judgment to every member of the group. We are careful not to manifest the blatant, socially reprehensible prejudices. It is the small prejudices that create difficulty. We may be convinced, for instance, that a receding chin denotes a weak character or that failure to maintain eye contact implies shiftiness.

Sometimes the dislike is based on more objective considerations. Anybody tends to dislike the people who make satisfactory completion of his job more difficult. Some interviewees assist the interviewer in his work and make his job easier; some impede the interviewer and make his job more difficult. The good interviewee helps the interviewer feel competent and adequate.

Interviewers have a clear idea of the kinds of people they prefer to interview. The ideal interviewee generally possesses those attributes which make the interviewer's job easier and enhance his pleasure in a job well done. They tend to be people who are persistent, intelligent, articulate, nondefensive, psychologically open, anxiously introspective, and willing to accept blame. On the contrary, the interviewee who is erratic, inarticulate, passive, defensive, dogmatic, dependent, demanding, and who projects blame is generally disliked. People with limited pathology and maximum discomfort about their difficulty are preferred. The good interviewee is healthy enough to be able to use the interview productively and uncomfortable enough to be highly motivated to cooperate (134, 246, 249, 275). Here, liking is based on objective interviewee characteristics that make life less difficult for the interviewer, that pose less threat to the interviewer's self-esteem.

Most interviewers, in response to their professional responsibilities and obligations, make efforts to mobilize themselves to do a good job of interviewing with all interviewees. But with some interviewees more effort is required and there is a higher probability of failure. As might be expected, when facing a difficult client the interviewer often acts so as to cut the interview short (137, p. 242).

Obtaining intimate information regarding the client's life may be necessary in order to help him, and therefore the interviewer is entitled to enquire about such matters. However if the interviewer feels doubtful about his ability to help, he is robbed of the feeling that he is entitled to the information. Consequently, doubt about his capacity to help increases the interviewer's hesitancy to intrude into the client's personal life.

The same is true for particular items of information the agency asks the worker to obtain, but about which the worker himself has no conviction. It is hard to ask the client to discuss material which the interviewer does not think is necessary. For example, adoption workers in a denominational agency who are themselves agnostics may find it difficult to explore seriously the religious practices of adoptive applicants. They lack conviction that such information is significant. The introspective comments of a 26-year-old, white, female social worker assigned to a terminal cancer ward of a large city hospital provide another illustration.

As I review the tape of the interview, I am struck by how frequently I introduced a question or a comment with an essentially apologetic preface. At one point I said, "You probably don't see much sense in this question." Another time I said, "You might not want to answer this question," and again I said, "Would you mind if I asked you . . . ." I even went so far as to say at another point, "I am supposed to ask you . . . ."

I think it's because I am new to the agency and I have a feeling that there is nothing we can do. The fact that these people are dying is the overwhelming consideration, and I am not sure talking to them and getting them to talk to us serves any useful purpose.

Some interviewers are highly sensitive about the pain occasioned for the interviewee in asking about his failures and personal tragedies. "Inexperienced doctors or nurses sometimes give an injection so slowly and gently that instead of avoiding pain they cause it. Student social workers, too, are sometimes too gentle to probe into (or even to allow the client to probe into) sensitive areas and they offer reassurance or change the topic. The more honest of them will admit that, in truth, it was pain to themselves that they were anxious to avoid" (91, p. 45).

When under pressure of making decisions on many cases, the social work interviewer may fail to ask questions or to hear answers that are likely to make it more difficult to expedite the case decision. Jacobs (141) details this tendency among social workers in a public welfare department. Although information on relatives available to help was needed, workers recognized that relatives were rarely able or willing to help. If legally responsible relatives were acknowledged, they must be contacted; meanwhile the case decision must remain open. It made expediting the work load simpler if the worker failed to ask questions about relatives or did not listen to the answers, noting on the record there were no such relatives. The pressure of work can make a quick decision rather than the best assistance to the client the overriding influence upon interviewer behavior. An AFDC worker's comments show this effect.

I had a feeling of apprehension about asking how things had gone with Mrs. G. during the past week. I knew I had to ask, yet I was afraid of the answer. Aware that the situation had been precarious, I was afraid to find out that everything had fallen through. If she were having all sorts of problems, which I dimly suspected, I did not really want to know. Once I found out I would have to start working all over again putting Humpty Dumpty back together again. Just for once I wanted things to be nice and uncomplicated. As long as I did not ask and give Mrs. G. a chance to tell me, that's the way they were as far as I knew.

While one can confidently count on the interviewee's repeated efforts to present his concerns, if the interviewer consistently fails to listen the interviewee gives up. A tape-recorded study of mothers' interviews with pediatricians showed that "if the doctor fails repeatedly to heed her statements of some basic worry or of her main hopes and expectations from him, she may cease to try, as evidenced by the fact that she either becomes completely mute or reduces her answers to toneless 'hmms' and 'yeses' " (167, p. 864).

The interview encounter permits various satisfactions for the interviewer that do not contribute to the purpose of the interview. The interviewer can use her power and control of the interview to impress the client with her wide knowledge about, and experience with, the subject matter of the interview. This is a simple narcissistic pleasure. The power granted the interviewer, by virtue of her position, to ask questions about the client's life is generally used legitimately. However it might be used voyeuristically or to embarrass the interviewee or dominate him. The worker needs to be aware that her position can be exploited for these kinds of gratification.

The interviewee's explicit acknowledgment that an interview has been gratifying and helpful is a satisfying psychic reward for the interviewer, especially since objective evidence of interviewing competence is difficult to obtain. As expected, interviewers solicit such testimonials in many subtle ways. Beginning interviewers, particularly, need such reassurance to allay their own doubts about their performance. The interviewer may create a situation of reciprocal flattery or try to induce the client to like her by allying herself with the client against the agency, especially against those agency requirements about which she herself has doubts.

The interviewer responds positively to the client who offers professional satisfactions. A hospitalized 56-year-old male, recuperating from a serious operation, repeated to the worker something she said before the operation which had been very helpful in diminishing his anxiety. The worker notes her reaction as follows:

> His bringing this up surprised and touched me, that he had put this much stock in what I had said and that it was that close to him. It triggered in me feelings of tenderness, humility, and gratitude, and I suddenly felt much warmer toward him and closer to him.

Conversely, challenges to the interviewer's adequacy stimulate defensive responses. This is illustrated by the worker's introspective comments on the following interview:

Social worker in an institution for dependent and neglected
children talking with a 15-year-old boy about his contact
with the shop teacher, Mr. S.

CHARLES: Mr. S. is one of the best guys to go to with your problems. If you tell Mr. S. your problems, he works them out the best he can.

WORKER: He has many years of experience. I am feeling with him and showing that I share the same respect for Mr. S. I must admit that I felt a little envious of Mr. S.'s influence with the boy.

CHARLES: I think it's twenty-five years he's been a teacher. He puts himself in your position and, well, he thinks if he was in that situation what would he do and he gives you his advice.

WORKER: A lot of times what you'd want is not advice, though, but really to look into your situation so that you can make your own decisions. [My envy shows through in my response here. I wanted to show him that there were limits to what Mr. S. was capable of.]

This extract suggests that the interviewer also has his needs in the interview, satisfaction of which depends on the interviewee. A

worker's conception of the ideal client and the tendency to seek
and encourage continued contacts with such clients is an aspect of
the worker's attempt to ensure that such satisfactions will be available.

Social work interviews are concerned with the problems of
everyday living—marital interaction, parent-child problems, making a living and managing a budget, facing illness and death. Consequently, there is a great deal of interpenetration etween the
problems the interviewer encounters in his own life and those he
deals with on the job. What is discussed in the interview may re-
mind the interviewer of unresolved, or partially resolved, problems
in his personal life. If he feels discomfort about a certain problem,
an interviewer may be reluctant to pursue it even when the interviewee himself initiates discussion. He may also project onto the
interviewee his discomfort about a discussion.

*A 24-year-old disabled client, talking about his family's
reaction to his disability while he was growing up.*

MR. D.: They did not want the responsibility of a disabled person
in the house. There were always arguments over who was going
to put my shoes and socks on, which I couldn't do myself.
Things like that you know. It really hurt.

WORKER: How many brothers and sisters do you have?

The worker comments:

I was aware that I did not follow his lead about his strong feeling reaction to his experience. I demonstrated fright for what
was for me a painful subject. I heard echoes of my own family's
arguments about who was going to take turns in pushing the
wheelchair of a paralyzed grandmother.

As Sullivan says, when interviewers communicate a reluctance to
discuss some particular feeling or problem, "the records of their interviews are conspicuous for the fact that the people they see do
not seem to have lived in the particular area contaminated by that
distaste" (292, p. 69). For instance, the interviewer who has some

personal difficulty regarding expression of hostility is less likely to permit, or encourage, such expression on the part of the interviewee. Bandura obtained independent ratings from peers on interviewers' level of anxiety about hostility. Interviews were analyzed to determine how interviewers with high anxiety about hostility dealt with it. The results indicated that interviewers "who typically expressed their own hostility in direct forms and who displayed low need for approval were more likely to permit, and encourage, their patients' hostility than were therapists who expressed little direct hostility and who showed high approval seeking behavior" (11, p. 8). When the interviewer, out of his need to avoid this material, indicated disapproval or discouragement of expressions of hostility, the interviewee was likely to drop or change the topic. Interviewer deflection was accomplished in a number of ways (11):

Disapproval:
CLIENT: So I blew my top.
WORKER: Just for that you hit her?

Topical transition:
CLIENT: My mother annoys me.
WORKER: How old is your mother?

Silence:
CLIENT: I just dislike it at home so much at times.
WORKER: [Silence.]
CLIENT: So I just don't know what to do.

Ignoring hostility:
CLIENT: I lose my temper over his tardiness.
WORKER: What are the results of the tardiness?

Mislabeling hostile feelings as nonhostile:
CLIENT: When are you going to give me the results of those tests? I think I am entitled to know.
WORKER: You seem almost afraid to find out.

Conflict for the worker involves more than evocation of personal problems. Many social work situations call attention to a worker's unresolved position on moral or ethical questions. For instance, a young student in a public assistance agency is struggling to define his attitude toward a client's entitlement to a full public assistance budget when a man living in the house is contributing some support. He feels that the client is sufficiently deprived and should, in any case, get more than the official budget. He knows, however, that what is happening is in some respects illegal, and he is further troubled by the fear that another client, or prospective client, may be thereby denied some assistance because available public funds are limited. Ergo, a bothersome ethical conflict. The problem manifests itself in the interview by the interviewer's unwillingness to ask questions about significant areas of the client's functioning. He and the client become involved in a conspiracy to avoid any mention of the boyfriend or the use of the grant, since an honest discussion of these topics would break open the question of the additional support and would require some response to an unsettled ethical question. The interview, then, is full of strange gaps and abrupt transitions as both participants detour around "unthinkable" areas. The worker is not aware of the pattern until later when, listening to a tape of the interview, he says:

Mrs. M. gave a nervous laugh because the subject of Frank [the boyfriend] is a rather touchy one and we both kind of shy away from it.

I suddenly started asking about John [client's 7-year-old son]. Why did I start talking about John when I was thinking about Frank? I wanted to avoid Frank because of the bad vibes I got every time the interview headed in his direction.

Interviewers may falter, avoid areas, and fail to follow up many worrisome, debatable questions. The worker may have convictions about the desirability of some women's working but worries about the negative consequences for the children in the instance at hand. Torn between supporting the right of women to work and a feeling of responsibility to the children, the worker would rather not find

out too clearly that in this instance the children may, in fact, be reacting negatively to the experience. In the interview this area is
quickly glossed over with platitudes and solicitation of confirmation that things are going well, through the use of questions that
answer themselves.

Your children seem to enjoy the day-care center, don't they?

You haven't had any trouble with Gordy's going to the center,
have you?

Stanley seems to be all right since your working, isn't he?

Questions may remain unanswered and certain content unex-
plored because of fear that the attempt to introduce the material
will evoke hostility toward the interviewer. The interviewer may
be reluctant to confront an interviewee with inconsistencies in the
material she has shared, avoiding a possibly hostile reaction. But
beyond this there is a hesitancy to challenge even when the interviewee is obviously lying, because it suggests mistrust and disrespect. For many interviewers such a challenge seems like checking
up, demeaning to both interviewer and interviewee. This topic will
be discussed at greater length in chapter 6.

Experienced interviewers face some special hazards. Spontaneity
lessens after repeated interviews with different clients about the
same general problem, and there is a resulting increase in bore-
dom. It is hard to maintain the same level of attentiveness and interest after five years and a thousand interviews with as many unmarried mothers about their plans for the unborn child. There is
also a feeling of *déjà vu*, of having heard it all before, which makes
it difficult to separate each interviewee clearly in all her individuality. Clients tend to merge. The hopeful optimism of the enthu-
siastic beginner is likely to be gradually modified to a cautious
pessimism as the interviewer develops an appreciation of the limits
of his influence and skill.

Interview Dimensions

There are a number of special dimensions to the interview, and an interviewer's decisions about them tend to determine his characteristic style. Among the dimensions are:

1. Balance between interviewer control and interviewee control of interviews.
2. Balance between maximum and minimum interview structure.
3. Balance between activity and passivity in the interview.
4. Balance between bureaucratic and service orientations.

INTERVIEW CONTROL

Control does not imply coercion. Skillful control of the interview involves giving direction without restriction; it implies stimulation and guidance without bias or pressure. It involves a confident flexibility that permits granting the interviewee temporary complete control if this expedites a more efficient accomplishment of purpose. In general, "control" has negative connotations that are really not applicable here. In this context it more aptly means "Who is in charge here?"

Many different aspects of the interview are subject to control. They include the topics to be discussed, the sequence in which they are discussed, the focus within each topic, the level of emotionality with which the material is discussed, the person initiating the transition from one topic area to another.

The degree of interview control involves not only a technical decision but also a philosophical one. Those who feel that the needs and desires of the client have priority, that the client should have the right to determine the content and conduct of the interview, will opt for granting the interviewee the greatest measure of control. This group of interviewers believes that only the client knows where she wants to go and how to get there. Those who believe that the interviewer must serve the best interests of the client rather than the desires of the client, that acceding to the wishes of the interviewee in every instance is professionally irresponsible, would opt for greater control of the interview by the interviewer. This group of interviewers believes that the client knows where she wants to go but is not clear on how to proceed; the worker, once she knows where the client wants to go, can help her get there.

Control also implies a nonegalitarian relationship, which is antithetical to some interviewers' conception of the most desirable client–social worker relationship. In actuality, however, all professional relations are nonegalitarian. This does not suggest that the participants are unequal as people but only in terms of the specialized knowledge that brings them together. If the patient knew as much as the doctor, the student as much as the teacher, the client as much as the lawyer, there would be little need for the professional contact.

Even yielding control to the interviewee is a contravention of the interview as an egalitarian enterprise. The interviewer, in effect, asserts his dominant position, since only those who have control can grant it to another. A truly egalitarian relationship might well produce anxiety for the client. He looks to the worker to help him find some answers, to make available greater knowledge. He may feel he is denied support if the worker communicates the feeling that he is equally powerless. At the very least, the relationship is unequal because the worker has skills to help the client find the answers he cannot find by himself. In the most egalitarian professional relationship the worker remains first among equals, based on his superior knowledge of interview content and process.

The ultimate purpose for which control is exerted is important. If the interviewer is acting in accordance with professional dictates, she exerts control for the purpose of meeting the interviewee's needs. It is an action taken with an intent to be helpful and in response to the interviewer's best professional judgment as to what will be optimally helpful to the interviewee.

Following the client's lead is a defensible procedure if it derives from the interviewer's conscious recognition of how, and in what way, this lead might contribute to a productive interview. If the interviewer follows the client's lead because she herself has no real direction for the interview or in abrogation of her responsibility, the results are not as likely to be helpful.

The philosophical question which affects the decision on the balance of control accorded the participants in the interview can be discussed interminably, like all philosophical and value questions. However, from a technical point of view, one might note that conducting an interview is a complex procedure. The interviewer presumably has greater expertise in this matter than the interviewee. To ensure successful attainment of the interview's purpose, it may be necessary to grant the interviewer some degree of control of the process.

Control must be exercised lightly and flexibly if it is to ensure a productive interview. The following excerpt and worker's comments illustrate the shortcomings of too rigid an exercise of control:

A social worker in a home for the aged, interviewing an
82-year-old white woman.

MRS. A.: I fell on the bathroom floor on my back.

WORKER: Um-hum.

MRS. A.: And I hurt the end of my spine, and it's just gotten well this week.

WORKER: Well, I see. One of the purposes of this interview is to find out if the names of your correspondents or the people who visit you, if the names and addresses are the same or if they have changed. Do you have visitors often?

In retrospect the worker comments:

Listening to the tape, it was clear that my concern with the interview guide had been given overriding importance. I failed completely to respond to the poor woman, became extremely direct, and made an abrupt change of topic. I should have taken into consideration here Hamilton's suggestion that the essence of the interviewer's skill is to ask questions responsive to what the client is already saying. I could have said, "You have gone through a great deal. I hope you are feeling better now," or "It must have been pretty painful, and I am glad you are feeling better now." Something, anything to show I had been listening and had some feeling for her. I then could have gently gotten back to the principal purpose of the interview.

By virtue of her coming to the agency for help, the client has conceded some leadership responsibility to the interviewer. The interviewer must not only accept this responsibility, she is in fact held accountable for implementing it. If the interview is a failure, the fault is attributed to her. It is manifestly unfair to the interviewer to hold her responsible, and accountable, for interview outcome and at the same time deny her significant opportunity to determine the interaction. Furthermore, it appears that the interviewee herself appreciates skillful control of the interview by the interviewer. It is an indication of the interviewer's competence and increases the interviewee's confidence that the encounter will be productive rather than time wasted.

INTERVIEW STRUCTURE

The interviewer must decide what degree of interview structure she prefers. The degree of structuring indicates how explicit the interviewer is in explaining what is expected of each of the participants. A greater degree of structuring implies that the interviewer will state the ground rules for interaction, explaining to the interviewee what to expect during the course of the interviews. A lesser degree of structure suggests that the interviewer will say nothing about these matters but passively permit whatever is said to develop freely; here structure grows out of the interactional experience. The degree of structuring is related to the dimension of control, more explicit structuring being associated with greater interviewer control of the interaction.

The following is an example of minimal structure:

PATIENT: Where shall we begin?

THERAPIST: Wherever you feel like.

PATIENT: Is there anything in particular that you'd like me to talk about?

THERAPIST: No, I just want you to talk about anything.

The excerpt below is from an interview offering a moderate degree of structure. It is followed by the same interview as it might have been conducted by a worker who preferred minimal structure.

Interviewee: male, 23, white, lower class, Veterans Administration psychiatric outpatient clinic.

MR. K.: Well, I'm not sure. I have this leg pain, and they gave me all the examinations they could give me, but they don't find anything wrong. So I don't know. They said maybe it's just nerves and they sent me here. What am I supposed to do here?

WORKER: Well you can talk about anything that's bothering you. You know any troubles you are having?

MR. K.: Well, I'm not much of a talker.

WORKER: I'll be glad to listen to anything you care to bring up.

MR. K.: Well, I don't know.

WORKER: For instance, since you came to the Veterans Administration about your leg trouble, we can talk about that.

MR. K.: And what happens then—you just listen?

WORKER: Well, I listen, but I also try to help you get a clearer idea of the things that are bothering you. For instance, you said they thought it was nerves. What do you think?

The same interview, conducted by an interviewer who feels that structure should evolve primarily on the initiative of the client might have gone something like the following:

MR. K.: Well, I'm not sure. I have this leg pain, and they gave me all the examinations they could give me, but they don't find anything wrong. So I don't know. They said maybe it's just nerves and they sent me here. What am I supposed to do here?

WORKER: What would you like to do here?

MR. K.: I'm not sure.

WORKER: What ideas do you have?

MR. K.: I don't have any ideas, but I sure would like to get rid of the pain in the leg.

WORKER: How do you think we can help with that?

MR. K.: Well, they said it's nerves [pause].

WORKER: [Expectant silence.]

Preference for degree of structure is related to the interviewer's perception of himself in relationship to the interviewee in the interview situation. Here, as with regard to the control dimension, some feel that structuring violates the client's integrity and falsely presupposes that the interviewer knows best not only what needs to be done but how it should be done. However, the whole process of structuring, of instructing the interviewee on the nature of reciprocal role responsibilities and behavior, has the effect of increasing the interviewee's confidence in the interviewer. It is a demonstration of competence.

Control and structure reduce the ambiguity of the interview situation for the client. As a result of clear leadership from the interviewer and a clear sense of the ground rules, the client is less anxious. He knows better how he needs to act in fulfilling the role responsibilities of interviewee. Research relating levels of interviewee satisfaction with structure has shown that there is more satisfaction with interviews in "which the therapists' verbal activity is highly structured" (173, p. 185). When the interviewer did not make clear to the interviewee what was expected, the situation provoked anxiety and uncertainty for the interviewee. The client's response was to talk more but to be hesitant and cautious in her speech. The client talked more because she needed to search more widely for feedback from the interviewer to indicate that she was doing the right thing.

One of the principal conclusions from discussions with forty former AFDC clients about their experiences was their frequent confusion because of caseworkers' failure to structure explicitly the purpose of the interviews (179). When there was little structuring by the interviewer, clients expressed uncertainty about the purpose of the interview and about what they were supposed to do in the interview.

Schmidt (263) studied clients' responses to social workers' differences in communicating an interview structure. One structural element was selected for examination, namely, the purpose of the interview. Some workers clearly and explicitly structured the purpose of the interview and shared the statement of purpose with the client for her to accept or reject. Other workers made no mention of purpose. The workers who refrained from structuring confused their clients; the clients did not perceive what the workers had in mind. The expectation that the client would select a purpose was not fulfilled. As Schmidt notes:

One thing is clear. . . . A worker's silence on the subject of the interview's purpose in no case conveyed his actual intent to the client, namely that the focus and content of the interview should be shaped by what was then most important to the client. . . . It is sometimes assumed that when workers inject no direction, or make no attempt to formulate their own objectives, then clients are free to choose (or in some way indicate) how the sessions will be used. There appears to be some basis for questioning the validity of this assumption. Unless a client knows clearly how his worker views their respective roles in determining interview content and direction, he is not free to make a choice. (263, pp. 80–81)

An interview with very little structure is not likely to be anxiety provoking, however, if minimal structure is what the interviewee expects. Clemes had interviewers deliberately vary the degree of structure with which they conducted interviews (53). The interviewees were asked beforehand about the kind of interview they expected and then were tested for level of anxiety experienced during the interview. Compatibility with expectations, rather than level of structure, was the crucial variable relating to level of anxiety in the interview. Interviewees who expected little structure experienced low anxiety when that was what they encountered. Interviewees who expected considerable structure were not made anxious when they experienced it. The interviewees were most anxious when they encountered an interview that was contrary to their expectations.

ACTIVITY-PASSIVITY DIMENSION

Control and structure are related to a third important variable, the relative balance between activity and passivity of the interviewer. Preference for low control and limited structure suggests lower levels of activity by the social worker. The relationship between greater interviewer activity and greater interviewing directivity or control is confirmed in Mullen's study of social work interviewers (211).

The following is an example of an interviewer with low activity level:

PATIENT: [Clearing throat.] Do you think we are getting anywhere, doctor?

THERAPIST: What do you think?

PATIENT: First of all, today I'd like to ask, uh, if you have any evaluation to make of myself as a patient. Is, uh, there anything wrong with my, uh, attitude, conscious or unconscious, that I can possibly do something about? Uh, is, uh, has anything I said worked anytime as far as you know, uh, or have I been trying to get at the right thing so far?

THERAPIST: Well, uh, may I ask how you feel about this?

PATIENT: [Laughs.] That's what I expected.

Lower levels of worker activity increase ambiguity felt by the interviewee, which increases uncertainty and anxiety. This effect may help explain the results of Lennard and Bernstein's study of tape-recorded interviews. Low therapist activity was associated with patient dissatisfaction with communication (173, p. 107). "Dyads in which the therapists were most active showed the least signs of strain" (173, p. 114).

Heller and his associates had interviewers vary their behavior in some specific way (130). Interviewees' reaction to the variations were studied. Active-friendly interviewers were liked best and passive-hostile interviewers were liked least. Interviewer passivity, resulting in lack of communication and lack of orientation cues, was felt by the interviewee to be a punishing situation. In general, when measured by such factors as volume of interviewee verbalization, level of interviewee satisfaction, consistency of meeting interview appointments, and continuance in treatment, the more active therapists had a better showing than less active therapists.

As with other factors, the effects are not linear—more is not always better. Control, structure, and activity appear to have more favorable effects on the interview than abrogation of control, lack of structure, and passivity, but only up to a point. If the interviewer goes so far that the result is authoritarian domination and inflexibility, the interview is adversely affected. When the interviewer limits the freedom of the interviewee to introduce material, when he restricts the interviewee by asking specific questions requiring specific answers, when he forces the introduction of content without regard for the interviewee's preference, when he specifically excludes content of interest to the interviewee and specifically limits the range of the interviewee's response to any question, he carries control and structure beyond the point where it yields positive returns.

Optimally, choice of emphasis toward either end of these dimensions—control, structure, and activity level—should be determined by the content of the interview and by the needs of the particular interviewee at one or another point in the interview. Some interviewees might need more or less control, more or less structure, more or less interviewer activity. And the same interviewee may need more or less control, structure or activity at different points in the interview. In general, most interviewees might need more structure at the beginning of an interview, when they have not yet learned what is expected of them. When they are concerned with content that is familiar, when they are ready, willing, and able to discuss topics, they may need minimum interviewer control and activity. When the interview is concerned with highly subjective areas of content, maximum initiative might be transferred to the interviewee. Greater interviewer activity may be desirable at those points in the interview when the client is ambivalent about discussing significant material and needs encouragement to do so.

The interviewer thus needs to have considerable flexibility and a willingness and capacity to modulate these dimensions in terms of the client's needs and interview requirements. This is a heavy burden, since the interviewer has his own needs and works more (or less) comfortably with greater or lesser structure, control, and activity. In addition, the interviewer is anxious to conduct a good interview so as to receive the approval of the colleagues and superiors who, in his thoughts, share the interview room with him. When an interviewer feels most anxious about an interview, when it seems to be going nowhere, he is likely to become more active, extend a greater measure of control, and enforce a tighter structure in response to these pressures.

The need for control, structure, and activity varies with the interviewee's age, intelligence, and experience in the role. Children, mentally deficient clients, and clients who are seeing a social worker for the very first time may all warrant more structure, more control, and more activity on the part of the worker.

The purpose of the interview also influences the level of structure and control. The social study interview and the assessment interview require that certain content be covered. Consequently, such interviews may need to be directive. Situational factors may be determining. At times of crisis, when some emergency action needs to be taken, or when the interviewee is very upset, there may be need for more worker control and activity.

We have, then, a complex relationship between the needs of the two participants, individually and in interaction, in a particular situational context. An interviewer who finds high control and firm structure congenial to his mode of operation is likely to be successful in interviews with clients with similar predispositions. With a client who needs less control and a flexible structure, the skill of this interviewer may be shown by his ability to modify his approach to meet the client's needs. Recognizing that both parties bring preferences, the hallmark of the good interviewer is the extent to which he can relinquish his own preferences in favor of the client's. The axiom might be that the interviewer should provide the least amount of structure and exert the least amount of control and activity necessary to achieve the purpose of the interview.

In general, the research available suggests that social work clients respond to, and appreciate, clear structuring on the part of the worker and a moderate level of control and activity.

BUREAUCRACY-SERVICE DIMENSION

Yet another dimension, of a somewhat different nature, requires a decision from the interviewer and further determines his interview behavior. Most social workers conduct interviews as agency representatives in the course of implementing agency functions. The interviewers must take some stand along the continuum between total concern for the agency's administrative needs and concern for the client's needs. This is true particularly for the public welfare agencies, where case loads are high and the pressure of work is great. In such an agency, an extreme bureaucratic orientation in the intake interview would dictate an approach that was concerned with answering, as efficiently as possible, the question of client eligibility. Only content that contributed directly to the answer would be explored. Anything else would be discouraged as irrelevant. The agency requires rapid disposition of an application, one way or another, so that it can go on to additional pending applications and to the other applications that will be made tomorrow and the day after tomorrow. Unless the interviewer sticks to the necessary business, the system risks being overwhelmed. Content is therefore sharply focused, and worker control of the interview is high.

The bureaucratically oriented worker is concerned with procedures, is inclined toward a strict interpretation of agency regulations, and is sharply task focused. By contrast, the strongly client-oriented approach gives primacy to client-initiated content, whether it is directly related to the task of determining eligibility or not. Rules are liberally interpreted, and greater client control of the interview is granted.

The difference is between a task orientation and a person orientation, between giving priority to meeting the needs of the system or meeting the needs of the client (141, 205, 342). The following worker in a public assistance agency expresses a client-oriented approach to the intake interview:

I always try to avoid [placing a strong emphasis on eligibility] unless somebody really begins to give me a hard time. You have to point out to them that we have only so much time to work on this; this is what must be done. But I never throw it at them the first time. I know persons in this office who have a very small case load because they are so cold and abrupt to people that they make them withdraw. . . . In the first interview I have the feeling that this seems awfully cold and abrupt, just to get names and addresses and information and never listen to the real reason they have come in. I have heard workers on the phone say, "Now Mrs. Smith, just a minute. You listen to me. I want you to get this. One, two, three," and this is no exaggeration of their tone of voice. [She had affected a severe, sharp tone of voice.] To me that isn't the way to treat people, but it is more efficient.

A second worker expresses the bureaucratic orientation:

If someone wants to go into "My mother comes over and we fight," and "My husband I think is going out with this person," and "I think my child had this problem in school," they are not really pertinent to the intake. Many workers will sit two and a half, three hours in an intake [interview] and just listen to that crap. (342, p. 256)

Although such pressure for completing assigned work tasks is perhaps obvious and pressing in a public agency offering assistance to meet emergent needs, every social agency faces similar demands. Foster-home and adoptive applicants are made anxious by long delays in processing their applications. Court calendars set time limits for probation studies. Scheduled diagnostic conferences impose constraints on social studies in mental hospitals and clinics.

Agency scheduling and demands for completion of clearly defined tasks within time limits tend to determine workers' behavior in the interview. If the worker is applicant-service oriented, she will tend to take the time to explore each of the client's problems to the point where she is confident that she understands the client's needs. However, such an orientation lengthens the time she must allot to interviewing a client. If she persists in trying to implement such an orientation, she finds herself falling further and further behind in completing eligibility studies or social studies or intake interviews. She risks censure from the agency administration. A worker is thus under pressure to modify the applicant-service orientation to the interview in the direction of a case load–management orientation. This means that the worker approaches the interview with the idea of directing the interaction so as to permit her to make the necessary decisions in the most expeditious manner.

Cold and businesslike as this approach may sound, it often is in line with the client's own preference. The public assistance applicant wants to know as quickly as possible if he can get a check, the adoptive applicant wants to know as quickly as possible if he will be granted a child. The more precise and efficient the interview leading to a disposition of the request, the greater the satisfaction of many interviewees.

Interviewee Tasks and Preferences

The interviewer is only one half of the dyad and only partially determines the success or failure of the interview. The willingness and capacity of the interviewee to perform his role competently is also an important determinant. Although the interviewer takes responsibility for providing the psychological atmosphere in which a good relationship can be initiated, the interviewee has to have the capacity to engage in a relationship.

The role of interviewee does make some minimal demands. The person occupying the position has to have some capacity for communicating, some ability to translate feeling and thinking into words, and some ability to organize his communication. He has to be able to understand and respond to the intervention of the interviewer and to follow her leadership. The capable interviewee also derives satisfaction from successfully implementing the role. His sense of personal adequacy is increased.

In addition to motivation and capacity, the interviewee's perception of the situation is important. He acts in response to his perception rather than the "true" and objective situation. The worker can, in fact, be accepting, interested, understanding, and noncoercive. However, she may not be perceived in this way, much to her disappointment and chagrin. The interviewee's ability to perceive the interviewer's communication of the essential conditions of a relationship may be as important in the success of an interview as is the interviewer's ability to actually provide these conditions. In one study, interviewees who had been identified as being highly dogmatic by the Rokeach dogmatism scale had more difficulty perceiving interviewer expressions of desirable attitudes than did low-dogmatism interviewees in contact with the same interviewers (296).

Studies indicate that client-interviewees have their own image of the ideal interviewer: he does not engage in behavior that indicates a lack of respect for clients, such as being "aloof, insincere, in a hurry, interrupting, yawning, lacking warmth, being late for the interview; [clients] said they would not like the [interviewer] to do most of the talking but stated significantly more annoyance at the idea of his doing little of it" (228, p. 550). Clients show a preference for interviewers whose "actions suggest that they can help them *do* something about their problems" (225, p. 552). The interviewer's "warmth" was perceived as self-assurance, sensitivity, and competence (7, 245).

The interviewees' concern may be focused primarily on the interviewer's capacity and willingness to help them. Yet they are gratified when she acts in a manner that indicates personal interest and respect and when she takes the trouble to personalize even interviews that have a restricted, instrumental purpose (179).

A client discussing her experiences with welfare interviewers

She's supposed to ask, "How are you doing? What do you need? What can I do for you?" My investigator she is always in a rush. There's only two things she ever asks—"Where is your light bill?" and "Where is your rent receipt?" Then she rushes out.

An investigator like that has no appearance. There are a few good ones. Like a friend of mine, she has an investigator when he sees her on the street he stops and says "Hello!" He says "How are you? When did you see your mother last? How is your sister?" Now that's mighty fine of him. An investigator like that makes you feel good. It can't help making you feel good when someone talks to you like that.

Like, I had an investigator once—a man. If he came in and there were people around, he'd say, "Is there someplace where we can talk?" And then he'd go into another room with you and ask you how you were doing. But most of them they come in and tell you what to do. They treat you like a child; no, worse than that, they treat you like a doll, like a nothing. You have to beg and whine and it makes you feel—well, terrible. (316)

Another client describes his picture of the "good" social worker:

[One] who in your first acquaintance lets you know by his or her expression that he's in your home to be of service to you if possible; and to show trust because most people are trustworthy if one shows trust in them; to be able to understand reasonably well problems concerning the family as a whole; not to criticize but to analyze why a person or a family is in unfavorable cir-cumstances; to give helpful advice in a way that isn't demanding but that lets a person feel that it's his own idea; one who has a sincere desire to help people, feeling that it might have been her as well as they but for the grace of God; one who encourages you to go above the capabilities that you thought you possess; one who guides you and makes the way possible but insists that you do for yourself what you're capable of doing. (221)

Repeated interview reports from a group of clients in psycho-therapy indicated that they experienced the most satisfactory inter-view when the interviewer was "actively collaborative, genuinely warm, affectively expressive," and humanly involved, rather than when she displayed an impassive, detached, studied neutrality (217; see also 291). There is a preference for interviewers who share their own experiences when these are pertinent. It makes the interviewer less distant, more human, easier to identify with. Personal examples suggest that the worker can understand since she herself encountered similar experiences (179).

As might be expected, client preferences for interviewer characteristics tend to vary with the kinds of problems they bring. Grater found that interviewees with personal-social problems regarded the interviewer's affective characteristics (warmth, friendliness, kindness) as more important than cognitive skills (logic, knowledge, efficiency). Interviewees with primarily educational-vocational problems were more likely to prefer interviewers who demonstrated cognitive skills (113). It is likely, although there is no research available on this, that clients whose problems are primarily related to a deprived social environment would show initial preference for interviewers with strong political power who command access to jobs, housing, an increase in income.

Preference is also related to personality characteristics of the interviewee. Egalitarian interviewees prefer a client-centered, nondirective interviewer; the more authoritarian interviewees prefer a more directive, more structured interview approach (284).

One important factor determining the interviewee's behavior is the need to communicate a favorable image and to maintain self-esteem. A good relationship that offers acceptance and immunity from rejection tends to mitigate the need, but it still exists. Social work interviewees may feel they need to project an expedient as well as a favorable image. A welfare recipient expresses this feeling during a discussion at a community action center:

> Mrs. C. abruptly interrupted, "Who says being on welfare is not work! You've got to learn how to act just right when you go down for an interview for welfare." She stood up, unbuttoned her coat and rebuttoned it, skipping one button-hole so that the material bunched up and the hem hung unevenly. She hunched over, lowered her head and raised her eyes to make eye contact with the rest of the group and with a dramatically forlorn expression explained, "You've got to make sure to keep your head down and look sad and not speak up and all that." The group

laughed and Mrs. C. began to laugh with them. She added: "It takes real training to be on welfare. I don't mean to fake, that's not what I mean. I mean when you need welfare you still can't go in there and look too proud because you're liable to get a bad time. You know the people who have you fill out the forms expect you to look a certain way. Well sometimes it takes work to look that way." (343, p. 213)

In sum, then, both interviewer and interviewee bring their reference group, primary group, and biopsychosocial backgrounds to the interview. The influence of any specific variable brought to the interview is modified in the interaction. The interviewer's own feelings, preferences, and needs pose problems for effective interviewing. In addition, the interviewer has to make decisions regarding interview control, interview structure, level of activity, and the balance between bureaucratic and service needs. The interviewee, in turn, has his own tasks, preferences, and problematic needs in implementing his role.

Chapter 4

The Interview Process:
Introductory Phase

Each interview in a sequence of interviews is part of a process, a series of steps that, over time, implement the goal of the contact between agency and client. Each interview, however, viewed as a discrete unit in the series, itself embodies a process with a beginning, a middle, and an end. The interview process is the consciously implemented, dynamic movement through successive stages in accomplishing the purposes of the interview.

The sequential steps in the social work, problem-solving process —study, diagnosis, and treatment (or data collection, data assessment, and intervention)—are not clearly demarcated. Similarly, in a given interview the introductory-phase activities are not sharply differentiated from those of the middle or development phase, which in turn are not clearly demarcated from those of the closing or termination phase. Process is somewhat like a symphony. Although at any particular time one phase, one theme, may be dominant, the other steps in the process can be heard, muted, in the background. For the purpose of more explicit analysis, we will artificially separate the steps in the process and discuss each in turn.

The Path to the Interview

The interview begins before it starts. It begins before the two participants meet, in their thoughts and feelings as they move toward the actual encounter. The client's decision to contact the agency for an interview is often the result of a series of complex, interrelated decisions. The residuals of these decisions may affect the client's initial behavior in the interview.

The prospective client first has to recognize that she has a problem, one that she cannot resolve on her own. She may choose an informal, nonprofessional source of help, such as a friend or relative or the local bartender (190, 191). Some people have neither friends nor relatives in whom they can or would like to confide, or find that their friends and relatives have neither the competence nor the resources to help them. At this point the prospective client has to make another decision. Having decided she has a problem which she cannot resolve alone and having decided that the informal sources of help are either not available or not effective, she must turn to the more formal, professional channels for the help she needs and wants. She now must choose among the numerous professional resources that are available. The kinds of social, interpersonal problems that are brought to social agencies are brought, with even greater frequency, to family doctors, local clergy, etc. (117, 166). The prospective client who contacts the agency to schedule an interview has then made a decision which is the end result of a series of prior decisions, namely that she has a problem with which she wants the help of some professional person and has further identified the social agency as the source of such help.

For many social agency clients there are few options available, and consequently the decision-making chain is relatively simple and direct. Social agencies have a monopoly over important social resources needed, and wanted, by the client, and the need for contact with the agency is apparent. This situation is particularly true for the client needing financial assistance, but it is also somewhat true for the prospective client needing foster care, homemaker services, a child for adoption, or a maternity shelter.

The route to the agency is not mandatory, however. People borrow money from friends, relatives, and loan companies. They make informal arrangements for child care when they are working or hospitalized. They adopt children through independent channels and find jobs and housing on their own. Although situational imperatives may not make coming to an agency the only alternative, they limit free choice, that is, if the client wants to eat or meet other strong needs.

For another group of clients, coming to an agency is more clearly an imposed, involuntary choice. Abusive or neglectful parents may be ordered by the court to obtain agency service; the delinquent may be required to maintain such a contact.

In some instances the interviewee does not take the initiative to make the first contact. Rather, the agency represented by the interviewer makes contact with the client. "Outreach" programs and "aggressive" casework programs are examples of such agency efforts to initiate contact (222).

An interview scheduled after the prospective client has made the sequential decisions listed above is apt to be different from the interview which begins after only some, or none, of these decisions have been reached. The correctional client may appear for the interview as requested, but if he has not decided that he has a problem and wants the interviewer's help, it will be difficult to establish an understandable, mutually acceptable purpose for the interview.

The prospective client whose decision to come to the agency was forced by limited options is apt to be more resentful, initially, than the client who felt he made a voluntary choice.

In each instance, then, the interview is affected in some measure by the events preceding it. The start of each interview in a series is affected by what took place during the last interview and by the intervening experiences encountered by the client.

Motivations Related to
Interview Participation

Different paths to the interview suggest differences in levels of motivation to participate. Clients may even go beyond lack of motivation to positive resistance. They may see the agency as having no legitimate right to an interview with them and the scheduling of such an interview as an act of coercive authority (35, 127).

Initial motivation or lack of motivation is, however, a transient factor. While it is admittedly easier to get a successful interview started with an interviewee who is motivated to engage in the encounter, this is no guarantee of success. The client might lose his initial motivation during the course of the interview because of the way it progresses. Conversely, clients who come with very tenuous, limited motivation may, and often do, develop the motivation to participate because of what goes on in the interview. There is empirical confirmation of these observations. Successful outcomes have been reported for interviews in which the interviewee was initially an involuntary participant; other studies have failed to show a clear relationship between high initial motivation and outcome of therapy (246, 248, 276, 305).

A group of young female probationers who were "directed" to accept treatment by a family service agency showed a favorable outcome as compared with a randomly selected, untreated group of probationers. The report notes that "these data would seem to cast considerable doubt on the assumption that voluntary initiation of casework treatment is required for successful involvement of the client" (313, p. 572).

The consequences of compulsory referral for treatment were studied by Gallant and co-workers (98). Male alcoholics paroled from a state penitentiary were randomly assigned to either a voluntary or a compulsory treatment group. Those assigned to compulsory treatment were told that failure to attend even one weekly psychotherapy session at an alcoholism clinic over a six-month period would constitute a violation of parole. The voluntary group was required to attend only the first appointment, all subsequent appointments being voluntary. A follow-up study initiated a year after the first clinic visit indicated that the compulsory treatment group showed clearly superior performance in terms of abstinence from drink, subsequent arrest record, work record, and general social adjustment. While the results do not argue for the advantage of compulsory referral, they do clearly indicate that it may be followed by very good results in the treatment contact. Similar positive results were obtained by Margolis and his associates in a study of voluntary and compulsory referrals of probationers to psychotherapy (186).

These data suggest that initial motivation is neither a necessary requirement for a successful interview nor a guarantee of one. They emphasize the interviewer's responsibility to nurture whatever motivation the client brings and to develop motivation in those clients who come without it. Concern with motivation is a necessary and obligatory task of the interviewer. Motivation energizes behavior and gives an impetus to action in a particular direction. Motivation to participate cooperatively and collaboratively in the interview is the result of social and psychological forces that encourage the client toward cooperative-collaborative participation and social and psychological forces that make for opposition and resistance to such participation.

People will be motivated to participate in the interview when they anticipate that the inducements and incentives, the gains and the pleasures, will outweigh the penalties and the pains. The task of the agency and the individual interviewer is to initiate and conduct the interview so as to enhance and intensify the magnitude of factors that motivate the client to participate and to reduce the factors that result in opposition and resistance.

In general, motivation will be higher if psychological penalties are reduced by agency procedure and the interviewer's behavior. For instance, some stigma is associated with becoming an agency client, although it varies with the presenting problem. Studies establish this feeling very clearly for the clients of the public assistance agency (127). As one public assistance client noted, "The hardest part of [being on welfare] is getting up the nerve to go up to somebody and say 'I'm poor and I need help.' That's very hard to say and its real work to say it because no matter how you try to say it, it still seems to come out 'I'm no good' " (343, p. 213).

Marital problems and parent-child problems are still regarded by many as evidence of personal failure and inadequacy; somewhat less stigma is associated with services related to physical illness and disability. Consequently some of the prospective client's hesitancy to contact the agency is due to the stigma which he and others see attached to the role of social agency client. The sense of shame, guilt, and inadequacy which afflicts the prospective client may be manifested in the interview.

The psychological penalties that result when a prospective client defines herself as inadequate because she must seek help from a social service agency are reduced if the worker's attitude is one of respect for the individual. Fear of rejection by others because of inadequacy is reduced by an atmosphere of acceptance in the worker's approach. Fear of loss of autonomy and independence as the interviewee becomes dependent, in a measure, on the agency and interview is reduced by the worker's respecting the client's right of self-determination to the degree that this is possible and permissible. Fear that the community will learn of her problem and that she might be shamed and rejected as a consequence is reduced by the promise and actuality of confidentiality. Fear of self-exposure, of learning about the more unpleasant aspects of oneself, is reduced in the context of an accepting relationship. Thus the interviewer's behavior designed to establish a positive relationship also has the effect of increasing the client's motivation to participate by reducing the negative aspects associated with participation.

More positively, however, the extrinsic rewards and the intrinsic gratification in the interview contact itself are prime considerations motivating the client to participate in the interview. The more the interviewer can prove his utility to the client by helping him solve his problems and by providing a socially and emotionally satisfying experience, the greater the likelihood that the client's motivation will be enhanced. Our competence to help must be as great as our desire to be helpful.

The pull of hope and the pressure of discomfort are powerful complementary factors motivating the interviewee to cooperative participation. Cooperative participation is admittedly more difficult to achieve with some client groups than with others. Freud recognized that the treatment motivation of the poor may be less strong than that of the middle class since the life to which they return after giving up the comfort of their neurosis is less attractive than the life of fantasy. The drug addict needs to be convinced that the unexciting routine of daily existence is better than the euphoria of temporary blissful withdrawal, the hassle of getting the means to pay for the drugs, the cycle of arrest and release, and the probability of an early death.

Approaching the Interview

Having decided to come to an agency and having scheduled an interview, the prospective client prepares for the interview and rehearses it in his mind. Prospective clients talk to other clients, find out about agency procedures, what the social workers are like, what to say, what to avoid saying, how to present their story. A wealth of gossip about many of the social agencies is available to people living in neighborhoods where a high percentage of the people have had agency contacts.

Interviewing that takes place in a closed social system where prospective interviewees are in close contact with former and currently active interviewees faces a special hazard. There is an active informal communications network among the people in prisons, hospitals, schools, and institutions of every kind. A frequent item of information for sharing is the interview habits of the social work staff.

The interviewee may come prepared to manipulate the interviewer into a favorable response to his request. Clients who have some sophistication about the factors that determine the worker's decision about their request are likely to engage in managing the impressions received by the worker—as would anybody in a similar situation. For instance, many adoptive applicants have not only discussed with already adoptive parents how they should behave but may also have studied what the agency is looking for in books such as *Adopting a Child Today* by Jean R. Isaac. One section of the book is in effect a perceptive tip sheet on how to behave to ensure favorable assessment by the agency interviewer. The author advises a couple to use the pronoun "we" not "I," to confess to quarreling on occasion, confess that infertility posed a problem for adjustment but "then go on to say that they adjusted to the situation through talking the matter out with each other." Both should indicate that they are "happy in their jobs but the wife should not be too happy," seeking fulfillment in motherhood; they should present a picture of a "reasonably active social life and be active in community affairs—but not too active" so that they will have time for children, etc. The suggestions are presented as a practical guide to a couple seeking to convince the agency that they have the capacity for adoptive parenthood (140, pp. 6–24).

The interaction also begins before the two people meet, in terms of the events around scheduling and the immediate pre-interview situation. Prospective clients face frustration in trying to find the agency's listing in the telephone directory, in being shunted on the telephone from one person to another, and in having to repeat their request to a number of different people. This recurrent difficulty is confirmed in the following report:

A group of well-educated volunteers, competent in the use of the telephone and with easy access to it, tested the information system for us by calling agencies in a designated order, making standard, set inquiries. Many inquiries required a number of phone calls and much persistence before help was given. Many other inquiries led to a dead end. In fact, one-third of all attempts ended without conclusive answers or offers of help. The average request required 3.5 telephones calls and considerable time, thus reflecting agencies' specialized functions and rather narrow conceptions of their responsibilities. Agencies rendering one specific type of service often seem to know nothing about other fields of service, even related fields. In fact, even within a given field an agency may know little about services other than its own. (154, p. 48)

An initial irritating experience in scheduling an interview might cause the prospective client to develop a negative attitude that contaminates the beginning of the actual interview.

The client may come to the interview after having experienced a number of false tries because he was not certain which agency offered the service he required. A process of sorting goes on between clients with particular needs and agencies with particular services. Some sorting is accomplished by the agency's name—Family and Children's Services, Society for Prevention of Cruelty to Children, Traveler's Aid. Some is accomplished as a consequence of agency auspices—Catholic Social Service Bureau, Jewish Child Care Association. Some is achieved because an agency is located as a social service department in a particular hospital or a particular school. People make mistakes, of course. Sometimes the agency title or auspices or location does not clearly communicate the kinds of people and problems to which it offers services. When this happens, the referral procedure is a second screening device to direct the applicant to the proper agency.

The physical accessibility of the agency is a determinant of the client's attitude at the beginning of the interview. Many clients have to come long distances dragging fretful children with them in subways or buses, to centrally located agency offices. It is, therefore, understandable that some prospective clients resist scheduling interviews or begin the interviews physically exhausted and emotionally enervated. Some agencies have responded by decentralizing their operations, opening district offices close to the client group, often in storefront locations in the immediate neighborhood.

The location of the agency, its physical appearance, and its state of repair (or more often disrepair) say something to the client about the community's attitude toward the service and the client group. Very often, particularly for public welfare agencies, the building suggests that the service has low priority among community concerns and that, inferentially, the client group which the agency serves need not be given any great consideration. This is disheartening and depressing to the interviewee and reinforces the suppliant attitude which many clients bring to the agency.

Of more immediate impact and potential for carryover is the experience encountered at the agency, while the client waits for the interview to begin. In public welfare agencies, clients wait for long periods in noisy, unattractive reception rooms, sitting uncomfortably on crowded, hard benches. Even a half-hour delay may seem interminable to an anxious person, uncertain whether he will be granted the help he badly needs. When the interviewer and interviewee finally meet, it takes some time, and effort, to dissipate the frustration and resentment generated by the period of waiting. The interviewer may be successful in communicating a genuine feeling of respect. Nevertheless, his job is made more difficult by the need to counter the disrespect inherent in the agency procedure that results in people having to wait for an interview. Administrative problems, shortage of staff, and constant heavy intake may make delays inevitable and, beyond a certain point, irreducible. An attractive, comfortable waiting room with easy access to lavatories and with a friendly, understanding receptionist may help to get the interview off to a good beginning.

Interview Scheduling

Agency time schedules affect the beginning of the interview. The client who can be accommodated at a time when it is convenient for him is less apt to be resentful and hurried than the client who has to fight for time off from a job, with possible loss of pay. The availability of an evening or Saturday morning interview, although an imposition on the staff, may pay dividends in a more effective interview.

Promptness without undue rigidity in starting and ending not only is a necessary manifestation of courtesy and respect to interviewees but also permits participants in the interview to know clearly the time alloted for the work they have to do. It enables them to plan their work with some assurance of having a given block of time available.

Scheduling should allow for the fact that some interviews will run over the alloted time. It should also allow for some break so that the interviewer can catch his psychic breath. A pause between interviews allows time for clearing the mind, changing the mental scenery, making the transition. It permits the reverberations of the last interview to die away and the mental and emotional preparation for the next to occur. A loose schedule of interview time is thus far preferable to a tightly scheduled program which squeezes production. Fewer interviews may be conducted, but those that are completed will be better.

Respect for time is respect for the interviewer's time as well as the interviewee's. The worker might best resist a temptation to yield readily to a client's sudden demand for an emergency appointment, or to the intrusion of an aggressive client who wants an appointment at will. Courtesy and firmness as well as an explanation may be required. Holding an interview at a time when the interviewer is preoccupied and distracted with demands of other scheduled obligations would not, however, be giving the interviewee a good hearing. Flexible scheduling may be needed in response to unavoidable emergencies, but this does not warrant a masochism which invariably puts a client's need ahead of every other consideration.

If it is impossible to keep to the scheduled interview time and the interviewee has to wait, an explanation should be made and assurances offered that she will be seen within such and such a time. If she has waited a long time, it might be helpful to recognize explicitly with her at the beginning of the interview that she is likely to be annoyed for having been kept waiting.

Worker about client, female, 38, white, lower class, homemaker service.

> As she sat down, I said that I knew that she had been waiting for an hour and a half and she might be feeling sore and irritated. She sighed in a kind of resigned way and said she is used to waiting. It always happens and by now she is prepared for it. She brings along some knitting and this helps to pass the time. She showed me the knitting she brought in the interviewing room with her, and we discussed knitting for a while.

Interviewer Preparation
for the Interview

The interview begins for the interviewer when she prepares, in advance, in a general way for all the interviewees she will encounter in her office.

One aspect of preparation is the physical setting for the interview; it should optimize the possibility of undistorted communication and minimize the possibility of distraction. A comfortable but unobtrusive setting suggests that you are treating the interviewee as one might a respected acquaintance. Since an interview is not a social visit, however, the setting must also suggest a businesslike purposefulness. A quiet office with privacy is ideal. Chairs for all participants should be pleasant enough that people are not conscious of physical discomfort, which would be distracting, and yet not so comfortable that they are lulled into passivity. The temperature should be comfortable. There should be sufficient light that the participants can clearly see any nonverbal communication but not so much as to hurt the eyes. While privacy is desirable, isolation may not be, particularly in those instances where one of the participants is male and the other a young female. The intrusion of telephone calls is an inevitable hazard unless explicit instructions are given to hold all calls.

Fortunately, the human capacity for adaptation to a less than ideal environmental situation permits one to conduct interviews effectively under all sorts of adverse conditions. But it would be best to reduce the distractions imposed by environmental irritants.

If clients of an agency are likely to be accompanied by children, a playroom and toys should be available; otherwise the interview may be constantly interrupted by the child or disrupted by the mother's anxiety about what the child is getting into.

The physical distance which separates the participants should not be so great as to preclude the interviewer's reaching over and touching the interviewee if this should prove desirable. Distance might also make for difficulty in seeing subtle changes of expression. Nor should there be physical barriers to nonverbal communication. A desk between the interviewer and the interviewee means that half of the interviewee's body is nonobservable. Any gestures of the lower part of the body—tapping feet, knees clamped together, tensely clasped hands in the lap—are masked from view. However, some people need the limited protection from interviewer observation which the table or desk permits. They are made anxious if too much of themselves is accessible to observation.

A definite block of time needs to be cleared for the interview so that the interviewer can appear unhurried. A reasonably uncluttered desk helps confirm the impression that, in effect, the worker has cleared his desk so as to make his time and energy exclusively available to the client.

The esthetics of the interview room have significance for the interview. Mintz studied the effects of the esthetics of work surroundings. Over a period of three weeks, two interviewers met with subjects in an interview-like situation. They alternately used two different rooms for these meetings. One room was "pleasantly decorated and furnished to give the appearance of an attractive comfortable study." The other room was "arranged to appear as an unsightly storeroom in a disheveled unkempt state" (208, p. 459). Observational notes showed that in the second, ugly room the interviewers reacted with "monotony, fatigue, headaches, sleep, discontent, hostility and avoidance of the room. By contrast in the first 'beautiful' room they had feelings of comfort, pleasure, enjoyment, importance, energy and a desire to continue their activity" (208, p. 466). Pictures in the interview room should be neutral and calming in their effect. A picture of, for instance, Michelangelo's *Moses* is likely to excite guilt and anxiety, since it appears accusatory.

For many social workers, the reality of the physical interview setting is, however, often far from ideal.

The new professional social worker's home base is usually a district office. His desk is one of many on an open floor. There is little or no privacy. He is surrounded by other workers, welfare assistants, clerks and supervisors all crowded together with one desk adjoining another. Telephones are constantly ringing and there is a steady hum of conversation, typewriting and people moving from place to place. The office is not an environment in which a worker can think clearly and calmly about the complex and painful situations he faces and the fateful decisions he must sometimes make. There is no quiet place where one can go to think for a few moments or consult with colleagues. Interviewing clients, which occasionally takes place at the agency, is carried out in small open cubicles. There is no privacy. In sum the setting is not one usually conceived of as professional; in fact the environmental image is more industrial than professional. (312, p. 95)

Preparation for the interview involves more than concern with scheduling and with the physical setting of the encounter. It involves the personal and professional preparation of the interviewer himself for the experience. It involves a review of whatever material is available on the interviewee. There may be a voluminous record of previous contacts or only the face sheet obtained by the receptionist. In any case, no one appreciates being asked questions she has already answered for the agency. Ignorance of essential data that have been previously shared communicates a lack of interest. If the interviewer knows, as a result of such preparation, that the client is married and has three children of such and such ages, the interviewee's confidence in the concern and competence of the interviewer is increased.

Interviewer preparation involves some effort at anticipatory empathy, an effort by the interviewer to imagine she is in the place of the interviewee coming to the agency for help. What does it feel like to be in such a position? What might one be thinking about? What kind of interviewer would one like to meet if one had her problem? What kind of help would one hope was available? We often say that the interviewer should start where the client is. Following this precept requires considerable thought as to where the client is, or might be.

Preparation may involve doing some homework. The interviewer needs to know what information she needs, what purpose the information would serve if she obtained it, how it can be used to help the client. The interviewer needs to be aware of the premises which guide selection of information. This kind of preparation gives the interviewer a cognitive map of the area in which she will be traveling. It permits her to obtain a sense of the unity of the interview, a sense of its coherence. An interview without some such guidelines is more apt to be disorganized.

The problem may be a mother's concern about a child's bed-wetting. If the interviewer has not recently conducted any interviews concerned with enuresis, she might do well to read some of the recent literature on the cause and management of the problem. If the medical social worker is scheduled to see a patient who has had a serious heart attack, it may be helpful to review the literature on the psychosocial consequences of this. If the assertion of the interviewer's need for knowledge has validity, preparation for an interview does involve a mental review of what the social worker knows about the problem of concern to the client and a search of the relevant literature.

Preparation involves getting specific information that might be needed, the addresses and telephone numbers of places to which the interviewee might be referred, the forms that might be used (with the social worker having some assurance that she knows how to fill them out). It involves a review of the requirements and technicalities regarding procedures that might be discussed during the interview—applying for vocational rehabilitation, making a job referral, dealing with housing regulations, getting into a retirement home, applying for assistance.

The interviewer's preparation must involve a clear idea of what she hopes to accomplish in the interview. The worker needs to make the purpose of the interview explicit to herself before she can communicate her perception of this to the interviewee and before she can hope to establish a mutually acceptable purpose. Some thought must therefore be given to what the interviewee's purpose might be and how the worker's purpose and the interviewee's purpose, if they are likely to differ, can be made more congruent.

Preparation involves operationalizing and specifying the interview's purpose, translating objectives into the specific items that need to be covered. How, in general, can the purpose be achieved, what questions will need to be asked, what content will need to be covered, and what is the most desirable sequence with which such content might be introduced? The following preparatory introspective comments illustrate the process:

Worker: female, 22, mental retardation unit.

> The purpose of the interview was to get a clear picture of the re-action of the family to learning that Bobby was seriously re-tarded and not likely to change much. But that's a global sort of thing. I needed to know about reactions that related to specific aspects of their lives. I tried to list these in my mind as I drove out to the house—changes in Mrs. L.'s relationship to the other children, her changed perception of herself as a woman, the change in relationship between the siblings, changes in the mari-tal relationship, changes in the family's goals now that finances had to be allocated differently, changes in family routines and allocation of roles and tasks in the family. I wondered what their reaction was to learning about the retardation. Did they feel mad, sad, guilty, frustrated, inadequate? Were they relieved to at least know definitely what the situation was? What was their feeling about Bobby—ready to abandon him, so sorry for him that they wanted to make restitution by breaking their backs for him, sore at him for spoiling things? These were some of the things I thought about, some of the things I might ask about in the interview.

The interview guide is, of course, to be lightly and flexibly applied in the actual interview, modified in response to what the inter-viewee says and does. This does not, however, diminish the impor-tance of advance preparation. There is an important difference be-tween planning an interview and inflexible adherence to a routine.

Developing an interview guide requires some decision as to how much can be covered during a specific, allotted time period. Just as beginning teachers try to teach all they know in the first period, beginning interviewers are apt to plan to cover too much during any one interview. Whatever the ultimate goal of the contact, each interview must have a proximate, immediate purpose which is clearly defined and limited enough to be achievable within the time set for the usual interview.

Preparation involves a recognition and resolution of some of the anxieties that every interviewer brings, in a measure, to every interview: Will I like the interviewee? Will he like me? Will I be able to help him? Will I be able to understand him? Will I be able to handle the demands he might make? Will I conduct a good interview? What areas are likely to present the greatest difficulty for interview management? What kinds of feelings is the interview likely to arouse in me which may make for difficulty?

Preparation involves something more subtle as well—an effort to delinate who one is in this interview. The interviewer acts in response to different images of what he thinks is his appropriate role, in response to his image of the client. A public assistance worker might see herself as the guardian of public funds, protecting the community from unwarranted raids on the public treasury. Or she might see herself as representing the community's conscience in aiding the needy. The correctional social worker may see the delinquent as tough, bad, ruthless, and lacking in control, or as a deprived, pathetic child, a victim of a stressful home life. He may see the delinquent as needing control and punishment or needing love, nurturing, and protection (52, 110). The interviewer might see himself as an all-forgiving father confessor, as a crusader correcting social injustices, as a professional helper, neutrally and objectively assessing what is feasible in a situation, as a rescue worker snatching the child or dependent adult from disaster, as society's avenger, seeing that the deviant is brought into line, as an expert who subtly helps the client find the answers the worker knows are correct, as an impartial judge.

Clients also perceive the social work interviewer in a variety of different images—as a bleeding heart to be worked, as a lover to be seduced, as an ally against a hostile world and personal enemies, as a source of influence with access to establishment resources, as an antagonist to be outwitted or placated, as a source of help or absolution or punishment, as an authority figure representing society's sanctions, as a parent protector. The setting and auspices with which the interviewer is identified tend to define the client's selective image of him. The school social worker is apt to be regarded as a teacher; the social worker in the court setting tends to be perceived as authoritarian, the medical social worker in the hospital as a nurse and comforter, the child welfare worker as identified with children.

The fact is that we all have an image of ourselves. We have, indeed, a variety of images, each of which we regard as more or less appropriate for some specific situation. Preparation for an interview requires some self-explication of who we think we are and who we think we represent in this particular situation.

There may be different conceptions of the nature of the service to be provided. One adoptions intake worker may see her responsibility as selecting, out of the pool of applicants, those offering the most desirable qualifications. Another may see all applicants as acceptable and the interview as an opportunity of helping the applicant resolve any problems or ambivalence about adoption.

Preparation involves some thought about the nature of the service and the extent to which one may feel coerced into the scheduled interview. Just as there are degrees of voluntarism with which the client engages in the interview, there are kinds of interviews and kinds of interviewees that the worker more or less dislikes and others with which he is comfortable. If he had his choice, he would never engage in some interviews or interview certain groups of people. But he is obligated, coerced by his professional conscience, to conduct such interviews.

Preparation requires developing awareness of what we confidently, but unwarrantedly, presume to be true about the interviewee. One reason some questions are not asked in the interview and some essential areas not covered is that the interviewer presumes he knows the answers. Since we know many things about sick people, or delinquents, or older citizens, or unmarried mothers, we think we know them, as well, about this particular sick person or older citizen. As Mark Twain said, "It isn't what we don't know that gets us into trouble, it is what we know which is not so."

The ultimate significance of preparation for the success of the interview can be easily exaggerated, although it needs to be noted. Being prepared is not as good as not being prepared is bad, since not being prepared suggests to the interviewee that this is not of importance. Once the interview actually begins, the nature of the interaction takes precedence over any of these preparatory considerations.

But adequate preparation increases the interviewer's confidence, diminishes anxiety, and ensures a more positive start to the interaction. Since many routine problems to be encountered in the interview are thought out and resolved in advance, the interviewer's mind is freed to deal more adequately with unanticipated problems during the interview. Being at ease yourself, you are less likely to stimulate anxiety in the interviewee.

Every interview is likely to be difficult. The interviewer is asked to be a member of the cast in a play which is being written while it is being performed. It is said that the interview is analogous to learning to play the violin in public while composing the music being played.

Concern with preparation can, however, be excessive. As Oldfield suggests, the interviewee may be made "uneasy by his perception that the interviewer is trying to set him at his ease" (216, p. 56). The admonition is to try not to try too hard.

The Place of the Interview

The social agency office is only one of a number of possible places where the social interview can take place. Each setting has a different effect on the beginning of the interview, and each presents its special hazards. Social work interviews may take place, for example, in the home of the client, in hospital wards, on street corners, or in institutions.

Office interviews have the advantage of permitting control of the physical setting to provide the features that are desirable for interviewing. There is continuity and familiarity with the same place from interview to interview. The technology which assists the work of the interview is available there—telephones, forms, record data, etc.

The client's home as the interview setting furthers our diagnostic understanding of him and his situation. As a consequence, the interviewer is in a better position to respond empathically to what the client says. Family interaction *in vivo,* in the natural setting which shapes the client's daily life, and the expression of his individuality in the way he arranges his home are open to educated observation (16, 87, 295). Verbal descriptions are often misleading, and home visits have frequently resulted in changes in diagnostic thinking as the worker sees the home situation as it actually is rather than as it had been thought to be. They give the worker the opportunity "to supplement what people say, by seeing what they do" (222, p. 56).

The home visit offers the interviewer more opportunities for actually entering into the life of the interviewee as a participant and consequently being perceived as less of a stranger. Holding a crying baby, opening a stuck window, moving a heavy box, and having coffee together are the kinds of participating events encountered in home visits.

Clients may be gratified by a home visit, since it suggests that the interviewer is sufficiently interested to inconvenience herself to make the trip. However, the additional investment of working time which travel requires must be recognized as a disadvantage of home interviews.

The home visit may be somewhat threatening to the social worker. A measure of control is transferred from the interviewer to the interviewee who hosts the interview. The interviewee is in familiar, friendly territory; the interviewer is now in an unfamiliar setting. The interviewee controls seating arrangements and interruptions; she can temporarily move out of the interview psychologically, and physically, by making some household excuse for moving.

The interviewee can exercise a measure of self-protection by "arranged distractions" such as a radio or TV going at full volume, a warm welcome to neighbors who drop in, or vigorous rattling of pots and dishes which are washed during the interview. Since it is the interviewee's home, she has to take the initiative in turning down the radio or TV, although the interviewer can request this for the sake of the interview. Of course the interviewer can, somewhat more subtly, gradually lower her voice until the interviewee is prompted to turn down the radio in order to hear. Visitors often persistently intrude in the interview. The interviewer, having listened to their comments, equally persistently must direct all of her responses to the client.

During the home interview a woman may not be entirely free of competing role responsibilities as mother, wife, and homemaker. This multiple role assignment may lessen the woman's concentration on and concern with the interview, to its detriment.

Invitations to a cup of coffee or a meal, which social workers handle without difficulty in their personal lives, pose a problem for them as professionals. In accepting these simple gestures of good will, is one in danger of converting an interview into a purely social occasion? What effect will it have on the interaction?

A correctional social worker visiting a female probationer.

BARBARA: Could I give you a cup of coffee? God, I gotta have one!

WORKER: Well, uh [pause] yes, maybe I will have a cup.

The worker commented afterward:

> My first response to Barbara's question was the feeling that I had been caught off guard. For a brief second I was trying to recall the so-called professional "dos" and "don'ts." None came to mind! I then thought about the actual situation I was in and how the results of my response would add or detract from our already well established relationship. I felt that Barbara and I had established a strong relationship, and yet I knew she needed constant reassurance of acceptance. I sensed that my not accepting the coffee would seem as if I were not accepting her. I really did not want coffee because I had just had a cup at the office. However, *in this situation,* want it or not, professional or not, I felt it was best to accept.

The home visit, like the family-therapy session, poses the risk of having to respond to family conflict while it is being enacted. A public assistance social worker visits a 27-year-old white mother, receiving AFDC, about whom complaints of neglect and possible abuse have been made.

MRS. W.: [To her 3-year-old daughter who is saying "Want a cookie."] What? No, you don't need another cookie. [The child repeats her request.] I said no; you just had one. [In the background the child again says "Cookie."] No! [Again, "Cookie."] Don't open! [Child is saying "Open."] I said no. [Child still saying "Open."] No. [Again says "Open."] What did I say? [Child says "Mom." Mother takes object from child and the child cries.] There's your bedroom in there, young lady [angrily]. [Pause, child is crying very hard, mother gets up and takes child's arm.] Now pick up this stuff. [There is a great deal of noise and crying and scolding in the background.] You stay in there and play, unless you can behave yourself. [The child is whining.] Do you want to go to bed? [Harshly.] All right, in there and go to bed, because I'm not gonna listen to it. [Mother takes the child by the hand and takes her into the bedroom; the child is crying.] Stay there too. [Mother closes the bedroom door and leaves the child in the room, crying at the top of her lungs. Long pause.]

The worker comments:

The incident followed a discussion with Mrs. W. of an upsetting visit to another child in placement. Mrs. W.'s response to the child is affected by her anxiety and anger about this visit, but it also suggests the general unhealthy relationship between Mrs. W. and her daughter. The problem for me at this point in the interview was deciding what to do about the whole incident to which I had been a witness and about which I was developing some strong feelings. It was clear that Mrs. W. was harsh and rejecting and at the same time unhappy about the situation. Choking a little bit on it, I swallowed my growing dislike for Mrs. W., made a conscious deliberate effort to separate the person and the behavior, and decided to respond to Mrs. W.'s unhappiness.

When she came back into the room, after the long pause during which we both tried to pull ourselves together, I said something about it's being tough to be both a father and a mother to the children.

A home visit is sometimes regarded as regressive since it may feed into the client's inability to mobilize himself to come for an office interview. Accepting the opportunity of coming to the office is seen as a sign of responsibility and interested motivation.

Some interviewers feel uncomfortable about home visits because they suggest spying on the client. The sense of intrusion is intensified if the worker drops in without previously making arrangements by telephone or letter. Home visits, initiated without such advance preparation, may start with a greater measure of anxiety, suspicion, and resistance on the part of the interviewee. These initial responses are transitory in most cases. On the basis of experiences with both announced and unannounced home visits in an "aggressive" case work program, Henry says:

We have become increasingly convinced that unannounced visits to those families whom the referral source has not prepared not only are less disturbing to most of these clients but that sometimes they give the caseworker an opportunity to deal more effectively with the client's initial anxiety than is true when he is informed in advance of the worker's visit. (131, p. 131)

In scheduling an appointment time for a home visit, it is necessary to keep the client's home routines in mind. Visits early in the morning and late in the afternoon are inconvenient, since they interfere with meal preparation. Many older people have favorite radio or TV programs and therefore resent having visitors at certain hours.

Respect for the interviewee requires that the worker come on time for a scheduled home interview. This might necessitate checking how to get there, knowing the route to take by auto, bus, or subway, and starting out early enough to arrive on time. Social workers tend to schedule a series of home interviews when out in the field. Delays and longer-than-anticipated interviews frequently make adherence to the schedule difficult. It may be necessary for a worker to call, in order to let a client know that she is likely to be late. Sometimes the client may have forgotten the scheduled interview or needed to leave the house unexpectedly. In such instances it is advisable for the worker to leave a note that she has made the visit.

Interviews also take place in hospitals, in institutions and, as in the case of the Life Space Interview, in a variety of other settings. The Life Space Interview permits the clinical exploitation of life events as these events take place. Such interviews take place wherever the significant event occurs—in a cottage, at the waterfront, on the street corner (233, 304, 333).

When S., a thirteen-year-old youngster, was adamant in refusing to return to her group and marched up and down the institution's "campus," it was her [caseworker] who joined her in the march. The material handled during this time was not at all dissimilar to the content of their interviews; the child's feeling that she was too sick to be helped, that her rejection by the family was devastating and motivated these overwhelming feelings of hopelessness. When she marched past the gate, she said she could not control herself and not even the worker could control her. On the ensuing three-mile hike through neighboring towns and the final return to the grounds of the institution, the child received not only the demonstration of the worker's ability to control her, which diminished her feelings of anxiety, but also some insight into her current concern about her mother's illness and its relationship to the incident. (274, p. 322)

Interviewing patients in a hospital ward requires a knowledge of hospital routines, a recognition that such people have less energy for a standard-length interview, the ability to hear low voices and to talk understandably in a low voice.

In an institution or hospital ward it is difficult to keep confidential the fact that a person has seen the social worker. If the inmate's or patient's group derogates those who see a social worker, the prospective interviewee may hesitate to make an appointment or may be uncomfortable when the social worker comes to see him. Clients are explicitly aware that the interviewer has ties to other clients. If there is any feeling of possessive sibling rivalry about the interviewer, these observations outside the interview will reverberate in it.

In an institution, interviewer and interviewee are likely to meet and interact outside the context of the interview. They have a relationship in which they occupy other roles vis-à-vis each other. It is difficult to keep these out-of-interview experiences from intruding into the interview relationship. The interviewee may have seen and spoken to the interviewer on the grounds, on the ward, in the prison yard. As a consequence, even before the first interview contact, he may have developed some attitude toward the interviewer.

The social worker has probably been seen talking to and laughing with the executive director or the warden or the hospital administrator. His relationship with those who are responsible for running the institution or prison is thus firmly established. The interviewee brings this perception into the interview, and if he has any feeling about the establishment and its representatives, the feeling will affect his initial interview behavior. Particularly in correctional institutions and residential treatment centers there is apt to be strong identification with the inmate subculture in opposition to the administration.

Interview scheduling may be simpler in institutions, where the interviewee is an inmate or where patient time is at the disposal of the administration. In an institution an interview may be a welcome break in the boring, monotonous routine or a sanctioned short vacation from a job. These secondary gains help to make an interview a desirable event.

Some of the difficulties of interviewing in a prison setting are perceptively reviewed by Johnson.

Many interviewers, though they have been in an institutional setting for a number of years, are very little aware of what the inmate goes through simply in coping with the mechanics of arriving for the interview and returning to his assignment. The searching by guards, the wisecracks of guards and inmates, the annoying red tape, a long wait in a stuffy anteroom, possibly changing clothes, being late for a meal or missing a recreation period because of the interview—these and other small things may make the prisoner less than anxious for the interview and may bring him to it in a bad frame of mind—antagonistic and irritable.

The physical facilities for the interview itself are frequently poor, and undoubtedly affect the quality of the interview in many ways. For example, because of the internal routine of prisons, more often than not prisoners have a long wait in unpleasant surroundings prior to the interview. They may be sitting on benches in a stuffy hallway, subject to curious stares and deprecating remarks by passers-by. The talk among the men waiting for the psychiatrist or social worker frequently takes on a negativistic, cynical tone, probably a collective reaction against feelings of embarrassment and concern over contact with the "bug doctors," as all such professional workers are usually called. The writer has frequently overheard younger inmates affect an air of braggadocio upon leaving the interview, undoubtedly calculated to convince their cohorts that they are not a "bug" or a "rat" but, to the contrary, have put something over on the "doc." Such remarks can hardly be expected to put the waiting inmates in a receptive and constructive frame of mind for their interviews. . . .

The stigma of staff contacts for the inmate likewise should not be underrated. Many prison officers and a great majority of prisonors look upon the frequent visitor to the "bug doctor," to the front offices, to the chaplain, or to the social workers with considerable suspicion. (143, pp. 44–45)

The Interview Begins

There comes a point in time at last when the interview actually begins; interviewer and interviewee meet face to face and the flow of communication between them is initiated. It is helpful if the interviewer can greet the interviewee by name. She invites her in, goes through the familiar, social amenities—taking her coat, offering her a chair, and demonstrating her concern that she is reasonably comfortable. The interviewer gives the interviewee a chance to get settled—to compose herself, to absorb first impressions, to get her bearings, to catch her breath. She needs a little time to get used to the room and the interviewer.

The ritualistic noises we make at each other at the beginning of a contact have been technically labeled phatic communications. "How are you," "Nice day," "Howdy," "What do you say," "How does it go," all mean "I see you, I greet you, I acknowledge you, I am friendly."

It is helpful, particularly at the beginning and the end of the contact, to make general conversation rather than engage in an interview. At the beginning we are making the transition from the way people relate to each other in an everyday social relationship, to the formal interaction of the interview. At the end we are making the same transition in reverse—this time from formal interview interaction to the informality of an everyday social relationship.

During the initial conversation the roles of interviewer and interviewee have not yet been officially assumed and the rules which normally apply to conversational interaction are observed. Any event or situation which is widely shared may be the subject of this transitional period. The preliminary chit-chat may be about the weather, parking problems, cooking, baseball, or the high cost of living.

This socializing is not wasted time. It eases the client's transition from the familiar mode of conversational interaction into a new and unfamiliar role which demands responses for which he has little experience. The conversation has the additional and very important advantage of permitting the interviewee to become acquainted with and size up the interviewer as a person. This opportunity makes for a more comfortable start to the formal interview, which demands, by implication, that the client trust himself to the interviewer. Small talk establishes the interviewer's interest in the interviewee as a person and reinforces a sense of human mutuality as they discuss matters of common interest and concern.

If the transition to the interview is too abrupt, it may be disconcerting and throw the interviewee off balance, as the following hypothetical interview beginning suggests:

CLIENT: Where shall I hang my coat?

WORKER: Where do you want to hang it?

CLIENT: Where shall I sit?

WORKER: Does it make a difference to you?

However, too long a period of conversation robs time from the interview. It also tends to puzzle the interviewee and make him anxious. He recognizes that although the interview is a social situation, it is not a social visit. Prolonged conversation makes him wonder what the interviewer has in mind. Undue prolongation might be regarded as disrespect for the urgency of the problem the client brings.

Even in the initial informal social conversation, an effort should be made to indicate the direction of attention of the interview. The emphasis is on the interviewee's experience: "Did *you* have trouble getting the car started in this freezing weather?" "Did *you* have any difficulty finding the office?"

Smoking along with conversation may help to break the ice. It is for many people a familiar, comforting activity; it keeps one's hands occupied and permits pauses without awkwardness. Offering a cigarette, or granting permission to smoke, bridges the gap between strangers and is a simple gesture of hospitality. When both participants smoke, the shared activity reinforces a feeling of mutuality.

The opening interview gambit, which signals the end of the conversation and the beginning of the interview proper, should be a nonthreatening general question to which the interviewee is capable of responding easily and one that serves to develop the mutuality of interaction. "What do you want to see us about?" "What do you have in mind?" "What do you think we can do for you?" Words like "problem" and "service" in the opening questions are less neutral, are somewhat more technical, and may have negative connotations. "What's your problem?" may be resented. "How can we be of service?" may sound too formal.

A general, unstructured question grants the interviewee the decision on the content and manner in which she chooses to communicate. An opening question that can be fielded successfully encourages the interviewee's confidence in her ability to perform creditably in her role.

Subtle differences in the opening question may determine differences in the direction the interview takes. One might say "What brings you here?" or "Why have you come here?" or "What would you like from us?" The first puts the emphasis on a description of the trouble itself, the second on the explanation of the trouble, the third on the treatment. The first question, in itself, can be delivered to focus on three different concerns. "*What* brings you here?" focuses on the problem; "What brings *you* here?" focuses on the interviewee; "What brings you *here?*" focuses on the agency.

The opening question might be phrased so as to force greater specification in response: "Could you tell me what problems prompt you to see a social worker?" This question specifies that what brings the person are problems and that she is seeing a social worker.

The initial phase of the interview should clarify the purpose that will engage the participants during the course of the interview. The purpose needs to be of manageable proportions and should be stated in such a way that its achievement is objective and identifiable. Frequently the stated purpose of an interview is either far too ambitious or far too ambiguously stated. The following statements of interview purpose from social work interview protocols exemplify some of these difficulties:

My purpose in this interview was to become acquainted, to get to know Mrs. P.

During this interview I planned to help him with his anxieties.

The purpose of this contact was to get to understand the client's situation.

My visit with the client was to establish a relationship.

In contrast, the following statements of interview purpose are circumscribed and the objectives are definite. There is a greater probability that such purposes can be achieved and their achievement identified.

The purpose was to help the client more adequately budget both her time and her money.

To determine what service the client wanted from the agency.

The purpose was to help Art with his feelings about leaving the foster home.

My purpose was to establish Mr. Y.'s level of motivation for job placement and, if time permitted, to explore what type of work he felt he was suited for.

To determine the problems this family faced as a consequence of the mental retardation of their preschool-age son.

To obtain the information which would help the agency make a decision regarding future placement plans for Jenny.

To help Mrs. C. handle her discouragement about Joe's schoolwork.

The purpose was to obtain the needed information to make a decision on relicensing the foster home.

Not only should the purpose be clear to both participants, but they should also make every effort to formulate the purpose in operational terms. What specifically are they attempting to achieve by the meeting, what will be accomplished, what will be changed —arrange for housing, find a job, select parents for adoptive children, prepare a mother to place her child in day care, resolve ambivalence about an operation, help a child to stop truanting, arrange a maternity-home placement for an unwed mother? If the participants know clearly and unambiguously the definite operational purpose of the encounter, they can know when the purpose has been more or less achieved.

If the interview is being conducted at the initiative of the interviewer, she needs to make clear as early as possible what her purpose is. "I asked you to meet with me today because the teachers are having a difficult time with Robert." "I scheduled this interview because I would like to discuss with you a possible job for one of my clients." "I wanted to talk with you because Dr. ⸺ indicated you had some questions about your medicare entitlement."

In addition to stating her purpose, the interviewer must obtain some agreement on the part of the prospective interviewee that he wants to engage in an interview directed toward this purpose. In interviews with collaterals, and in advocacy interviews, the statement of purpose might also include the reason for choosing this particular interviewee for achieving the purpose. The statement should be simple and concise.

Interviewer: female, 23, white, school social worker.

I visited Tommy's second grade teacher. I said I had made this appointment because I should like to find out more about how

Tommy behaved in contact with other children. I said I thought that she had a good chance to observe this, since this was the second year she had had him in class, and I thought her observation could be helpful to us in getting to understand him better.

Special Aspects and Tasks

Certain aspects of the interview are more prominent in the introductory phase than in other phases. During the introductory phase the authority of the worker's position is more important than the personal-relationship authority, since the latter takes time to develop. The interviewee's uncertainty, unfamiliarity, and confusion are likely to be greater, and the interviewer may have to offer greater direction and structure at this point.

More attention also needs to be paid to the expressive aspects of interview interaction. It is at this point that the interviewee is apt to be most anxious and most uncomfortable with the newness of the situation. Affect is likely to be high not only with regard to the client's problem but also with regard to bringing the problem for agency help. Consequently the demands for encouragement, support, and empathetic understanding are likely to be greater in the early part of the interview. During the body of the interview there is relatively more concern with instrumental problem-solving activities.

The opening phase of the interview is likely to include open-ended, general questions. The interviewer is trying to find out what the situation is as seen by the interviewee. He does not have enough information to warrant asking specific questions or responding to details.

The form for the entire interview is that of a funnel—nondirective, open-ended questions early in the interview, more detailed explanation and discussion of specific areas of content later. The sequence with which material is introduced is an important aspect of planning interview strategy. In general, material at the beginning of the interview should be concerned with more impersonal, more recent, more familiar material having lower affective importance for the client. The movement over the course of the interview is from impersonal to more personal, from recent to developmental history, from the overtly conscious and familiar to content of less explicit awareness.

Because there is less actual as well as vicarious exposure to the role of social work interviewee as compared with, let us say, medical patient interviewee or legal client interviewee, many people come to the social work interview with ambiguous or erroneous expectations. Relatively few people have ever participated in a social work interview and few have seen or heard a social worker doing social work in a movie or on the radio or TV. The client is therefore not clear about what content is appropriate and relevant, who will take responsibility for introducing the content, the sequence in which participants will talk, or how long they will talk. In short, there are questions about who does what to whom and "who shall speak, how much, about what and when" (173, p. 154).

Because the interviewer is the expert on interviewing, the one who knows the regulative processes of the interviewing system and the rules of communication which are appropriate to the social work interview, it becomes his responsibility to teach these to the interviewee. This process of socialization to the role of interviewee is illustrated in the following extracts:

Client: male, 27, white, lower middle class, family service–marital counseling.

WORKER: Just a little while ago you were telling me about this argument you had with your wife about the way she spends the money and the trouble you two have in budgeting. How does it make you feel the way she spends the money?

MR. R.: You want me to tell you how I feel?

WORKER: Well, yeah. What happened is important, but how you feel about what happened is important too.

MR. R.: So I am supposed to say how I feel.

WORKER: Well, it would help to understand the situation.

Client: female, black, upper lower class, child guidance clinic.

MRS. E.: Well, I have been talking since I came in here but you haven't said hardly anything at all.

WORKER: [Laughs.] What did you want me to say?

MRS. E.: At least more than you have been saying. Am I supposed to do all the talking? Doesn't anything come back from you?

WORKER: Like what?

MRS. E.: Well, like if we are doing anything wrong and advice about what to do.

WORKER: I am not sure that advice would be much of a help.

MRS. E.: You don't give advice?

WORKER: Not in the way you mean it, no.

Client: female, 58, white, lower middle class, ward interview (client has been talking about results of recent blood tests).

MRS. P.: I never talked to a social worker before. Are these the kinds of things you want me to talk about, the kinds of things you talk with a social worker about?

WORKER: Yeah, sort of, any kinds of troubles, difficulties you have because, you know, because of the diabetes.

As part of the process of socialization, the worker is engaged in encouraging the development of some aspects of the client's role behavior as appropriate and discouraging others as inappropriate. Social chit-chat and overtures directed toward personalizing the relationship are discouraged, and a focus on the problems and expression of feelings is emphasized. The interviewee thus learns what content is relevant to the interview. The interviewee also learns some of the presuppositions of social work—that feelings are facts, that the past is structured in the present, that it is better to express feelings than to deny them, that behavior is purposive, that the interviewee generally makes some contribution to his problem situation, that ambivalence is ubiquitous.

The interviewee expects to use words much as he has habitually used them in communicating with other people—as a defense behind which to hide, as a means of maintaining distance between himself and others, as instruments in making a favorable presentation and impression. The interviewer expects the interviewee to use words as a bridge to communicate what he honestly thinks and feels.

Frequently the interviewer has in mind a relationship characterized by mutual participation and collaboration. The prototype is a near-peer relationship between two consenting adults. The client, on the other hand, might expect a guidance-cooperation relationship in which the more knowledgeable professional advises and the client cooperates by following the prescription. The prototype is more like the parent-child relationship.

Mayer and Timms interviewed lower-class clients regarding their experience at a family service agency (192, 193). For many, the worker's relative passivity, his reluctance to give advice, and his general orientation to the client's problem were disconcerting. The clients were unaware that "the worker's approach to problem solving was totally different from their own. The clients tacitly assumed that the workers shared their approach" (192, p. 30). They tended to explain the worker's interview behavior in terms of lack of interest, failure to understand, confusion as to how to proceed, or lack of power to help. Some explicit explanation of what the worker was about would have allowed the clients to understand better the situation in which they found themselves.

A limited number of both clients and workers from a variety of social agencies were intensively interviewed by Silverman regarding their respective experiences in the social work interviews (277). The clients, low-income blacks, felt that it was their obligation to inform the worker about their problems. The worker's obligation, in turn, was to "organize this information, explain what it means and tell the client what to do." One client said, "I thought if they found out what was wrong they would explain the situation to me. I thought they would tell me what will work and what is bugging me" (277, p. 627). The workers, however, were oriented to forming a "therapeutic alliance" with the clients so that the interview would be devoted to helping them solve their own problems. "The workers wanted the clients to learn through the interview experience that it is helpful to talk to somebody who understands and cares" (277, p. 632). The clients, on the other hand, distinguished between talking and helping. They saw talking as an expressive release but one that did not correct or ameliorate the situation for which they were seeking help. The differing conceptions held by worker and client of the way they would work together in the interview made a barrier to communication which was never explicitly discussed.

It might be argued that the social worker is correct in her view of what the interview can accomplish and how she can best help the client deal with his problems. The elementary fact is, however, that she owes the interviewee a clear explanation of her conception of what the interview is all about and also some help in learning to play his part in an interview organized in accordance with such expectations.

It is necessary to stress the importance of beginnings. There is a good deal of truth in the folk saying that well begun is half done. A good beginning starts the interaction spiral in a positive direction. It is easier to establish a good first impression than to reverse a bad one. First impressions are strong and persistent; later perceptions tend to be assimilated to earlier ones and to be consistent with them.

Interviewers tend to be involved in grating, a process of selective attention whereby the perceiver attends to an increasingly narrow range of stimuli as the sequence of perceptual activity proceeds from initial to final stages. The kind of information to which the interviewer has greatest selective sensitivity is apt to be that which tends to confirm the direction of the earliest established, tentatively formulated decision.

The importance and pervasiveness of the initial impression are substantiated in a study of its impact on diagnostic assessment. Psychiatrists were asked to view movies of actual interviews. At the end of the first three minutes the movie was interrupted, and each psychiatrist was asked to tape-record his impressions up to that point. Showing of the interview was then continued and a diagnostic assessment was made at the end. In a very high percentage of cases, assessment at the end of the interview agreed with the assessment made after three minutes (257).

Summary

Many decisions need to be made and much happens before the interview starts which affect how the interview will begin. The nature of the problem, the motivation regarding help, the physical and psychological accessibility of the agency, and the nature of expectations influence the course of the scheduled interview. Interviewer preparation involves both physical and psychological considerations. Both the office and the home present special advantages and problems for interviewing. The beginning phase of the interview is of special importance. Supportive and socialization responsibilities of the interviewer are prominent in this phase.

Chapter 5

~·~

The Interview Process:
Developmental Phase

The introductory phase of the interview is concerned with getting acquainted, initiating the interview process, deciding on some mutually acceptable purpose for the interview. The next step in the process, the main body of the interview, is concerned with accomplishing the agreed-upon purpose. Content is focused and the sequence of actions is guided toward the goal.

The interviewer has to employ his technical skill to move the interaction toward achievement of interview purpose while at the same time he intervenes in other ways to maintain the ad hoc social system resulting from the coming together of the participants. He has to keep the emotional interaction comfortable and satisfying and to establish and maintain a positive relationship.

In achieving these instrumental and expressive tasks the interviewer faces a number of problems which we will discuss in turn. He must help the interviewee to talk about the broad *range* of concerns that are relevant to the achievement of interview purposes, help the interviewee to discuss some of this content in greater emotional *depth*, and make *transitions* when it is necessary to move the interview from one content area to another.

Range

One of the principal difficulties encountered during the main body of the interview is to stimulate the interviewee to discuss freely all the relevant aspects of the problem for which he wants agency service. The interviewer needs to help the interviewee to cover adequately the range of material which might be pertinent to the problem-solving process. In appraising what needs to be covered, the interviewer again needs an expert knowledge of the particular social problem involved.

For any one interview, range and depth are antithetical. If the interview covers a lot of territory, it cannot deal with any one question in depth. If sharply focused on one area, it may sacrifice a discussion of other pertinent topics. The interviewer needs to plan the strategy of each interview to balance range and depth in achieving the purpose of the interview.

The interviewer may employ a variety of techniques to encourage the client to talk and to maintain the flow of communication. The following techniques will be presented for discussion: expressions of understanding and interest, reflection, clarification and interpretation, summary or recapitulation, and questioning.

EXPRESSIONS OF INTEREST

The simplest techniques to encourage communication are the various expressions of interest in, and attentiveness to, what the interviewee is saying: "uh-huh," "hmm," "I see," "go on," "yes," "good," "that's interesting," "I understand," or a nonvocal head-nodding in response to the interviewee.

By rewarding the interviewee with such proofs of our interest and attention, we encourage her to continue sharing with us. Certainly the continued absence of any response on the part of the interviewer actively discourages continuation of communication. Studies of verbal conditioning (330) indicate that nodding, smiling, leaning forward, and saying "mm-mmm" all act as verbal reinforcement, conditioning the interviewee to continue to talk about whatever topic is currently under discussion.

The recurrent nonverbal vocalizations, such as "uh-huh" and "hmm," are neutral, ambiguous responses. They tell the interviewee little or nothing about the interviewer's reactions other than that she is interested, attentive, and acknowledging what the interviewee is saying. The responses of "yes," "go on," "I see," "I understand" also are ambiguously encouraging. "Good" and "that's interesting," on the other hand, suggest more explicitly that the interviewee should continue focusing on the kinds of content she has been discussing.

These responses also are delaying tactics. They keep the interviewee talking and give the interviewer the opportunity to build up a picture of the situation. The responses permit the interviewer to refrain from committing himself before she knows enough to decide what is best to do, yet suggest that the interviewer is with the interviewee and is not ignoring her. Shepard and Lee recapitulate some additional functions served by "hmm-hmm," as follows:

[Hmm-hmming] allows the patient to hear the sound of the therapist's voice; allows the therapist to hear the sound of his own voice; provides the therapist with a feeling of usefulness; provides the therapist with an outlet for stored-up energy; makes the therapist sound non-committal and therefore extremely professional. . . . When the patient hears 'hhmmnn' he knows for certain that he is in therapy and getting something for his money. (273, p. 65)

These interventions are one step beyond an expectant and receptive silence. They are somewhat selective, whereas silence is indiscriminate. They emphasize a response to some content, highlighting and encouraging elaboration of the material to which there is an "uh-huh" response.

REFLECTION

The reflective comment indicates that one is ready and willing to hear more about a particular topic. But the choice of word or phrase which is reflected indicates to the interviewee what the interviewer thinks is important and what he wants to hear more about. The fact that the interviewer has selected this item rather than others to which he failed to react indicates that the interviewer understands the significance of this content. His echoing response suggests "Yes, this is important, and I would like you to continue." Sometimes the reflection is a simple echo of a word or a phrase.

MRS. L.: It seems like he always wanted me to work, so when I had kids and quit, he was disappointed.

WORKER: Disappointed.

GEORGE: All the kids were together on this when we decided about breaking into the store.

WORKER: Breaking into the store.

Sometimes the reflection is a selective restatement. From a number of different things the interviewee has just said, the interviewer selects a particular phrase for reflection. In doing so, he does not repeat exactly what the interviewee has said but some accurate approximation.

MRS. W.: We were all right until my husband deserted. We could have made it. He worked pretty steadily. But since he took off, seems that things just fall apart.

WORKER: Since he left, it's been much harder.

Reflective responses are formulated as statements, not as questions. The reflecting statement is affectively neutral, indicating neither approval or disapproval. The interviewee's thinking or feeling should be reflected as much as possible in his own words.

One danger in the use of reflecting techniques is that it may lead to finishing the interviewee's thoughts for him. Instead of reflecting accurately and without distortion, we add some gratuitous interpretive comment without intending to.

CLARIFICATION AND INTERPRETATION

Clarification and interpretation go a step beyond mechanical reflection and selective restatement. Clarification mirrors what the interviewee has said but translates it into more familiar language so that it can be more clearly understood; it amplifies without falsifying. Clarification involves helping the client restructure his perceptual field. Unlike interpretation, in clarification all the elements of such restructuring are already within the interviewee's level of awareness. Clarification is often concerned with distinguishing subjective reality from objective reality and with presenting various alternatives for consideration, with a delineation of the consequences of different choices. The dominant note is cognitive understanding.

Interpretation makes explicit that which the interviewee had communicated at such a low level of awareness that he was not aware he said it. It is often a latent affective message translated into words. Fromm-Reichmann defines interpretation as the translation of the "manifestations of that which is barred from awareness into the language of consciousness." The dominant note is emotional understanding.

Interpretive statements should be offered very tentatively. They have the greatest probability for acceptance if they result from a collaborative effort in which the interviewee has actively participated. If this is the case, they should have interviewee antecedents: "Am I to understand that you mean. . . ." "Are you telling me that. . . ." "Did I hear you to say that. . . ." "Did you mean. . . ."

In the following instance an interpretation is offered without sufficient preparation. A correctional social worker is talking to a 32-year-old white inmate.

MR. R.: But I just go on resenting authority.

WORKER: Why do you resent authority?

MR. R.: I don't know. I can't answer that.

WORKER: Was your old man pretty tough on you when you were a kid?

MR. R.: No, he was pretty easy on me. That may be why I didn't like authority. My father never gave authority to me so why should I take it off of these people. [Short pause.]

In the following, the interviewer recognizes the danger of making interpretations for the interviewee. The client is a teen-age, single, pregnant white girl.

RUTH: Like, at a party I can talk to people, but inside I am afraid.

WORKER: Of what? [pause.] Maybe you're afraid that people won't like you?

RUTH: [Blowing her nose.] Yes, I guess so.

The worker comments:

I think I could have waited out a longer pause before giving an interpretation. Perhaps she might have stated this reason herself —or maybe another reason—if I had let her.

Every interpretive statement has an element of inference. The interviewer is establishing some connection between thoughts, feelings, and attitudes which previously had not been perceived as being related. It is often, in effect, a translation of "manifest behavior into its psychodynamic significance."

Every inference is more or less conjectural. The best interpretation is the one that has fewest components of conjecture, that is most clearly substantiated by evidence from the client's communications. It is what the client has almost said but has not yet said. The interviewer anticipates him by just a little.

SUMMARY OR RECAPITULATION

Partial or detailed summaries and recapitulations help to extend the range of communication. The interviewer briefly reviews what has been discussed and gives the interview its direction. A summary tends to pull together a section of the interview, make explicit what has been covered and, by virtue of this, indicate what has not been covered. It clears the agenda of items which have been adequately discussed so that attention can be devoted to items which have not. It also indicates to the interviewee that the interviewer has been listening attentively and knows what has been going on.

The interviewer, in moving into a summary or recapitulatory statement might say, "Let me make sure I understand you. As I hear you, your situation is like this," or "To sum up what we have been talking about . . ." or "During the past 10 minutes we have been discussing —— and it seems to me that you are saying. . . ." The interviewee is invited, at some point, to react to the summary to see if it accurately reflects his own view of what has been going on. The following excerpt illustrates such a summary:

You describe—I'll tell you how it sounds to me and you can correct me if I've misunderstood—you describe to me a little boy who was deserted by his mother and who was adopted. Things didn't go very well, especially between you and your adoptive mother. You felt pretty much rejected and alone. You felt thrown out to whoever would take you—that maybe you were the forgotten child. I get the picture of a really unhappy little boy.

QUESTIONS

The most frequently employed technique for encouraging the interviewee to communicate relevant material is the question. One might doubt the appropriateness of questioning as a technique in social work interviewing. Interaction based on a persistent question-answer format tends to confirm a kind of relationship between interviewer and interviewee which contradicts the co-operative–collaborative–mutually participative atmosphere that is most often helpful. Despite this danger, however, asking questions is often necessary in achieving the purpose of the interview. The social work interviewer might make an effort to keep questions to a minimum and at the same time develop greater skills in using alternative procedures for helping the interviewee maintain a free flow of communication.

Questions are asked not only to obtain information, not only to help the interviewee communicate more fully with himself as well as the interviewer, but also to help the client tell his story. Good questioning helps the interviewee to organize his presentation and ensures that he will include all the relevant material.

The nature of the response is shaped, in some measure, by the question asked and the way it is formulated. Questions also direct the focus of the interviewee's attention. They select for attention, from the many possibilities, those which are deemed maximally important and relevant. They should, however, be formulated so as to offer direction without unnecessary restriction on the response. Further, we might ask questions in a Socratic manner so that the interviewee, in answering the series of questions, informs himself of the difficulties or advantages of some course of action.

The attitude with which a question is asked is perhaps as important as the question itself. The context and spirit of the question should reflect the emotional tone of the interviewee at that moment. If the interviewee is depressed, the question should indicate a supportive understanding; if she is anxious, reassurance; if she is hostile, recognition and acceptance of her hostility. In each instance the interviewer demonstrates that she is paying attention not only to the content of what the interviewee is saying by asking a relevant, appropriate question but also to the feelings which accompany the interviewee's statements.

Male, 78, white, lower middle class, Old Age Assistance.

MR. Q.: At our age we have to depend on each other. As long as I'm around, she has somebody to depend on. But I don't know. . . .

WORKER: It worries you. [Pause.] How do you think your wife would manage if she survived you?

Male, 19, white, upper lower class, probation interview.

MR. D.: And my mother is another one. She gives me a stiff pain in the ass.

WORKER: She really makes you sore. What does she do that gets you so mad?

Where the subject matter is unfamiliar to the interviewee, it might be best to introduce the question by offering some essential information.

The mothers' group has about six to eight people, all in their early thirties, meeting for two hours every Wednesday evening to discuss the problem of how to live on a public welfare budget. What is your reaction to the idea of joining such a group?

A series of questions act as successive approximations, as progressive specifications. The successive questions should act as a funnel, moving from general to more specific aspects of the content being discussed. As discussion of one area is completed at the more specific end of the funnel, the new content area introduced for discussion should start with another general, open-ended question. The movement is from "Could you tell me what it is like for you to live on an AFDC budget?" to "What did you do about food for the children the last time you ran out of money before the next check was due?"

Question Dimensions. Questions may be classified in terms of a number of dimensions. One is the amount of freedom or restriction the question offers the interviewee. By focusing on specific aspects of the situation, the closed question restricts the scope of the answer which the interviewee can offer. The open question, on the other hand, gives the interviewee the responsibility, and opportunity, of selecting his answer from a larger number of possible responses. The interviewee has the opportunity of revealing his own subjective frame of reference and of selecting those elements in the situation which he regards as of greatest concern. Open-ended, nondirective questions also communicate clearly that the interviewee has considerable responsibility for, and freedom in, participating in the interview and determining interview content and direction.

"What brings you to the agency?" "What would you like to talk about?" "Where would you like to begin?" and "What seems to be bothering you?" are all relatively open-ended questions. "What seems to be bothering you about the children?" "What seems to be bothering you about what the doctor told you?" and "What seems to be bothering you about school?" are all more restricting questions that define the frame of reference for the content of the response.

The following series of questions moves from an open to a progressively more closed format. The setting is a child guidance or family service interview.

"Before this happened, what was your life like?"

"What was your life like as a child?"

"When you were growing up, how did you get along with your family?"

"When you were a child, how did you get along with your parents?"

"When you were a child, how did you get along with your mother?"

"When you were a child and you did something wrong, what did your mother do in disciplining you?"

"When you were a child and you got into fights with your brothers and sisters, how did your mother handle it?"

"When you were a child and you got into fights with your brothers and sisters, how did you feel about the way your mother handled the situation?"

Each question successively narrows the area of the interviewee's experience to which attention is directed. The first question is open to any period prior to the event which brought the client to the agency. The second question restricts the scope temporarily to childhood but permits the interviewee to select for discussion any sector of childhood experience—relationship with parents, with siblings, with peers, school experience, leisure time activities, attitude toward the community, economic situation at home, etc. The last questions direct attention to one particular relationship, during one time period, i.e., the mother-child relationship during child-hood, in a very specific context, disciplining in response to sibling conflict. The scope of answers solicited by the last questions is more narrow than that permitted by the first questions. The next to the last question calls for an objective description of the mother's handling of the situation. The last question calls for a subjective emotional response to the same situation.

The spontaneous, unrestricted response to a broad question yields the greatest amount of undirected material. Having helped the interviewee say what he wants and needs to communicate, through a few broad open questions, the interviewer then can use more restricted, closed questions to fill in details. Even later in the interview, as a new subject area is introduced for discussion, it is best to start with an open-ended question to give the interviewee the choice of approach to the new content.

The appropriateness of open or closed questions varies with the interviewee. Nondirective, open questions may be very appropriate with sophisticated interviewees who have a clear grasp of their role and the capacity to implement it. They need very little direction and structure from the interviewer to fulfill the purposes of the interview. Open questions impose heavy demands on the interviewee to select and organize his responses, demands that experienced interviewees can meet. The same kinds of questions may be inappropriate with interviewees who need direction and structure because they are not sure what is wanted or what they are supposed to be doing.

If the interviewee responds to an open-ended, nondirective question with a detailed account of some relevant significant aspect of his situation, the interviewer has no problem. However, the answer to a beginning question such as "Could you tell me about the situation which brings you to the agency?" may be "Well, I really don't know where to begin." The interviewer then faces the problem of helping the interviewee to tell his story. A more specific general question is required, such as "What has been troubling you recently?" or "What made you decide to come here?"

As is true for most interview techniques, the different kinds of question formulations are not, in themselves, good or bad. They are merely appropriate or inappropriate at different stages of the interview and at different stages with different kinds of interviewees.

Nondirective, open questions are generally more appropriate in the early part of an interview. At this point, when the interviewee knows everything about his situation and the interviewer knows nothing, maximum freedom should be extended to permit the interviewee the opportunity to talk about whatever is of concern to him. Later, as the interviewer develops some picture of the situation, she may need to ask more specific, closed questions to fill in significant omissions or to check her understanding of particular aspects of the situation.

Controlled, nondirective interventions are designed to motivate the respondent to communicate fully but to control the interaction by focusing it on a particular content, accomplishing these results without introduction of bias. "How did your children manifest concern about your disability?" The question is "controlled, nondirective." Although it clearly specifies the area which is the focus for response, it does not restrict the intervieweee in any way within the focus.

Leading and neutral questions are also differentiated on the dimension of freedom or restriction. Leading questions incorporate an expectation in the formulation of the question. The communicated expectation constrains the interviewee's freedom to respond and influences the nature of the response. Leading questions may influence the response not only by the nature of their formulation but also by intonation used. Intonation restricts, since it emphasizes the interviewer's choice of focus. Thus one can ask: "How do *you* feel about that now?" or "How do you *feel* about that now?" or "How do you feel about that *now?*" In each case, a different question is asked, and a direction has been given which prescribes the scope of the response.

Questions may further be classified in terms of the dimension of responsibility. Direct and indirect questions are differentiated in this way. Direct questions ask about the interviewee's own response to a situation, a response for which he takes responsibility. Indirect questions solicit a response for which responsibility is diffuse. The following questions are presented first in the direct and then in the indirect format:

How do you feel about your job?
What's the feeling in your unit about the job?

What's your feeling about applying for assistance?
How do you think most people feel about applying for assistance?

Questions are also differentiated by the level of abstraction to which they direct attention. A question such as "What hobbies do you have?" is somewhat more abstract than "What do you do in your leisure time?" "How do you discipline the children?" is more abstract than "Think back to the last time one of your children did something which made you mad. What did you do then?"

Questions may be classified in terms of antecedents. Those questions that derive from interviewee communications are said to have interviewee antecedents. Questions that derive from what the interviewer has said might be labeled questions with interviewer antecedents. Whenever possible and appropriate, once interaction has been initiated, the interviewer's questions or comments should derive from and respond to what the interviewee has said, his interests and preoccupations. Furthermore, questions and comments are most understandable when they use the interviewee's own words or phrases.

Questions can be classified in terms of differentiated focus. For example, they can focus on different time periods. The interviewer can ask about past events, current events, or future events. Questions can have the thinking, feeling, and behavior of the interviewee as their point of reference, or they can focus on the thinking and behavior of significant other persons related to the interviewee. "How does your husband feel about having a homemaker in the home?" (time: now; person focus: other; activity: feeling). "Once the children are placed in foster care, in what ways do you think your husband's feeling towards you might change?" (time: future; person focus: other; activity: thinking). "What was your feeling when you learned your wife had been hurt in the accident?" (time: past; person focus: interviewee; activity: feeling). "What do you think is the cause for your reluctance to go to school?" (time: present; person focus: interviewee; activity: thinking).

Questions may be differentiated in terms of whether they can be answered with a very brief response or require a more extended response. In general, closed questions can more frequently be answered in a few words than can open questions. Questions which start with "is," "did," "have," or "does" are more likely to permit a simple yes or no answer and a limited response yield. "Have arrangements been made for maternity-home care?" "Is he generally this way when his mother visits [the foster home]?" "Did you ever make application for adoption previously?" "Does the fact that you have been in prison make for difficulty in applying for a job?" Similar questions starting with "what" or "how" are likely to require more detailed communication of the interviewee's experience. "What arrangements have you made for maternity-home care?" "How does he generally behave when his mother visits?" "What contacts have you had with adoption agencies previously?" "What difficulties have you encountered in applying for a job as a result of your having been in prison?" Similarly, to avoid encouraging a yes or no answer, the formulation is not "Does he like his sister?" but "How does he get along with his sister?"; not "Did retirement from the job lessen your contact with people?" but "What contacts with people have you had since retiring from the job?"; not "Is it difficult for you to manage on this budget?" but "How have you managed on this budget?"

Probing. Probing by the interviewer ensures that significant but general statements are not accepted as such. It is not a cross-examination technique. It is rather a judicious explication which permits the interviewee and interviewer to see the situation in greater, more clarifying detail. If an adoptive applicant says that she loves children and gets pleasure from her contacts with them, the interviewer tries to fill out this statement through probing. What kind of contact has she had with children? Under what circumstances? What exactly did she do with them? What was pleasurable in the contact for her? What was difficult? What kinds of children did she like best? Which children did she find hardest to take? How did the children react to her? What were her feelings at the termination of contact? What initiative did she take to bring her in contact with children? What kinds of volunteer work does she do that involves children?

A school asks the protective agency to visit a mother whose children come to school hungry and inadequately dressed, and the mother says, "That's a damn dirty lie; my kids are as well taken care of as anybody's." The worker replies, "Perhaps you're right," but then goes on to probe the behavioral aspects of the mother's statement. "What did the kids eat yesterday?" "How regular is mealtime?" "Who takes responsibility for preparing the food and seeing that the children are fed?" "What do you consider a decent meal?" "What problems do you have in giving the children the kinds of meals you think are desirable?" "What kinds of cold-weather clothes do the children have; what kind of rainy-weather clothes?" "What difficulties do you have in getting proper clothes for the kids?"

The words "probe" and "probing" tend to evoke a negative reaction among social workers. The words suggest to them the very antithesis of the kind of emotional response to the client which they regard as proper and desirable. Probing implies an active interviewer and a passive interviewee who is involuntarily required to answer questions. The probed interviewee implies an object, valued as a source of answers to questions.

Despite the negative reactions which are likely to be invoked by the term, social work interviewers very frequently engage in what is technically termed probing. Questions are directed toward clarifying ambiguities, completing a picture of the client's situation, obtaining more detail on the interviewee's thinking and emotional response to the situation. All probes are designed to encourage the flow of relevant communication. While probe questions may often be circumscribed and direct, they do not have to be asked in a demanding manner or in a way which denies the interviewee the right to refuse a response.

Completion probes are directed toward neglected or inadequately covered content and call on the interviewee to elaborate and amplify details and to fill in omissions. They include such questions as "And then?" "What else can you think of about this?" "Does anything else come to mind?" "What happened then?" and "Could you spell that out a little more?".

Probes for clarification are designed to reduce ambiguities and conflicts in details; they help to further explain the situation. They include questions such as "Can you help me? I don't understand that." "Could you explain that a little more?" "Could you give me an example of that?" "What prompts you to say that?" "What do you mean by that?" "Could you tell me what you think leads you to feel this way?"

A psychiatric social worker discusses a mentally retarded 4-year-old girl with the mother.

WORKER: What problems did you have with her during this past year?

MRS. M.: No problems, but only that I feel she was too good a child, that there had to be something wrong.

WORKER: Well, when you say too good a child, could you give me some examples?

Some clarity probes permit further specification of response so that the interviewee, with the help of the interviewer, more clearly defines his situation. "When you think about the shoplifting incident, what feeling seems dominant, shame or guilt?" "Do you feel anxious about Roger [a mentally defective child] only when he is out in the street or when he is in the house as well?"

The use of completion probes suggests that the interviewer senses that the interviewee might say more if given additional encouragement. The use of clarity probes suggests that the interviewer is sensitive to the ambiguities, contradictions, and qualifications of the interviewee's response.

Woman, 44, white, lower middle class, AFDC because of husband's disability, vocational counseling service.

WORKER: How does your family feel about your going back to work?

MRS. H.: Well, the kids are all for it.

WORKER: All for it? [Clarity probe through reflecting.]

MRS. H.: Well, they think it would be good for me. I would get out and be less concerned about the house and have some interests. They know it will mean more cooperation on their part in the housekeeping. They say they are ready to do this.

WORKER: And your husband? [Completion probe—question was around family reactions, and interviewee had answered in terms of children only.]

Reaction probes focus on the interviewee's own thinking and feeling and serve to increase the emotional depth of interview content. "How did you react to it?" "What do you think about it?" "What are your own feelings when this happens?" "How did you feel while this was going on?"

Hypothetical probes pose hypothetical, but realistic, situations for reaction. "Suppose she did. . . ." "Suppose you had. . . ." "What do you think would happen if you said. . . ."

Worker in a correctional agency is talking to a 17-year-old white male.

BILL: They urged me to try it [shooting heroin] and so I thought, what the hell.

WORKER: Suppose you had refused. What do you think would have happened?

Errors in Question Formulation. Questioning is a much abused art. It appears to be very difficult for interviewers to ask a clear, unequivocal, understandable question and then be quiet long enough to give the interviewee an unhampered, uninterrupted opportunity to answer.

Questions need to be understandable, unambiguous, and short enough that the interviewee can remember what is being asked. Any question of more than two sentences is apt to be too long. One sentence may permissibly set the context for the question, or explain the reasons for it or prepare the interviewee for the question, or motivate him to answer it. The second sentence should be the question itself. After which the interviewer should stop and wait, expectantly listening for the response and comfortable in the period of silence between the question and the response.

Among the recurrent errors in question formulation are the following: the suggestive question, the yes-no question, the double question, the garbled question, the "why" question.

A frequent error is formulation of questions so as to suggest or encourage some particular answer. The formulation of a leading question is based on a premise by the interviewer of what the answer should be or on a strong expectation of what the answer might be. Leading questions make it difficult for the interviewee to respond freely. He has to oppose the interviewer's question-answer if he is offering a response that contradicts the anticipated answer implied in the question. Leading questions are not really questions at all, but answers disguised as questions. The interviewer is not asking for an answer but soliciting a confirmation.

A school social worker talks to a 7-year-old girl about her relationship to classmates:

WORKER: You play just with these two girls in the class. But you want more friends, don't you?

The worker's introspective comment follows:

As soon as I said, "But you want more friends, don't you?" I wished I hadn't. I felt I was putting words in Helen's mouth. It is true that she wants more friends, but I shouldn't be telling her; she should be telling me.

The context in which the question is framed, rather than the question formulation itself may suggest the interviewer's answer.

Do you think Roger and Ruth [client's preschool children] receive enough attention and care from your neighbor while you are working when she has three children of her own to take care of?

*Family service worker, talking to an 18-year-old girl
who has been dating an older, married man.*

But don't you think that your parents, with all their accumulated
years of experience in living, might be able to make a better,
more reasoned decision than you?

A leading question may influence the response on the basis of
the associations it seeks to evoke. "As a mother concerned about
the welfare of her child, do you think it would be good for him if
you go to work so soon after his birth?" "As a considerate son, do
you think your mother would be happy in an old-age home?" "Do
you, as a good husband and father, help your wife with the care of
the children?"

Sometimes selective emphasis suggests the answer. "Do you
really feel that your plans to keep the baby and find a job and
housing are realistic?"

Questions may prejudice a response by communicating the interviewer's annoyance. "What made you think that spanking Billy
was going to do any good?"

Sometimes, however, a question which suggests a response is a
result of the interviewer's desire to be helpful. Rather than impose
on the interviewee the burden of formulating his own answer, the
interviewer makes it less difficult by offering both the question and
the answer simultaneously.

The following are some question-answers taken from social work
interviews, with the more desirable neutral formulation of the
question offered:

Question-Answer Formulation	*Neutral Formulation*
If you leave Mark at the day-care center now, won't he act up again?	How do you think Mark will react to the day-care center now?
Won't Sue be the most difficult one to care for?	What difficulties do you think you might have with Sue?
Well I see you're making good progress. Don't you think so?	What progress do you think you are making?

I suppose Mrs. A. [the foster mother] treats all the kids the same?	How does Mrs. A. treat the different kids?
You feel pretty comfortable with younger children?	What's your reaction to younger children?

The dangers of such kinds of question formulation can be exaggerated. Leading questions can be and are appropriately employed by highly competent interviewers, and when used properly they do not result in a distortion of the interviewee's true response. Clients with well-crystallized points of view and with some self-assurance are not likely to be intimidated by the statement of interviewer preference embodied in a leading question (68, 69, 71). However, the research just cited was conducted with a general group of respondents. Social work interviewees are a particular group of respondents—particular in a sense that most of them want something from the agency. The power differential in the relationship is clearly in the interviewer's favor, and the interviewee is vulnerable. Consequently his readiness to disagree, to oppose, to contradict is likely to be somewhat more attenuated in this situation than it might be in other interview situations.

Leading questions are least appropriate with those interviewees who are anxious to please or "con" the interviewer, who are afraid to disagree with the interviewer, or who have little motivation to participate actively and responsibly in the interview. In these instances the interviewee will be ready and willing to parrot back whatever the interviewer suggests he expects to hear. For such interviewees, this is the least painful way of fulfilling what is required of them.

Leading questions can be useful in communicating the social worker's position. They consequently tend to ally the worker with that aspect of the client's ambivalence which favors the alternative supported by the directive question. The worker may deliberately select the leading question "Don't you think it might be better to consider other methods of discipline than refusing to talk to Sally?" rather than the more neutral "What methods of discipline would you consider, other than refusing to talk to Sally?" because she wants to emphasize that she favors an alternative procedure.

Beginning interviewers often make the mistake of formulating questions in a manner which permits a simple yes or no answer without any requirement for further, useful elaboration.

Yes-No Formulation	*Formulation Requiring Elaboration*
Do you feel that when you go home your visits with your family are successful?	Tell me about your visits with your family.
Did you have to miss work a great deal?	What about absenteeism on the job?
Do you think there are some advantages in having this operation?	What do you see as the advantages in having this operation?
Do you ever do anything together with your children?	What kinds of things do you and your children do together?

The beginning interviewer also frequently asks more than one question at the same time. Having heard his first question, the interviewer decides that it is not really what he wanted to ask. Before the client can begin to answer it, the interviewer asks a second question. The situation is confusing because the interviewer asks his question, then qualifies it, then explains it, then qualifies the explanation. By the time the interviewer is through nagging at the question, there is not much of it left. Frequently, the second question changes the frame of reference, or shifts the content, or asks something quite different from the first question. The interviewee then has the problem of deciding which of several questions he should answer. Given a choice, he often answers the easiest question, ignoring the others. The least difficult question to answer is often the least productive since it encounters the least emotional resistance. For the interviewer, multiple questions pose another hazard as well. Having asked a series of questions, he may forget that the original question was not answered. He may remember only that the question was asked and write it off his interview agenda. Often it is not clear which question has been answered.

WORKER: Are you managing better with your crutches, and how about your glasses, do they fit?

MR. W.: Oh my, yes.

The following are some examples of double questions asked during social work interviews.

Have you found the changes in customs from your country hard to deal with? How have you gone about adjusting to them?

Would you like to tell me a little bit about your thinking around adoption? What do you see yourselves adopting? I notice you mention two children or one child. You mentioned twins on the registration form?

What happened when you had a nervous breakdown? By the way, what do you mean by a nervous breakdown?

Are you at all concerned about making application at the Department of Welfare? Is there anything I can clear up for you?

Sometimes a single sentence can involve a double question because it offers more than one frame of reference for response.

Since coming home from the hospital what difficulties have you had in finding a job, or finding housing, or even getting back in with your friends?

Were you angry at what you were doing then or at the way you were treated then?

When the interviewer is unclear what he wants to ask, the message is more or less garbled. The interviewee would be justified in asking "What did you say?" or perhaps, less kindly, "Would you please get the marbles out of your mouth." The following are verbatim examples from tape-recorded social work interviews:

A worker discussing choice of substitute-care placement
with a 15-year-old girl at a child welfare agency.

We wouldn't want to, uh, move you, and if things, you didn't get
along there and it, uh, there were too many problems, you know,
then it would be a . . . then what would we do?

A worker discussing marriage planning with a 17-year-old
girl in a group foster home.

What kinds of thing do you think, uh, do you think a person
should be, like you know what kinds of things do you think a
person should be ready about before they get married? Like
what kinds of things about themselves should be ready?

A social worker in a divorce-court setting, interviewing
a 40-year-old male with regard to a possible reconciliation.

What do you think, what do you suppose she wants to do, like
why do you suppose she's acting the way she does?

The worker comments about this question as follows:

My response was uncertain to the point of being incoherent. I
felt something should be brought out and clarified, but I wasn't
sure what and so I stumbled around. I am not sure what point I
wanted to make—possibly something about his wife's deeper
motive for [sharing his infidelities with the children], to justify
herself or punish him, or erode the children's loyalty to him.
What? I guess I had several ideas in mind but wasn't clear
about how I wanted to develop this.

One kind of question that is used more frequently than it should
be is the "why" question. This is a very difficult kind of question
for the interviewee. It asks for a degree of insight and understanding which, if possessed by the interviewee in the first place, would
have obviated the necessity of coming to the agency. In asking
"why," we are requesting that the interviewee provide the insights
into his own behavior. But this discovery of explanation is often

one of the objectives of the therapeutic contact. The truth is, we often do not know "why."

Most people find it difficult to explain "why" they behave in the way they behave, particularly when the behavior is self-destructive and self-defeating. The "why" question increases their feelings of frustration, inadequacy, and defensiveness.

At best, "why" encourages a degree of falsification in which the interviewee becomes enmeshed. As rational people most interviewees feel a need to defend their rationality by devising a rational answer in response to the question—and one "why" question leads to another.

A school social worker, talking to an 8-year-old girl.

WORKER: What happens when you try to play with the other girls?

LIL: They say, "go away."

WORKER: They tell you to go away. Why do you think they say that?

LIL: 'Cause they don't want more people to play with.

WORKER: Why do you think they don't want *you* to play with them?

LIL: 'Cause they have too many friends, and I was just learning how to jump rope, and I can't jump good. I always hafta take an end. I never get to jump.

WORKER: Why do the other girls always make you take an end?

Psychiatric social worker in an institution for emotionally disturbed children, discussing attitudes toward institutional personnel with a 16-year-old boy.

WORKER: You just said you're not going to, uh, like anybody around here again.

WILLARD: I'm not [hostile tone of voice].

WORKER: Why do you feel that way?

WILLARD: I just feel that way.

WORKER: Have people disappointed you?

WILLARD: Nobody's disappointed me.

WORKER: Then why do you think you feel that way?

WILLARD: I just do [matter of factly].

The worker comments:

> I continue to try to get Willard to verbalize his reasons for not
> liking anyone. I make a serious assumption here, and probably
> an erroneous one. I assume that Willard understands, or at least
> is aware of, the dynamics of his behavior. I push him to reason
> on a cognitive level as to the origins of his feelings.

Instead of "why," it might be better to ask "what." "What" is easier for most people to answer than "why," which calls for self-anal-
ysis. "What" calls for explanatory description. Not "Why do you
have difficulty in telling your husband about the things he does
that annoy you?" but "What do you think would happen if you
told your husband about things he does that annoy you?" Not
"Why are you afraid of the medical examination?" but "What
scares you about the medical examination?" Not "Why didn't you
use contraceptives since you knew you might become pregnant?"
but "What prevented you from taking precautions so that you
would not become pregnant?"

Interview Depth

A second major problem frequently encountered during the developmental phase of the interview is depth. Having covered the general content areas of relevance to achieving the purposes of the interview, the participants have identified some particular areas that
need to be discussed at a more intense emotional level. The problem posed for the interviewer is to focus on a particular subject
and move vertically from a surface statement of the situation to the
more personal, emotional meaning of the content.

Depth refers not only to the intensity of feelings associated with events and people but also to the level of intimacy of such feelings. It encompasses those feelings which the interviewee regards as private and which are shared with some reluctance and resistance. In sharing this material, the interviewee feels a greater risk of self-revelation. Depth implies an affective response and a personal involvement with the content, as against impersonal detachment. Range is concerned with what happened; depth is concerned with how the interviewee feels about what happened.

The presumption is that "deeper" content is more valid content. This is a dubious assumption; it might be more correct to say that deeper content is different, rather than better. At some points in the interview it may be appropriate to explore the content at a more intense emotional level. At another point it may be entirely inappropriate.

The interviewee may differ from the interviewer in her definition of "intimate" material. Gordon gives a good example of this as applied to a social work situation.

A social worker was interviewing Puerto Ricans in New York to determine the need for Aid to Dependent Children. Three items of information were necessary to estimate the future budget requirements of certain social welfare agencies: whether the woman of the house was married, how many children she had, and the ages of the children. The social worker assumed that the best order of questioning would be as follows:
   a) Are you single, married, widowed, separated?
   b) (If ever married) How many children do you have?
   c) What are the ages of your children?
She had assumed that the first question should precede the second, because a woman would be embarrassed if she first answered she had three children and then was asked whether she was married. To avoid this embarrassment, it was assumed that the respondent with children would falsely report that she was married even if she were not. In this case, however, the interviewer's own cultural values prevented her from empathizing correctly with the respondent.

During a few exploratory interviews, the interviewer discovered that there was a large percentage of couples with children who were not legally married. However these couples did not have guilt feelings. If they lied about their marital state, it was usually to avoid embarrassing the interviewer. The longer the common-law couple had been in the United States, the more they were likely to lie about the basis of this experience.

The interviewer decided to reschedule the sequence and phrasing of questions as follows:
 a) How old is your oldest child? The next? The next? etc.
 b) Are you married, living common-law, or alone?
This order of questioning indicated to the respondent that the interviewer realized there was no necessary connection between having children and being legally married. If, in addition, the interviewer's attitude was not one of condemnation or shock, the respondent was assured that the interviewer "understood" the situation. (111, p. 47)

Various techniques have been developed to help the interviewee move from a superficial affective level to a more intense, more intimate level in discussing interview content. Encouraging the discussion of feelings by asking about or commenting on feelings is the simplest and most frequently employed technique for achieving depth. The "How do you feel about it?" response, which has almost become an identifying slogan of social workers, is a good example. Such questions or comments tend to focus the interviewee's attention on feelings and feeling contexts. They offer stimulus and invitation to discuss content at greater depth.

Female, 32, black, upper lower class, juvenile court.

 The mother had been describing at some length the experiences her son, 16, had with drugs. He had been recently arrested for possession and sale of heroin, and at this point the mother was detailing the arrest and the efforts she had made to obtain legal assistance.

WORKER: A lawyer is very important, and I am glad you were able to get such help. But what were your feelings when they told you that William was arrested?

Social work interviewers are sensitive to and quick to call attention to feelings.

Woman, 29, black, lower lower class, foster care agency.

MRS. Y.: So when the doctor said I needed the operation and I knew I had to go to the hospital, I thought what am I going to do with the kids? Who will take them, take care of them I mean, there's nobody. Half the people, like relatives, I know, far away, they can't come.

WORKER: You feel all alone.

In response, the interviewee shifted from the problem of child care to discussing her own feelings of fright at being alone and facing operation without the support of anybody close to her. The worker here responds not to the external details of the mother's problem but rather to the unexpressed feelings associated with it. The interviewer's comments on the emotional aspects of the situation encourage the interviewee to discuss them. The worker identifies the feelings, gives them recognition, and attempts to keep the interviewee's attention centered on her emotional responses.

A 30-year-old Mexican-American mother on public assistance, discussing her relationships with her children.

MRS. D.: And John more or less is inclined to favor Mary, and my mother-in-law favors the twins. Everybody favors the twins, and Mary. But then these two are left out. I guess I'm more or less inclined to favor Mary, too.

WORKER: What makes you feel this way?

MRS. D.: Well, we all love them the same. We buy them things, we buy them all nice things, but yet when that one's hurt or something, I just sort of ache more. I don't know why, is that selfish, or something? I don't know. I even feel guilty about that and maybe I'm doing wrong.

WORKER: You feel guilty?

MRS. D.: Yes, but as long as I try there's nothing wrong. Okay?

WORKER: I think so, but how do you mean wrong?

MRS. D.: Am I doing wrong because I favor Mary above the others? I don't try to favor her. Well, I think I have my own answer, really. But I hate to look at it sometimes.

WORKER: What's your own answer to what makes you feel this way about Mary?

Once the interviewee begins to discuss material with some intensity of affect, rewarding encouragement may help her to continue. "I know it is hard for you to talk about this, and it's a sign of your strength that you can discuss it"; "It must be painful for you to discuss this, and I admire your courage in making the effort." Part of what may be involved here is a process of modeling. The interviewer demonstrates that she is not afraid of feelings, is ready and willing to discuss feelings; she acts as a model for the interviewee to emulate by being open about her own feelings.

One of the barriers to self-revelation is that such sharing makes a person vulnerable to rejection by others. Content about which the client is sensitive, about which she has considerable feeling, is often content which is likely to seem, at least to the interviewee, to be self-incriminating, embarrassing, associated with shame, guilt, or blame.

One approach to such content is to sanction, in advance, feelings which might provoke shame or guilt. It makes acceptable the seemingly unacceptable and frees the interviewee to share that which she would have withheld. A legitimate explanation or excuse may preface the comment or phrase which is offered as stimulus to the exploration of feelings. Thus the interviewer might say to a mother of a large family, who is considering institutionalizing her mentally defective child, "It must be hard caring for the other children, given the extra burden of care that John requires. How do you feel about the care you have been able to give the other children?" Or to a daughter struggling with the problem of helping her elderly parents find a place to live, "I can understand that there might be a conflict between what you feel you owe your children and what you feel you owe your parents. How do you feel in looking for a nursing home for your parents?" Such prefacing has a face-saving effect; it softens the potential threat involved in self-disclosure of feelings.

Another sanctioning procedure is universalization of emotional responses which are known to be very common. Thus one might say to an unmarried mother, "Most girls are anxious about many things related to pregnancy. How do you feel about it?" Or to a woman recently divorced, "Many women feel lost and lonely right after the divorce. What are your own feelings about this?" Or to an unhappy wife, "All married people hate each other on occasion. How do you feel about your husband?"

Kinsey used such a procedure to encourage discussion of material about which the interviewee might otherwise have been reticent. Instead of asking whether or not the interviewee masturbated, followed by a question on frequency, his interviewers asked only, "How frequently do you masturbate?" The question incorporated the presumption that the practice was universal.

One can sanction socially unacceptable responses by prefacing which indicates the interviewer's awareness that people feel this way and that such feelings are understandable. What is involved here is projection of such feelings onto others and a depersonalizing of what are regarded as socially unacceptable feelings. "Some people feel that parents cannot always love their children. How do you feel about your child?" "Even happily married men think of extramarital adventures. Have you ever felt this way?" "Some people feel that going for an operation is scary even to adults, and they feel frightened. What is your reaction to this?"

The interviewer may explicitly sanction feelings and at the same time present herself as a model for emulation by indicating her own response to the situation. "If anybody treated me like that, I know I would really get sore." "I don't think I could face a situation like the one you mention without feeling depressed and upset."

Explicit expressions of empathy help the interviewee to verbalize feelings. "I can understand how anxious it might make you feel to know that Jim is getting into drugs and not knowing what to do to stop it." "I can imagine how frustrating it must feel to be ready, willing, and able to find employment, only to find no jobs are available."

By explicitly articulating the different kinds of feelings that might possibly be associated with some problem, the interviewer indicates that all are equally acceptable. "Some families do institutionalize their mongoloid children. Some maintain them at home. What is your own feeling about this at this time?" "Some unmarried mothers keep their child. Some unmarried mothers give up their child for adoption. How do you feel about it?"

The interviewee has no difficulty in sharing positive, socially sanctioned feelings. Encouraging the articulation of such feelings about some content under discussion might then make it easier for the interviewee to verbalize feelings that he perceives as negative and unacceptable. Having discussed what he likes about his marriage, the interviewee might be ready to discuss what he dislikes about it. The child might be ready to express his dislike for his parents after having described some of his affectionate feelings for them. The interviewer then moves gradually from focusing on the acceptable feelings to asking about less acceptable feelings.

The use of euphemism is helpful in moving into more sensitive areas. A mother who might be reluctant to discuss her feelings about "hitting" a child may be ready to discuss her feelings about "disciplining" a child. An adolescent who retreats from talking about his feelings associated with "stealing" may talk more readily about his response to "taking things." Euphemism and metaphors soften the threatening impact of the question, trigger less anxiety and resistance, and reduce the probability that the interviewee will avoid discussion of certain feelings. For example, in talking with an older client about a possible move to a group home, the worker refers to it as a "nursing home." The client reacts negatively to the connotations of such a term and shifts the interview to more neutral material. A little later in the interview the worker reintroduces this content but now refers to a "home for senior citizens." The client picks up on this and readily engages in a discussion of planning for the move.

One may approach personal emotional reactions gradually and indirectly. One way of doing this is by initially depersonalizing the discussion. Instead of asking a mother how she reacted to the experience of accepting a homemaker after her return from the hospital, the worker asks about her husband's feelings in response to the homemaker and about her children's feelings. Only after such discussion, desensitizing the mother to any reluctance to discuss the emotional aspects of homemaker service, does the worker ask the mother about her own feelings.

Sensitivity to and labeling of latent content is one approach to depth content in the interview. The latent content behind the manifest comment suggests the accompanying deeper, more intimate feelings associated with the content. The very sick patient who says to the medical social worker, "This has been a very hard winter. I wonder what next winter will be like," may be asking for assurance that she will live to see another winter. The 6-year-old child who asks the foster-care worker, "Did my brother cry when you took him to the [foster] home?" may be asking for acceptance of his own need to cry.

Although the interviewer may stimulate the interviewee to introduce more intense emotional content, she may also block further exploration of feeling. As is true to some extent for all of us, the beginning interviewer is more comfortable with concretely factual material than with affective content. The initial tendency, then, is to retreat from emotional material into the reportorial, factual "who," "what," "when," "where" kinds of response. The interviewer fails to respond to the feeling the client is attempting to communicate, thus discouraging further discussion of feelings.

A 13-year-old boy describing a family fight involving his parents and older brother to worker of family service agency.

PHIL: Jim wanted to go out; some one of his friends called him up and he wanted to go out. But Mom didn't want him to go out, and he pushed her away and he slapped her, and then they just started fighting and hollering, and it was all sort of scary.

WORKER: What day did this happen?

PHIL: I think it was Wednesday, no Thursday. I can't picture it in my mind.

WORKER: What time was it?

The following example illustrates the worker's feelings affecting an interview. The mother of an emotionally disturbed 3-year-old boy is discussing the child with an intake worker at a day-care center for disturbed children. She has just suggested, with considerable affect, that the child was unplanned, unwanted, and is rejected.

She feels guilty about her attitude as a possible explanation of the boy's behavior. She is leaning forward tensely in the chair, twisting her hands together, looking at the floor. The worker, in response, introduces a series of questions about the onset of walking, talking, and toilet training by saying, "Let me ask you some questions we need for our records." The worker says in retrospect:

> I felt that the mother and myself needed the emotional relief of a fairly objective line of questioning. But what made me feel that? As I think about it, she seemed ready to explore it further. Maybe I wanted out.

Asking about the emotional reactions of everyone but the interviewee is another evasive procedure. It permits discussing the issue but not risking any strong display of feelings by the interviewee himself, to which the interviewer will have to respond.

Correctional social worker talking to a 19-year-old white male charged with drug abuse.

WORKER: So when you dropped out of school, how did your parents feel about this?

GREG: Well, they didn't like it, of course. They were upset and hollered a lot and we argued.

WORKER: What was your girlfriend's reaction?

The worker fails to ask about Greg's feelings about his decision.
    The interviewer can also avoid discussion of emotionally laden material by shifting the focus to a person outside the interview.

MARY: I was over at my boyfriend's house, watching TV, and my father came busting in and said I had to go home with him. He was shouting and everything and made a big scene. I was so embarrassed.

WORKER: Why did he do it?

Interview Transitions

NATURE AND PURPOSE

At times during the interview the interviewer may decide that a change should be made in the material being discussed. The interviewer then faces a problem of engineering a transition without disturbing the relationship.

There are a number of reasons why the interviewer may decide that a change is advisable. The content under discussion may have been exhausted, and it would not be productive to devote further time and energy to it—there is a clear diminution in spontaneity and interest with which the interviewee discusses the material. The content area may have been introduced for exploratory overview by either of the participants but now proves to be a dead end. The interviewee may have introduced some clearly irrelevant material which cannot, in any conceivable way, further the purpose of the interview. Some material may have been introduced prematurely. The interviewee may appear to be distinctly uncomfortable, embarrassed, or threatened by the content and, rather than risk danger to the relationship, the interviewer may employ some transitional comment to move away from this material.

A transition may be initiated by the interviewer if she senses that the interviewee is sharing material of a more emotional nature than is desirable at this point in the interview contact. Recognizing that neither she nor the interviewee will be able to handle this much affect at this time, the interviewer might say, "You seem to be getting quite upset about this. Perhaps we can table it at this point and talk a little more about the job situation you were telling me about before."

Transitions frequently are initiated by the interviewer to serve her own purpose rather than the purpose of the interview. This is indicated in the following comments made by social workers in explaining transitions initiated by them during the course of interviews:

I was physically and mentally worn out from trying to keep up with the client. I introduced a somewhat neutral topic in order to give myself a breather.

I was feeling frustrated since the client hadn't been giving me any answer I could work with or had expected. I introduced another subject in the hope that I would have somewhat greater success.

This last reply she made should really have been probed for further elaboration, but since I really did not know what further to ask, I hastily moved on to another topic.

We were getting close to an area we had discussed before and about which I knew the agency, because of lack of resources, could do very little. I therefore made a transitional statement, taking us further away from the area I wanted to avoid.

At this point we got about as far as I was prepared to go with this. I wasn't sure about the admissions situation and/or procedure for local residential treatment centers. I therefore introduced a transitional summary and moved the interview on to the new content.

The cardinal operative principle violated by such transitions is that whatever is done by the interviewer should be done because it serves the purposes of the interview and the needs of the client.

The problem of transition derives from the time-limited nature of the interview. Out of respect for both participants, time available has to be employed most productively. Consequently no topic area can obtain truly exhaustive consideration. Limited time implies selective concentration. Interrupting the interviewee's flow of communication on material which is inconsequential and suggesting a transition to more meaningful material is not a derogation of the client or an exercise of arbitrary authority. It spares both the client and the worker a fruitless expense of time and energy and increases the confidence of the client in the worker's competence.

The catch, of course, is knowing what communication is inconsequential. Here, as elsewhere in the interview, the interviewer is stuck with the responsibility. He can share it, to some extent, with the interviewee—flexibly checking, keeping his decisions tentative, keeping alert and sensitive to the data he needs to know to make a reasoned decision. But ultimately the agency, the interviewee, and the interviewer look to the interviewer himself to decide how the interview should be conducted.

The interviewer should be aware that the need for focus that is served by use of transitions may be antithetical to the need for rapport. Transitions employed by the interviewer tend to restrict the spontaneity of the interviewee and emphasize that the contact is interviewer-controlled. In some instances it may be necessary to sacrifice focus for rapport and permit the interviewee a greater freedom despite the fact that this is clearly unproductive in achieving the specific interview purposes.

It is best not to make a transition to other content unless some time can be spent on the new material. Every time the context of the interview shifts, both participants have to readjust their perception of the situation. It takes a little time, and some psychic energy, to get accustomed to the change. Unless there is time available to work on the new content, there is no return on the investment.

Too rapid and too frequent transitions may indicate that the interviewer has no clear idea of how to conduct the interview, does not know what is most relevant to discuss, and is seeking some direction. It suggests a buckshot approach, trying many things in the hope that one topic or another will prove productive.

Before actually initiating a transition, the interviewer should mentally review the area under discussion to check for failure to cover any significant aspects. The interviewer then checks with the interviewee to see if there is anything else of relevance to the content area that he would be interested in discussing.

A transition is like a scene change in a play. One topic is ended, another is introduced. Sullivan, a psychiatrist, in a book on the psychiatric interview comments as follows:

When I talk about how to make transitions I simply mean how to move about in the interview. It is imperative if you want to know where you are with another person that you proceed along a path that he can at least dimly follow so that he doesn't get lost completely as to what you are driving at. . . . It is ideal, if you can, to go step by step with sufficient waving of signal flags and so on so that there is always something approaching a consensus as to what is being discussed. (292, p. 46)

Transitions which are abrupt, transitions for which there is no preparation, transitions which might appear to the interviewee to be illogical, are apt to be upsetting and confusing. The interviewee knows what he was doing and why; suddenly he is moved to something else, and he isn't clear how he got there or why.

If the relationship of the new content to the purposes of the interview seems clear, it may be talking down to the interviewee to note it. Frequently, however, the significance of the topic being introduced is not clear to the interviewee, no matter how obvious the relationship is to the social worker. Preparation for transition then should include some explicit statement of the relationship between new content and the purpose of the interview.

Couple, white, upper middle class, man aged 33, woman aged 28, adoption application interview.

WORKER: We have been talking about the different kinds of children for whom you both seem to have a preference. Perhaps we might discuss now your feelings about unmarried mothers and illegitimate children. You might wonder what relevance this has to your wanting to adopt a baby. You may know, however, that most of the infants we have available for adoption are illegitimate, so that your feelings and attitudes about illegitimacy are relevant to our meetings together. What comes to mind when you hear the words "unmarried mothers?"

In the face of a determined, non-stop interviewee, interruption to effect a transition may be difficult. The interviewer may need to be unequivocal in regaining the initiative. This may require a sentence like "Permit me, I know I am interrupting, but I wonder if I can say something about this," or "May I interrupt for a moment, please?"

In making a transition, even with the apparent agreement of the interviewee, the interviewer must be sensitive to any changes in interview interaction immediately following the transition. If the interviewee subtly reverts to the previous content area, if the flow from the interviewee seems to indicate a resistance that was not encountered earlier in the interview, if the interviewee seems to display some resentment, it may be necessary for the interviewer to reconsider the transition. It is more efficient for the interviewer to be flexible and follow the interviewee's lead back to the previous content area than to stubbornly dragoon him into discussing something else.

Transitions refer not only to a change in topic but also to a change in affect level within a content area.

Woman, 26, black, upper middle class, family service, marital counseling.

WORKER: Well, let me kind of see where we are now. You have been telling me about your husband, the kind of man you think he is, his education, his work, the kinds of interests you have in common, the kinds of things you do together or the kinds of things you hope he would do along with you. But I am not sure what the feeling is between you, what about him makes you glad, what about him depresses you, what about him that makes you happy, what makes you sore as hell. Maybe now we can talk about the feelings between you and your husband.

One can also shift the time reference. One can discuss the same relationship in the past as well as the present, making a transition from one time period to another.

Psychiatric social worker talking to 20-year-old male about plans for release from mental hospital and return to his home community.

GEORGE: The thing I really hate is, when you're in a place like this, you get out and people call you stupid and nuts and everything. Tease you about being here and all that.

WORKER: I imagine that makes you pretty angry. [Client nods. Pause.] That hurts. [Pause.] That really does. [Pause.] But how about before you came here, George? They couldn't say that about you then. [Client shakes head, no.] What was the trouble then in your relationship with the guys back home?

Transitions are not the exclusive prerogative of the interviewer. The interviewee often takes the initiative in making a transition. He may be bored by the topic under discussion; he may have something else to discuss that worries him more; he may want to flee the topic under discussion; he may feel a need to exercise some control over the interview situation.

With interviewee-initiated transitions, the interviewer has to decide whether to go along with the change and, accordingly, to modify his ideas about the content and sequence of the interview. He also has the problem of understanding what prompted the transition. Sometimes, of course, this may be obvious. At other times the emotional logic of the interviewee's thinking may not be apparent. Often an interviewee-initiated transition seems warranted. When the interviewer goes along with it, however, he needs to make a point of mentally filing for future reference the material he wanted to discuss but was now withholding in preference for the interviewee's choice of content.

When the interviewee introduces apparently irrelevant material, it is advisable to stay with it long enough to explore whether a transition is necessary. Sometimes apparently irrelevant material has a pertinence that only gradually becomes clear. The interviewee's interest in the material, manifested by his introducing it, acts as a constraint on rapid transition away from it. Rejection of the new content area is sometimes perceived as rejection of the interviewee. It may be necessary to accept the topic and by implication, the interviewee, in making the transition.

If it is unclear what prompted the interviewee-initiated transition and if the interviewer is uncertain about what to do, it might be helpful to raise an explicit question about the transition.

Male, 19, white, lower middle class, parole preparation interview.

WORKER: Help me out here. I think I lost you somewhere a little further back. We were talking about the guys you used to know at [the reformatory] who got out and made it. Now we're talk-ing about the changes your father plans to make around the farm. I don't get it.

GEORGE: Yeah, how did we get to this?

WORKER: As I say, I don't know, but maybe you could think back on this.

GEORGE: Well, I don't know either. [Pause.] What was I saying about this? [Long pause.] Yeah, oh hell, I don't know.

WORKER: Okay, maybe you don't.

GEORGE: It may be that those guys who made it, some of them got a lot of help from their family, money for things they wanted to do or needed, so if my old man puts all that dough in the farm, maybe he can't help me out so much, or maybe I feel I can't ask him because he won't have it, see.

The interviewer's comments on the exchange follow:

George had me puzzled on this. I really didn't know how we got from his reformatory peer group to his father's farm. I turned over a couple of things in my head as he talked, but nothing seemed to click. I didn't want to cut him off because he seemed to want to talk about it, but I couldn't see that this stuff about the farm was going to get us anywhere. That's when I decided to risk having it out with him. For a while I thought he didn't know either. The pauses seemed long, and he seemed to get more annoyed. He fidgeted a lot in his seat. That's why I de-cided to let up the pressure by saying "Well, maybe you don't [know why you shifted the focus]." But maybe my letting up on him by saying that helped ease his tension so that he was able to tell me.

If the digression is apparently unproductive, the interviewer may want to acknowledge it but not accept it as a focus for discussion. He might say, "That is very interesting and may be helpful. Per-haps if you like, we can come back to it later. However, it may be more helpful to you if we could talk about the way you get along on your job."

Sometimes the interviewee-initiated transition is designed to frustrate achieving the purposes of the interview. It is an attempt to evade painful work of the interview that must be done. In instances where an interviewee-initiated transition seems clearly designed to be an escape, it may be advisable to go along with a temporary digression to neutral material. This provides the interviewee with a breather, a rest break, during which he can pull himself together for another try at difficult content. But if the difficult content is relevant and important, the interviewer should try again. If he fails to make this return transition, the client may be pleased, but disappointed, at the interviewer's collusion in his evasion of painful material. He may be annoyed, but gratified, at the unyielding but compassionate interviewer who holds him to the purpose of the interview.

ROLE-REVERSAL TRANSITIONS

The role-reversal transition presents a recurrent problem for interviewers. The interviewee initiates a question, or series of questions, and becomes the "interviewer" temporarily. Although the interviewer might well ask herself what explains the interviewee's shift in role, she should respond by a willingness to share, simply and briefly, the information the interviewee wants. The interviewer should answer the questions asked, without apology, and should keep as much as possible to factual data.

As soon as it is feasible, however, the usual interviewing roles should be reestablished. The interviewer, if she is true to her responsibilities, has to reclaim her position, not to exercise authority or to emphasize the subordinate status of the interviewee, but because the interview exists to serve the purposes of the interviewee. They can only be accomplished if the worker interviews the client, and not the other way around.

Interviewers frequently feel uncomfortable with role reversal because it may mean sharing information that puts them at a disadvantage with the interviewee. Finding out that the interviewer is unmarried, or childless, or a student may erode, it is felt, some of the worker's potential for influence.

For the interviewee, such a reversal turns the spotlight away from him and onto the interviewer. It gives him a break from having to talk, having to consider his situation; it acts as a diversion and digression. It may be symptomatic of interviewee hostility and a desire to make the interviewer uncomfortable by asking personal questions. It may be a test of the worker's willingness to share. It may be a challenge to the interviewer's control of the interview or resentment at the inequality of the relationship. More frequently, perhaps, the role reversal is a response to the interviewee's need to know better the person with whom he is sharing so much of importance. Knowing more about the interviewer helps him "place" the interviewer. The interviewee may also want assurance that the interviewer is as human, as fallible, as himself.

The interviewee can engage in role reversal not only by asking the interviewer for personal information but also by frequently asking for greater clarification and specification about the interviewer's questions or comments. He may ask what the interviewer has in mind, or what use the interviewer will make of the information, or for a justification of the interviewer's questions. Interview reversal is sometimes effected by frequent and specific requests for advice or by soliciting the interviewer's opinion.

So when she said that, I just walked out of the house. What do you think I should have done?

We were all together in this and everybody was kinda feeling good, and when the marijuana came around again to me, I took a puff. What could I do? What would you have done if you were me in this situation?

KINDS OF TRANSITIONS

Sullivan (292) classifies interview transitions as smooth, accented, or abrupt; Merton (201) labels them as cued, reversional, or mutational. The smooth or cued transition is one where the interviewer adapts a remark that has just been made in order to effect a transition. There is no, or little, apparent break in continuity but the concern of the interview has been shifted as a consequence.

One form of cued transition is a short question or comment that leads the interview back from irrelevant to relevant material by linking the two. In effect such a question or comment makes the irrelevant become pertinent. The smoothest transitions are, technically, related associations rather than real transitions. The interview is really concerned with the same content, but in another context.

Transitions may result from the association between psychologically related topics. The classical transition from talking about one's father to talking about one's employer or supervisor is based on the emotional association of one's father with other authority figures on whom one is dependent.

Female, white, 36 years old, child welfare agency.

MRS. S.: Like, if I just told George to get on his bike and told him to go to church he would probably say, "How come I have to go and you don't have to?" Well, I think this messes a child up more in his own mind than anything else.

WORKER: Yes, it does.

MRS. S.: Well, I know George has wondered, "Where's my dad?" I told him. I didn't go right down to brass tacks, but I told him that his father found happiness someplace else, and this is where he went. I don't know whether he understood it or not, but he has never asked. I figure I told him as plain and simple as I could. As bad as Mike has been, I have never talked bad about him. I figured it might mix [George] up in school. I have always just told him that he found happiness someplace else and that's his privilege.

The connectivity between the two topics lies in the concern for honesty in relation to the child.

Reversional transitions employ content alluded to but not discussed at some earlier point in the interview. The interviewer ex-

ploits the comment previously made by using it to introduce the
new topic.

WORKER: You remember, a little while ago, near the beginning of
the interview, we were talking about the foster home you were
in before you came here. And you said it wasn't an easy place.
Remember that? What difficulties did you have there?

It is best wherever possible to use the comments and even the
exact wording of the interviewee. This suggests that she has shared
some responsibility for the decision and that it is being made to
some extent with her consent.

A mutational transition is a clear break with what is currently
under discussion. It has no obvious associational ties with the material which preceded it, as in a cued transition, nor with anything
previously raised in the interview, however briefly.

Interviewer responsibility for brief summaries and recapitulations of areas covered is related to the problem of transition. Such
a summary may be used as a means of transition or to accompany
a transitional comment. We will note later, in discussing termination, that summarization helps to consolidate material covered and
give participants a sense of accomplishment. Transitions signal, in
effect, a series of minor terminations during the interview, as one
topic is completed and another started. A summary here tends to
act as a closure to some section of the interview. It assembles and
synthesizes the material provided in the series of discrete ex-
changes that preceded it.

Sometimes a transition is achieved not so much by what the interviewer does but by what he fails to do. If he fails to respond to
what the interviewee is saying, if he displays no interest in it, his
inaction is likely to prompt the interviewee to attempt a change of
topic.

Hackeny and associates (119) perceptively divide the interview
into "islands" and "hiatuses." An island is a section of the interview
where both participants are mutually engaged in attending to some
content. Having momentarily said all they need or want to say
about this, they reach a hiatus, a respite. The hiatus is "a period of

negotiation between the counselor and the client, a negotiation in which new response classes or topics are sought" (119, p. 343). In short, it is a period of transition. The client may tentatively offer something as new content; the worker may tentatively suggest new content by a question or a comment. Each waits to see if the other responds with interest, acceptance, and approval, or disinterest and rejection.

Male, 20, white, parole interview.

WORKER: That's about it on the job situation then.

ANDY: Yep, that's about it. [Pause.] It's sure been hot lately.

WORKER: Yeah [pause].

ANDY: Good weather for swimming. Carol [girlfriend] and I were at the lake last night, and there sure was a big crowd out.

WORKER: I would imagine so.

ANDY: Saw a couple of guys from [the correctional school] there.

WORKER: What did they have to say?

In the above extract there is closure on the topic of the client's job. The client offers the weather, his relationship with his girlfriend, and leisure time activities as possible topics of interview continuation. The worker is indifferent to these possibilities. He picks up, however, on the client's contact with boys he knew previously in the institution. This became the topic on which the interview was focused during the next fifteen minutes.

Summary

Range, depth, and transition are frequently encountered during the developmental phase of the interview. Range requires skill in use of assertions of understanding and interest, reflecting, clarifying and interpreting, summarizing and recapitulating, as well as skill in asking questions. Frequent mistakes in question formulation include suggestive questions, yes-no questions, double questions, garbled questions, and "why" questions. Encouraging depth responses involves an explicit concern with feelings, sanctioning socially unacceptable feelings, universalization, depersonalization, appropriate use of euphemisms. Transitions are initiated when it is clear the client has exhausted the topic or it has been sufficiently covered, the topic under discussion is unproductive for achieving the purpose of the interview, or the topic occasions overwhelming anxiety for the client at this time. Transitions may be initiated by either participant, and are cued, reversional, or mutational.

Chapter 6

~·~

The Interview Process:
Development and Termination

Listening in the Interview

It is estimated that if the interviewer spends less than two-thirds of an interview listening and more than one-third talking, he is more active than he should be. A common error of inexperienced interviewers is to talk too much and give the interviewee too little opportunity to talk. Listening is deceptively simple; effective listening is difficult, an active rather than a passive technique. Good listening requires following carefully what is overtly said as well as the latent undertones (14, 214, 282). It requires being expectantly attentive and receptive. It requires a relaxed alertness during which the interviewer reaches out mentally to bring in what the interviewee is saying. Hearing is a physical process, listening a mental-emotional process.

Good listening requires an assumption and acceptance of ignorance. If a worker knew what the interviewee was going to say, she would not have to listen and would feel little motivation to listen.

True listening implies also a readiness to accept hearing what challenges our preconceptions. It involves the readiness to lower the psychic barriers that might impede undistorted perception of what the interviewee is saying.

The nature of spoken communication presents a special hazard, seducing the interviewer into an easy nonlistening. The hazard lies in the great discrepancy between the number of words that are normally spoken in one minute and the number of words that can be absorbed in that time. Thought is much more rapid than speech. The average rate of spoken speech is about 125 words per minute. We can read and understand an average of about 300–500 words per minute. There is, then, a considerable amount of dead time in spoken communication, during which the listener's mind can easily become distracted. The listener starts talking to herself to take up the slack in time. Listening to the internal monologue may go on side by side with listening to the external dialogue. More often, however, it goes on at the expense of listening to the external dialogue. The interviewer becomes lost in some private reverie—planning, musing, dreaming.

Client, female, 68, white, upper middle class, medical
Social work interview.

MRS. M.: So maybe because of the experience on the trip, Arnie has a better appreciation of how inconveniently crowded it might be with another person living in their relatively small house.

WORKER: Arnie?

MRS. M.: Yes Arnie, Arnold, my daughter's husband. I told you this before.

The worker's introspective comment on this follows:

I felt ashamed about this. I was caught woolgathering. Mrs. M. has been telling me about a trip her daughter's family had taken recently out West. It didn't seem particularly consequential to the problem for which she was referred [helping her accept a post-hospital living situation with her daughter], and so I began to think about my coming vacation and a trip we were planning. I just monitered the cadence of what Mrs. M. was saying but really was not listening. I was thinking about what needed checking on the car and some of the reservations that needed to be made yet. Somewhere along the line, Mrs. M. must have switched from the trip to the reactions of the family, living crowded together in motel rooms. Somehow I must have become aware that the content was becoming more relevant, but I surfaced slowly from my own trip plans, and when she said Arnie, for the moment I couldn't place the name. She generally refers to him as "my daughter's husband." When she had to explain who he was, she must have sensed I had not been listening, because she was irritated and annoyed. Not so good.

The supposition is that if you are not talking, you must be listening. Actually, one may not be talking and not be listening either—at least not to the interviewee.

The following analysis by a male psychiatric social worker of his pattern of listening is instructive:

I have become aware that I carry over to the interview some defensive listening patterns I have developed in general social interaction. It is a way of faking listening while permitting yourself the opportunity of enjoying your own private thinking. You look expectantly directly at the person, nod occasionally, or say "Yes, yes," smile when he smiles, and laugh along with him—at what, you don't know, because you haven't been listening. To protect my relationship with the speaker, I half-listen or listen sporadically. Every once in a while I'll really listen to check if I know what, in general, he is talking about. This is in case he should ask me a question. I listen for questions by the inflection. If the tone changes and I catch a rising inflection, I know I am being asked something. In social encounters, this gives me a lot of time for myself, and saves me from having to listen to an awful lot of BS. But I tend to slip into this pattern in the interview when the client bores me with repetition or with inconsequential detail. It bothers me because, unless I keep listening, how do I really know it's repetitive stuff or inconsequential?

The great possibilities for distraction from listening require considerable self-discipline from the would-be listener. Rather than becoming preoccupied as a consequence of the availability of the spare time between the slow spoken words, the good interviewer exploits this time in the service of more effective listening. The listener keeps focused on the interviewee but uses the time made available to the mind by slowness of speech to move rapidly back and forth along the path of the interview, testing, connecting, questioning: How does what I am hearing now relate to what I heard before? How does it modify what I heard before? How does it conflict with it, support it, make it more understandable? What can I anticipate hearing next? What do I miss hearing that needs asking about? What is he trying to tell me? What other meanings can the message have? What are his motives in telling me this?

Listening is a selective effort. If the interviewer felt compelled to listen to everything that was said, he would be overwhelmed with stimuli. The ear, like the eye, receives more than it can efficiently process. The good listener is attentive to the general themes rather than to the detail of each incident. The active listener does not passively absorb what he hears. He must have a clear idea of the purpose for which he is listening. This purpose then guides him in screening out what he decides is not relevant, accepting other content and trying to assimilate it to material previously accepted, or holding it in his mind to relate to other content that might come in later. Active listening requires considerable mental effort to catch and accurately decode the message that the ear hears. Rapid fading is a characteristic of spoken communication; unless one is attentive, the communication is lost.

After we have heard the first few words, we frequently fill in what the interviewee is saying by our anticipation of what he is likely to say. We can "see" what he is driving at. We listen quite differently to a foreign language. Because we are unfamiliar with it, we cannot easily anticipate what will be said. We have to listen to every word, and invariably think that the person is talking too rapidly. Because we make assumptions about what the interviewee will say, rather than listening to what he is actually saying, we often interrupt to finish his thoughts for him.

A 47-year-old man has been sharing his paranoid thoughts with a psychiatric social worker.

MR. A.: These things I've told you are—

WORKER: [Interrupting] strictly between you and me, confidential.

MR. A.: [Continuing] are the way I think most of the time, and I hope you don't misinterpret me.

Focused and attentive listening is made more difficult by virtue of the redundancy that all speech includes. To ensure that we will be understood, we say the same thing in several different ways. The listener, thinking she has received the message the first time, finds that her mind wanders as the message is repeated.

The client who tends to repeat himself is a special hazard; as soon as the worker recognizes that this is the second time around on some detail, she is apt to turn off her listening. The following introspective responses to taped interviews indicate this problem:

The tape shows that I am temporarily not aware of what is going on. The client is repeating a story he told me in the last interview, so the absentmindedness is understandable but still indefensible. Concentrate or else you risk many things—missing subtle changes in the repeated version; conveying an impression to the client of not caring much; losing an opportunity to respond to the client when he is making some effort to both talk to and interest you.

As the client had already gone into this earlier [the effect of her illness on her relationship with her husband] and is repeating the details, I only half listen and plan ahead to find out about other problems in the marriage. As a result I miss the cue she gives me that, while she doesn't want her daughter in a foster home, it is really nice when she's not around.

Listening, while comparable to reading, is a more difficult assignment. You can always improve the lighting or use a magnifying glass on small print. Frequently, you have to accept a poor hearing-listening situation as a given—poor acoustics, interviewees who have speech defects, or a difficult accent, or who talk at an inaudible level, or in rapid jerky tempo. These difficulties mean, however, the expenditure of more energy in merely hearing what is said, and therefore result in fatigue and a wish for relief from the work of listening.

External noise which masks speech is as distracting to listening as is the inner noise of absorption in a private reverie. Just as we try to control distraction from inappropriate internal digressions, we try to focus on the sounds coming from the interviewee. Looking at the interviewee while she is talking focuses our attention and concentrates our mind on the sounds coming from her. Lip reading, which supplements hearing, is possible only if we look at the interviewee.

Silence in the Interview

The principal therapeutic activity of most kinds of social work interventions involves talking. Even providing a social utility such as day care or homemaker service, a foster home, or housing involves a considerable amount of talk between client and worker around acceptance of the concrete service, preparation for use of the service, and adjustment to the service. All of social work, but particularly casework, may be listed as one of the "talking cures." Talk is the medium of exchange, the raw material for the work of the interview. Consequently silence, the absence of talk, gives the appearance of frustrating the achievement of the purpose of the interview.

The social work interviewer frequently perceives silence as a hindrance and a hazard to the progress of the interview, which needs to be removed or resolved. The professional presumption is that talking is better. Sometimes, however, silence may be more effective for achieving the purposes of the interview.

The American cultural emphasis on self-expression, on speaking one's mind, having one's say, makes silence seem an unacceptable form of behavior. In general social interaction, we feel compelled to talk even if we have nothing to say. The silent one is suspect and regarded as unfair for his failure to contribute to the conversation. The usual social meaning of silence is rejection. We use the "silent treatment" to punish by denying ourselves to others. Silence also is used to communicate the fact that we think so little of the other person that we will not exert ourselves even to talk with him.

Silence generates social anxiety, felt as embarrassment, in people who have come together with the intent of talking to each other. But the social worker, in addition, feels a professional anxiety at the thought that continued silence signals a failing interview. It is no surprise, then, that inexperienced interviewers tend to feel uncomfortable with silences and tend to terminate them prematurely. It takes some measure of confidence and security for the interviewer to permit a productive silence to continue. It also requires that the interviewer accept the fact that a silence is not necessarily an attack against him.

Sometimes a distinction is made between pauses and silences. Pauses are regarded as a "natural rest in the melody of speech," a kind of verbal punctuation analogous to a change of paragraphs or a new topic heading in printed communication. Silence, unlike a pause, is a temporary deliberate withholding of speech. Silence is the ultimate confirmation of the dictum that in the interview nothing never happens. Something is happening all the time, even when the participants appear totally passive in their silent interaction. It is a period filled with nonspeech, in which both interviewer and interviewee participate.

The interviewer's response needs to be predicated on some understanding of the meaning of the interviewee's behavior in maintaining his silence. Silence is itself a communicative gesture. Its meaning varies from interviewee to interviewee and may be different for the same interviewee at different points in the interview (55, 89, 142, 176, 182, 188, 317, 324, 341).

The interviewee might be silent because nothing further readily occurs to him to say about the topic. He stops to think things over, to review this content in his mind, to see if there is anything else that needs to be said.

Silence may be the result of normal difficulties encountered in enacting the complicated and demanding role of interviewee. The interviewee may have reached a point when it is not clear to him which of a number of different directions he might want to take. His silence is an expression of his indecision, and it gives him time to resolve his uncertainty.

Silence may have an organizational aim. The story is a complicated one; the response to the question raised is difficult; and the interviewee is silent while trying to organize his answer in a coherent fashion.

Sometimes silence permits the work of synthesis. Having talked about material that has considerable emotional meaning, the interviewee wants a chance to pull himself together, to reduce tension and to gain a measure of composure. He sits in silence to give himself an opportunity to sort out his feelings, to absorb them and assert control over them. The following illustrates the need expressed by the client for a period of silence following discussion of highly charged material. The interviewee is discussing possible divorce and breakup of the family.

*Client: male, 9 years old, white, middle class, child
guidance clinic.*

RICKY: If that happens, I don't know what I'm going to do, I'm just
   gonna keep. . . . If that hard to face, I'm just going to jump in
   the Susquehanna River, or, or. . . .

WORKER: Or just not face. . . .

RICKY: Or just go, or just climb in a hole, or. . . .

WORKER: Or cover yourself up.

RICKY: Yeah, just climb in a hole and maybe put a blanket there.

WORKER: Hide.

RICKY: Or just starve to death. Because I don't want to live in a
   world if the world is going to be like that when I grow up.

WORKER: Like what?

RICKY: Well, say, the way it is now, you know, it's not going to be too nice to face.

WORKER: What is not going to be nice to face?

RICKY: Well, say, if that . . . ah . . . if that ever happens.

WORKER: If what ever happens?

RICKY: If my mother and my father departed, well. . . .

WORKER: Yeah. . . .

RICKY: You know, I'm just a. . . .

WORKER: You're just a. . . .

RICKY: Where am I? I'm just a. . . . I'm just a. . . . I'm just nowhere. I would have been better. . . .

WORKER: You would have been better. . . .

RICKY: I would have been better. . . .

WORKER: You would have been better off dead?

RICKY: Yeah.

WORKER: Is that what you think?

RICKY: Yeah. I would be better off. . . . [R. is really agitated, and the therapist offers him candy.] No, thank you, I don't like candy.

WORKER: Why?

RICKY: Oh, I, well, I'm thirsty. May I?

WORKER: No. [Long pause.] How do you feel about my not letting you go for a drink?

RICKY: Well, I, I don't feel like you're punishing me, I could probably go and get a drink. I would just like to stop and review my thoughts. You have me kind of mixed up or under a barrel. (121)

Silence can be the pensive consideration of some interpretation, some explanation of the dynamics of his behavior, which the interviewee has encountered in the interview discussion. The interviewee needs a period of silence in order to think over the validity of interpretation.

Silence may be a deliberate effort on the part of the interviewee to solicit, or provoke, some response from the interviewer. The interviewee may have asked for advice, or a suggestion, may have requested information, or may have subtly solicited support or approval. His silence at this point is a pressure on the interviewer to give him what he asked for.

Silence may indicate an effort to frustrate the interviewer and hence has the nature of a hostile attack. The interviewee spitefully withholds what the interviewer needs in order to conduct the interview. The interviewee who is requested to come to an interview against his desire may demonstrate his opposition by frequent and prolonged silences. Here motivation rather than silence is the problem.

Silence may reflect an effort by the interviewee to exert control over the interview and the interviewer or an attempt to defend himself against control by the interviewer. In silence the interviewee is beyond any outside control. Silence, in these instances, is an act of protective antagonism and has a quality of anger not associated with other, more comfortable, silences.

Silence may be a defense against anxiety, a resistance to saying what should not be said. One series of studies empirically establishes an association between anxiety-provoking content and subsequent silences (107). Speech affirms, to ourselves and others, the existence of thoughts and feelings and makes perception of them more difficult to evade. To convert thoughts and feelings into speech, so that one hears oneself articulate them, is to intensify the conscious knowledge that one harbors them. Conversely, refraining from putting such thoughts and feelings into words makes them easier to deny. Silence is an act of refusal to give speech to some thoughts and/or feelings so that they cannot be heard either by ourselves or others.

The tendency is to interpose resistance to those thoughts and feelings which we are reluctant to recognize. Speech is interrupted and a silence maintained when the interview approaches such content. The interviewee needs time to think things over to consider whether or not he should divulge the things he came perilously close to saying. Thus a clue to understanding the silence may lie with the material which was being discussed immediately preceding the silence and with the associations and recollections such content might evoke.

It is the function of silence as a defensive withholding which suggested the frequent theoretical equation of silence with oral eroticism, words with feces, the mouth as a sphincter maintaining selective control over what is shared.

The following excerpt illustrates the use of silence to give the interviewee a chance to catch her psychic breath, after which the interviewer permits a transition. He then holds the interviewee to the anxiety-provoking material that she was reluctant to disclose and that prompted the initial silence. The interview excerpt not only illustrates the correct use of silence but also the correct use of transition. The interviewer permits the interviewee to make a transition away from painful material but then, recognizing the need for dealing with the evaded material, he moves the interview back to this material. The client has been discussing the causes for her conflict-filled marriage. Each pause is a substantial period of silence.

Patient: female, 30, white, middle class, psychiatric
outpatient clinic.
Interviewer: a psychiatrist.

PATIENT: [Sighs.] I don't think he's the sole factor. No.

WORKER: And what are the factors within. . . .

PATIENT: I mean. . . .

WORKER: Yourself?

PATIENT: Oh, it's probably remorse for the past, thing I did.

WORKER: Like what? [Pause.] It's something hard to tell, huh? [Short pause.]

PATIENT: [Sighs, moves around. Pause, sigh, pause.] I've had one psychiatric interview before, but it wasn't anything like this.

WORKER: Where did you have that one?

PATIENT: Oh down———. [Sniffs.] I was depressed, and this doctor took a history on me. [Interviewee, who is a nurse, gives some detail about the examination.]

WORKER: So, how is this interview different?

PATIENT: Oh, he asked me routine questions.

WORKER: Mmmmhnnn.

PATIENT: How. . . . Then he asked me how I liked the Army and so forth. But you know [sniffs]. . . . I dunno. I think I had a tendency to cover things up.

WORKER: Yeah. What is this thing you had so much remorse about? [Pause.]

PATIENT: [Sighs.] It seems to me I'm going around in circles. [Sniffs.] In 1946 I met a man. He was married but I loved him anyway. [Sighs.] I became pregnant. (101, pp. 194–198)

While resistance is frequently offered as an explanation for silence, studies tend to show that silence is more frequently used by interviewees for nondefensive purposes. The interviewee falls silent because there is nothing more to be said about the matter under discussion, or because he is organizing his thoughts, or because he is not sure which direction to go (242).

Interviewers' responses to pauses as they reviewed tapes of their own interviews suggest a recognition that bewilderment, uncertainty, and frustration may bring the interview to a halt.

I would like to say that this long period of silence was maintained because of its therapeutic, thought-provoking potential, but actually I felt frustrated because my questions weren't getting the material I thought we needed to discuss and I couldn't think of how I could get the client to discuss this.

This silence meant that we had reached the end of a thought and both did not know what to say next. I had lost my way temporarily and did not know how to proceed. This made me feel nervous and out of control.

More frequently, however, interviewer silence is deliberately employed. Silence on the part of the interviewer acts as a stimulus encouraging the interviewee to continue talking. The interviewee, who knows and accepts his role, is conscious of the fact that he has the major responsibility for talking. The major channel for interaction in an interview is verbal communication. If the interviewer refrains from talking, the interviewee feels a pressure to fill the silence in response to his recognition of his role responsibilities. The interviewer's silence communicates his clear expectation that the interviewee will interrupt the silence and accept his obligation to talk. The normal role relationship between interviewee-talker and interviewer-listener can then be resumed.

Interviewer silence is an ambiguous interventive technique. It gives the interviewee no direction, no specification of what is wanted or expected other than the general expectation that he will continue talking. If the interviewee needs some direction, a silence enhances anxious uncertainty. For the interviewee who is capable and desirous of taking the initiative, however, interviewer silence offers the freest choice of selecting the content he wants to discuss.

Since one can get lost in silence, and since too much is as bad as too little, impeding the work of the interview, the interviewer sometimes has to accept responsibility for ending the silence. Tension as a consequence of too prolonged a silence might make it difficult for the interviewee to continue. If the silence results from some uncertainty about what to say next or from the fact that the interviewee has said all he can say about a particular matter, there is little point in letting it continue. If silence is the result of hostility, prolonging it might engender guilt; if silence is due to resistance, prolonging it might solidify the resistance. In these instances, instead of a "pregnant pause" that leads to productive communication, one has an unproductive, embarrassed silence.

The problem for the interviewer is not only to help the interviewee resume the flow of communication but also to help him understand, if this is appropriate to the goals, what prompted the act of silence.

Wolberg has offered a series of graded responses to silence in psychotherapy that is equally applicable to the social work interview (335, p. 164). When an appreciable pause is encountered (more than five seconds) so that it might be regarded as a silence, Wolberg suggests the following:

    a. Say "mmhmm" or "I see" and then wait for a moment.

    b. Repeat and emphasize the last word or the last few words of the patient.

    c. Repeat and emphasize the entire last sentence or recast it as a question.

    d. If this is unsuccessful, summarize or rephrase the last thoughts of the patient.

    e. Say "and" or "but" with a questioning emphasis, as if something else is to follow.

    f. If the patient still remains silent, the therapist may say, "You find it difficult to talk," or "It's hard to talk." This focuses the patient's attention on his block.

    g. In the event of no reply, the following remark may be made: "I wonder why you are silent?"

    h. This may be succeeded by, "There are reasons why you are silent."

    i. Thereafter the therapist may remark, "Perhaps you do not know what to say?"

    j. Then: "Maybe you're trying to figure out what to say?"

    k. This may be followed by: "Perhaps you are upset?"

    l. If still no response is forthcoming, a direct attack on the resistance may be made with "Perhaps you are afraid to say what is on your mind?"

    m. The next comment might be: "Perhaps you are afraid of my reaction, if you say what is on your mind?"

    n. Finally, if silence continues, the therapist may remark, "I wonder if you are thinking about me?"

    o. In the extremely rare instances where the patient continues to remain mute, the therapist should respect the patient's silence and sit it out with him. Under no circumstances should he evidence anger with the patient by scolding or rejecting him.

Lying

Lying and fabrication by the interviewee present a difficult problem for the social work interviewer. The whole attitudinal stance of the profession suggests that we should accept, with respect, everything the interviewee says and that to question the interviewee's truthfulness is derogatory. Yet it is no tribute to a client's

membership in the human family to act as though clients are an-
gelic and never stooped to conning us. We feel stupid and imposed
upon if we suspect lying but continue to act as though everything
the client says is gospel. And we appear stupid and gullible and
weak to a client if she is lying, knows she is lying, and seems able
to put things over on us.

Social workers have conflicting feelings about doubting the
client. They feel guilty and unhappy because skepticism seems to
violate the professionally dictated need to be "accepting" and to
treat the client with respect. Yet they live in a real world with
clients who often do lie and they live with agency regulations that
require objectively accurate data. These conflicting feelings are reflected by a correctional social worker, listening to a tape of his interview with a recently released, 24-year-old rapist. At this point in
the interview the social worker was asking questions about the
kinds of drinking sessions the parolee had been involved in during
the previous week. The worker's response to hearing his line of
questioning follows:

> It bothers me to listen to this—it reminds me of the welfare
> snoopers who I deplore. All those damn questions. But then I
> felt if he wasn't being honest with me, we wouldn't get any-
> where. Also pride came into it. One hates to be conned. But
> pride does have a positive side to it in that if one lets oneself be
> conned, the relationship and ability to help is damaged. So I
> don't know. It's a compromise that requires your doing the
> things you don't really feel comfortable about doing.

We tend to suppose that we have to choose between maintaining
a working relationship and questioning the lie and threatening the
relationship. This is hardly correct. Not to question the lie means
maintaining a relationship which is ineffectual because it is built
on duplicity. A relationship built on lies and maintained through
lies, one lie leading to others, involves a complex mixture of feelings, none of which lead to good, easy, comfortable communication. The interviewee may feel guilt toward the worker, contempt
of the worker, shame in lying, anxiety about the possibility of

being found out, disappointment in, and resentment of, the worker for not being strong enough, or capable enough, to call a halt. Furthermore, lying robs the relationship of its reason for being. The relationship exists to enable the worker to help the client. But lies make it difficult, if not impossible, for the worker to help effectively, since he is denied the opportunity of knowing the client's actual situation. Consequently, one does not risk the relationship in calling for the truth when one suspects lying. A good relationship obviously has not existed and therefore cannot be lost.

In many instances the social worker does not know what is objectively true about the client's situation. One tests for plausibility and internal consistency. Is it likely, from the social worker's knowledge of similar situations, that something like this could have happened in this way? It is helpful to ask for details, which can be given readily if the story is true but are difficult to make available if it is a fabrication. Is the material consistent? Is one element congruent with others? The social worker can appeal to the interviewee to help her understand since the story doesn't seem to hang together and she wants to be sure she has correctly heard what she has been telling her.

If one suspects lying, one must ask oneself what prompts this behavior—what purpose does it serve, how can one understand it and, through understanding, discourage its continuance or reduce it?

One of the best defenses against lying is prevention. The client lies for a purpose. Our effort is to act in a manner which would deny him all reason for lying. Clients lie because they want to be accorded respect and acceptance; they want to present a socially desirable facade, hiding their imperfections. One effect of the non-judgmental, respectful approach is to communicate to the client that he need not lie to be accepted, that we are ready to offer him acceptance and respect even though we know about the imperfections he hesitates to share with us. In reducing threats to the ego, we reduce the motivation for defensiveness and lying. Similarly, the boast of accomplishments never really achieved is made unnecessary by an accepting attitude.

We prevent lying by indicating the acceptability of even the least "socially desirable" responses. We make some lies unnecessary by sharing, with neutral affect, information we may already know. We say matter of factly:

"I know from the school that John has been expelled for taking drugs. . . ."

"We know that you have had two previous convictions on charges of breaking and entering. . . ."

Yet often the interviewee has significant, realistic motives for falsification, involving possible punishments for not lying or rewards for lying. In corrections, in protective services, in public assistance programs, the interviewee is concerned with important, real consequences of what he says. We might anticipate that, being human, the interviewee will surely be tempted to lie.

The impact of "vested interest" on interviewee response was experimentally demonstrated by Braginsky and Braginsky (33) in a study of hospitalized schizophrenics. Patients in one group were told that the purpose of the interview was to see whether they might be ready for discharge; another group, that it was for deciding admission to an open or closed ward; a third group, that it was aimed at evaluation of their feelings and their progress in the hospital. The interviewees responded in a manner designed to accomplish their aims. Patients anxious to leave the hospital or get into the open ward presented themselves as "healthy"; those who wanted to remain in the hospital presented themselves as "sick."

Because the vested interest can be such a strong force favoring lying, confrontation may on occasion be necessary and justifiable.

Gee, help me out here. I am not sure I get it. The whole thing just doesn't hang together. A little while ago you were saying that your husband is indifferent to the kids, never helps you with them, couldn't care less for them, and now you're telling me that he brings John to the day-care center and picks him up at night. I don't get it.

You know, I am sitting here thinking you are trying to give me a snow job, that you're kidding me. What you're saying doesn't seem plausible. Here, let me show you what makes it difficult for me to swallow.

The admittedly very difficult, yet necessary, saving aspect of effective confrontation is to reject the falsification without rejecting the falsifier.

Nothing said here is meant to suggest the abrogation of common sense. If there is doubt whether the interviewee is lying, it is best to let the matter rest. If the content of the suspected fabrication seems relatively insignificant for the central purpose of the interview, it might be casually overlooked and not raised as an issue. Nor is it wise to ignore the fact that the impulse for engaging in a seemingly justifiable confrontation may stem from the worker's hostility toward and annoyance with the client.

The interviewer has to feel confident in her ability to call for honesty and responsibility without being punitive, however tempting this may be. Even more difficult to achieve is the requirement that the interviewer herself set a scrupulous example of honesty. Her honesty robs the interviewee of a powerful justification for lying and sets a positive example of behavior for interviewee emulation. Interviewer honesty implies never falsely reassuring, never making a promise without fulfillment, openly sharing one's position and responsibility as a community representative, as an agent of social control, sharing the limitations of one's helpfulness and responding with genuineness, when appropriate, in terms of the feeling evoked in one by the client (124).

Admittedly, some of what I have said must sound incredibly naive in the face of the counterculture's ideology, which sees falsified applications for welfare benefits as a legitimate "rip-off." The philosophy of theft-without-guilt is exemplified in Abbie Hoffman's *Steal This Book*, a guide on how to get away with as much as possible, as often as possible. The only response that the interviewer can make in defense of the legitimate needs of the eligible client group is a strict application of eligibility requirements and a conscientious review of the interviewee's qualifications for benefits.

Interview Note-Taking

The more notes taken during the interview, the less note-taking is required after termination. The most important caveat is that note-taking presents a possible distraction to interview interaction. While the interviewer is taking notes, he risks diminishing his contact with the interviewee and the attention he can devote to what the interviewee is saying. If he looks down to write, he breaks eye contact, indicative of a shift in his field of awareness. His focus in note-taking is generally on what *has* been said rather than on what *is* being said.

Note-taking also risks some increase in the interviewee's selective attention to certain content. If, after talking for some time, the interviewee says something which mobilizes the interviewer to take a note, the interviewee is apt to wonder about the significance of this content and to focus on it. This focusing may be good if the interviewer's deliberate intention is to reinforce concern with this particular content and to single it out for emphasis. However, focusing may be an inadvertent, unintentional byproduct initiated by note-taking.

As the interviewee sees the interviewer taking notes, he is unsure whether he should continue to speak. He hesitates not only because the interviewer is apparently not listening to him but also because he does not want to interfere with the interviewer's action. It may be necessary to assure the interviewee that taking notes does not affect the conduct of the interview and that he should continue to talk.

Note-taking is, in some measure, self-defeating. When the most important things are happening, when involvement in the interview is greatest, the amount of attention which can be devoted to note-taking is minimal. When what is happening is less significant, there is more time for notes. Hence the most complete notes may highlight the less important interchanges. There are exceptions. Some interviewers can take notes unobtrusively without looking away from the client and without seeming to shift their attention.

They have learned to set down key phrases or words that serve as adequate reminders of blocks of interview content. And they have learned to write without looking at the note pad. They take notes without discomfort and without much show.

Further, these considerations need to be applied differently with regard to different content. If the interviewee is offering specific, necessary information such as dates, names, addresses, and telephone numbers, it is essential that the interviewer note them. If he does not, the interviewee, recognizing that they will probably not be remembered, concludes that the interviewer is disinterested and indifferent. He might well wonder why the interviewer asked about these matters in the first place. Taking notes at this point validates the importance of what the client has said and indicates that it has been taken seriously. Notes about the actions the interviewer has promised to take are essential. If she has promised to obtain an interpretation of some regulation, make a hospital appointment, or check the availability of a home-maker, a note should be made.

If the interviewer is planning to take notes during the interview, this should be shared with the interviewee and her permission should be requested. Generally this is done in a manner which suggests that the interviewee will have no objections and includes some explanation of the purpose for note-taking. "You don't mind if I take some notes while we're talking? I'll need to do this if I am going to be most helpful to you." Especially with a suspicious interviewee, the request for permission may, further, include a statement of a willingness to share the notes if the interviewee wants to look at them. The interviewer may even encourage the interviewee to take her own notes on the interview. Notes should be taken in full view of the client rather than surreptitiously.

The effect of note-taking needs to be assessed periodically during the interview. If at any point the interviewee appears to be upset or made hesitant by note-taking, this should be raised for explicit discussion. If, despite the interviewee's stated assent, note-taking appears to be a disruptive tactic, one might best forget it.

If it is difficult to take notes during the interview because either person is hesitant, it may be necessary to take some notes immediately after the interview. To wait until the end of the working day risks a considerable loss of essential detail. It is easy, after a series of interviews, to confuse interaction that occurred in one interview with interaction in another.

Termination of the Interview

The final phase of the interview is termination. Preparation for termination begins with the very beginning of the interview. The interviewee should be informed explicitly at the beginning that a definite period of time has been allotted for the interview, that she is free to use some, or all, of this time but that going beyond the time limit is clearly discouraged. Unless an unusual situation develops, it is understood that the interview will terminate at the end of the allotted time.

Another aspect of preparation relates to the mutually agreed-upon purpose of the interview. The interview is an ad hoc social system created to perform a purpose. When the purpose is accomplished, the system should dissolve. The purpose should bear some general relation to the time available, so that it probably can be accomplished within the time scheduled. If this is not possible, the general purpose should be broken down so that some subunits are achieved in one interview, and an additional interview, or interviews, scheduled. In a sense, the interview has not been terminated at the end of the first meeting; it has merely been interrupted.

Research findings regarding long-term and short-term worker-client contacts may be applicable to the interview situation. Such research suggests that if the agency establishes a limited time period for contact with the client, both worker and client tend to mobilize their efforts more effectively to accomplish the tasks of the contact within the time designated (235). If there is a clearly limited time period for the single interview, similar mobilization of effort may take place.

Throughout the interview the social worker has to be aware of time spent and time yet available. Since she is responsible for seeing that interview purposes are accomplished, she needs to pace the interview so that there is some reasonable expectation of success. She may decide to make more rapid transitions; she may decide to focus less time on some areas; she may make less effort to evoke affect if time is growing short. If the movement toward accomplishment of purpose is more rapid than anticipated, she may decide to conserve the interviewee's time as well as her own by ending early. It might be well, in moving toward termination, if the interviewer occasionally checks with the interviewee.

It seems to me that we have done what we set out to do and that we are coming to a close. How do you see it?

It might be noted that the interviewee is as free as the interviewer to terminate the exchange. If she feels her purposes are accomplished or if she feels that there is little real likelihood that her purpose will be achieved, the interviewee may not want to waste her time further.

There is preparation for termination in the pacing of affect as well as content. In moving toward the end there should be a dampening of feeling, a reduction in intensity of affect. Content that is apt to carry with it a great deal of feeling should not be introduced toward the end of the interview. The interviewee should be emotionally at ease when the interview is terminated.

The interview should terminate before the participants become physically or emotionally fatigued and the interview suffers. An hour to an hour and a half is a long time for most participants. Highly charged emotional interviews may fatigue participants even earlier. If fatigue sets in, the risk of interviewer error is greater.

In a good interview, the participants together move toward the end of allotted time, both aware that the interview will terminate shortly and sharing the decision to terminate. A desk or wall clock, visible but unobtrusive, allows both participants to check the time periodically. If it is clear that the interviewer is conscious of limited time available but the interviewee is not, some gentle reminders may be necessary.

Now that we are coming to the end of the interview, perhaps you. . . .

In the limited time we have left, I wonder if you could tell me something about. . . .

I wish we could get into this more fully now, but given the time we have left it seems that. . . .

The verbal reminders are reinforced by nonverbal gestures which suggest that the interview is drawing to a close. The interviewer shifts forward in her chair, hands on lap getting ready to stand up. She collects the papers or forms used during the interview; she looks at her watch rather than glances at it.

If the interview is terminated abruptly and without considerate warning, the interviewer may be perceived as discourteous and re- jecting. Separation is easily confused with rejection; the inter- viewer should make clear that termination of the interview is not the equivalent of wanting to get rid of the interviewee—although sometimes the worker may want to do so.

While one cannot start an interview without some consensus of both participants, one can terminate it unilaterally. With a persis- tent interviewee, this sometimes needs to be done. There is the progressive movement of preparing to stand up, standing up, mov- ing to the door, opening the door, preparing to shake hands, shak- ing hands, and saying good-bye. But there needs to be concern for, and understanding of, the interviewee's reluctance to leave. Some- times this reluctance is a hostile gesture toward the interviewer. Sometimes it reflects the long time needed before the interviewee feels comfortable enough to bring up the most important problem. This may be delayed until the end of the interview to avoid having time to explore it fully. Sometimes the reluctance to end the inter- view expresses a desire to prolong a satisfying experience; some- times it is an expression of sibling rivalry and reluctance to share the interviewer with the next sibling-interviewee. The problem may result from different perceptions of how the interview has progressed—the interviewer seeing the purpose accomplished, the interviewee, from his point of view, seeing much that still needs to be done.

The interviewee's reluctance to terminate and the worker's diffi- culty in handling it is illustrated in the following account of the end of an interview:

She began to talk about the boys, and as I began to breathe in at a pause or start a concluding sentence which would indicate a termination of the interview, she became extremely tense, talking faster and in a dissociated manner. I asked what she thought of my getting hold of her again, and she replied that she would be able to hear the phone ring. I then stood up to indicate termination and she began to list relatives and their careers. I perhaps should have stated that I must return to other work, but I was rather cowed by her sudden extreme talkativeness, and so I just walked her to the stairs and she continued to talk all the way downstairs and as she walked out onto the street. I had avoided interrupting her or being firm—those are not my usual ways of dealing with people—and I also was afraid to, but I did no favor to her to allow her to become so anxious at that point.

Whatever the interviewee's reasons for failing to perceive the warning preparations for termination and for acting to prolong the interview, the interviewer needs to follow some desirable procedures in terminating. Here as always the worker would do well to recognize explicitly the meaning of the behavior.

I can see that you would like to continue longer.

It seems like you are reluctant to end the interview.

It appears to me that you wished we had more time.

While holding, without equivocation, to the need to terminate, the interviewer should indicate a desire to maintain communication. It is not that she does not want to hear more, it is that she does not want to hear it at this particular time. Consequently an offer is made to continue during another specified time period. The offer confirms the interviewer's continuing interest. If there is already an understanding that this is one of a series of interviews, there is an implicit promise of continued discussion. The interviewer might say, "I am very sorry but we have to wind this up. I would like to continue but it's not possible. I would be glad to schedule another appointment so that we could continue talking together about this."

In those instances in which another interview is scheduled, specific arrangements should be made for the next steps, such as time, date, and place of the next interview or the time, date, place, the person to see, and how to get there, if the interview terminates in referral to another agency. If the interview is with a collateral, or is an advocacy interview, it is advisable to thank the interviewee, recapitulate the significance of the contact, and reassure him about how the interview content might be used. An assessment interview should invariably terminate with some statement regarding the timing of the decision and the procedure for communicating the decision to the interviewee.

All these suggestions need to be applied flexibly, with sensitivity to the individual situation and with a generous helping of common sense. The interviewer should consider the interviewee's needs in moving toward termination. He must also give some consideration to his own needs, since they may indirectly affect the interviewee adversely. The interviewer's balanced concern for his own schedule is the highest courtesy to the interviewee. If the interviewer is too compliant, too yielding, too compassionate, and the interview runs beyond the scheduled time, he begins to worry about the next waiting interviewee, he begins to worry about the things that need to get done and will not get done if the interviewee continues to talk, he begins to listen to his own mounting anxieties and forgets to listen to the client. The extra time is then spent inefficiently and unproductively.

As part of the termination phase, the interviewer briefly recapitulates what has been covered in the interview, what decisions have been arrived at, what questions remain to be resolved, what steps for action, if any, are to be taken. A summary tends to consolidate the work of the interview and give participants a feeling of satisfaction as they look back over what they have done. If nothing much has been accomplished, however, it may lead to a sense of despair.

Summarization is always a selective process. Consequently a summary tends to highlight and emphasize those aspects of the interview which the summarizer, generally the interviewer, regards as most significant. For this reason the interviewee's response should be actively and explicitly solicited. She should be invited to revise the summary if it does not accord with her perception of what was significant during the interview. Or the interviewer may ask the interviewee to recapitulate what *she* thought was accomplished. Such recapitulations might include a statement of what still needs to be done in subsequent interviews. The summary should enable both participants to get a perspective on the interview, highlighting the relationship of the many different, perhaps seemingly unrelated, aspects that have been discussed. It is an opportunity to give a sense of coherence to what has taken place.

Just as the interview itself may be preceded by a short social conversation as a transition, the termination of the interview may be followed by a similar short conversation. It acts as a transition out of the interview. It helps, further, to restore emotional equilibrium if the interview has been emotionally charged. Such post-interview conversation permits the interviewee time to regain composure and restore his ego, which may have been somewhat battered during the interview.

A correctional social worker has been discussing the best fishing spots with a male client toward the end of an interview. He notes later, listening to the interview on tape:

> The content is pretty much small talk and the time may have been better spent had I summed up the topics we'd touched on, and terminated the interview. However, he seemed to need this neutral topic after expressing the previously emotional material. It also gave me an opportunity to learn something about his interests and show him I was interested in him as a person with hobbies, etc., and not merely interested in him as a probationer.

As at the beginning of the interview, if such a conversation goes on too long it tends to confuse a formal interview with a social encounter. Since there are different rules for communication in the two situations, the interviewee may be puzzled about which rules are appropriate. Even though the conversation may be pleasant, pleasure and gratification are not the factors that bring people together for the interview and should not be the determinants of when it ends.

The best termination is accomplished in a friendly, collaborative, and definite manner, indicating that the interviewer knows what she is doing. Adherence to the suggested procedures will ensure a greater likelihood that the interview will terminate rather than just stop or peter out.

Just as an interview starts before it begins, it terminates before it ends. Both participants carry something of the interview away with them, mulling over what was said, continuing the interview in their minds after they have separated. The interviewer may deliberately stimulate postinterview rumination by assigning some "homework." She might suggest that the interviewee think over something they discussed, in preparation for continuing the exploration of the problem. The following is an excerpt from a protective service interview:

WORKER: So that we can work on it next time, I'd like to ask you to put down anything Mike does that is a problem and also write down what kind of discipline you used in trying to deal with the problem. How does that sound to you?

MRS. P.: Yeah, I guess I'll probably forget, but I'll try.

WORKER: Well, try to do as much of it as you can. I think our time is about up now. Will this same time and day be convenient for you next week?

The interviewer needs to schedule some free time between interviews. We noted the importance of this in discussing the beginning of the interview, to enable the interviewer to clear his mind in preparation for the next interview. Time off also is necessary, however, to serve the needs of the interview just concluded. The worker may need time for review and evaluation of this interview, time to absorb some of the less obvious aspects before closure. Evaluation is a responsibility of the interviewer. The interview is not ended until the interviewer recapitulates the encounter in his mind and attempts to assess his performance critically. There are a number of questions that the interviewer may want to ask of himself in making such an evaluation.

1. In retrospect, what were the purposes of this interview—for the interviewee, for the agency?

2. To what extent were the purposes achieved?

3. What interventions helped to achieve the purposes? What intervention hindered the achievement?

4. What was my feeling about the interviewee?

5. At what point was my feeling most positive? Most negative?

6. How might these feelings have been manifested in what I said or did?

7. If I now empathize with the interviewee, how did he seem to see me? What seemed to be the reaction of the interviewee to the interview?

8. When did the interview seem to falter? When was it going smoothly?

9. At what point did the interviewee show signs of resistance, irritation? What had I said or done just prior to that?

10. At what point did it cease to be an interview and become a conversation, a discussion, an argument?

11. If I had the opportunity of doing the interview over again, what changes would I make? What justifies such changes?

12. What, in general, did this interview teach me about myself as an interviewer?

Recording

Having conducted and completed the interview, the interviewer is faced with the responsibility of recording it in some manner (126). Very considerable amounts of staff time and agency finances are absorbed in recording. Time and cost studies of agency expenditures indicate that for every dollar spent on interviewing, an additional three dollars are spent on recording (163, p. 253). In addition to actual time spent in recording by the worker, such expense involves clerical transcribing time, filing time and space, time in record reading.

Recording ensures a continuity of client-agency contact that transcends the client's contact with any individual social worker.

The case record also implements the agency's accountability to the community. It provides a permanent, documented account of services to clients.

The interviewer about to record the interview faces the essential question, What should be recorded and how should the recording be organized? Just as purpose guides interview interaction, so it guides selection for recording. Traditionally, social work recording has been designed to meet a number of different purposes. We record to achieve more effective practice; we record to meet the needs of supervision and administration; we record to provide material for in-service training and teaching; we record for the purpose of research. There is no consensus on the principal purpose of social work recording; consequently, recording has served these various purposes with limited effectiveness and has served no one purpose well.

Use of case records suggests that they are an integral aspect of practice and interviewing. The caseworker responsible for a case is the person most likely to use the records. Studies of record use indicate that their principal use has been in preparation and planning for direct or indirect service to the client (163). Records are used less frequently for supervision and administration, rarely for teaching and training, and even less frequently for research.

Miles' empirical study of usage of correctional case records further confirms that the use of records for teaching and research is minimal and that their use in supervision has been overemphasized (203). According to Miles, the worker uses the record "to organize his thinking about the case and to plan future courses of action. Through reading the record and recording his contacts with the case in the record, the [worker] organizes his thinking and prepares his plans for the case" (203, p. 290).

Social workers and supervisors frequently use alternatives to the records in getting their work done. Thus, supervisors use the worker's verbal recapitulation of interview activity and workers depend on memory and notes of the previous contact in preparing for the next contact (95). Records are used for administrative review and case assignment. The records are most likely to be used during the early phase of contact with the client (95, p. 61).

The recording purpose dictates form and content. If recording is primarily designed to serve the needs of the practitioner, it might include content which focuses on the extent to which the purposes of the interview were achieved, worker interventions which helped or hindered achievement of purpose, client strengths and weaknesses in relation to interview purpose, work completed, and plans for the next contact. The practitioner's record would include all the essential identifying data which would enable him to review the client's situation at a glance.

Record content and organization will naturally differ from agency to agency. However, at least one definite prescription may be justifiable. The agency needs to be clear and explicit as to the purpose, or purposes, for which it requires the records. The agency should be able to communicate to the workers its unambiguous expectations as to what is wanted, how much is wanted, why it is wanted, how it should be organized.

The time lag between the interview and the recording should be as small as possible. The longer the passage of time between the interview and the recording, the greater the danger that interview content will be forgotten or distorted (152). No matter what the purpose, selectivity is inevitable; even in the most detailed process records, a large part of what happens goes unrecorded. An hour's interview, when transcribed, generally covers thirty-five to forty typewritten pages. A great deal of selectivity is clearly involved in a process recording of six or eight pages, which is a long record by any standards. Selectivity and consequent distortion are empirically confirmed by comparing process recordings with tapes of the same interviews (326).

Experimental attempts have been made to standardize and reduce recording through forms of one kind or another (267, 268). An effort is made in these forms to record great detail briefly and concisely through categorization. Thus the Seattle Atlantic Street Center Recording System permits 151 diagnostic categories and 17 treatment-technique categories. The categories employed have been distilled from the theoretical and social work practice literature. Use of the form has cut recording time to less than one-fourth of that previously needed (268, p. 35).

Summary

Listening is an active, selective process. Concentrated listening is difficult because speech is considerably slower than thought. Listening, like silence, is an important interviewer activity. Interviewee silence might be maintained in order to further the work of the interview, as a hostile, controlling gesture toward the interviewer, or as a defensive gesture. More frequently it helps the client organize his responses, synthesize his reactions, integrate what has taken place.

Lying is frequently encountered. Like all behavior, it is purposive. If there is good reason to believe the interviewee is lying, there is little to be gained and much to be lost by ignoring it.

Note-taking during the interview is a hazardous distraction which, however, is sometimes necessary and appropriate.

Just as the interview begins before it starts, it terminates before it ends. The interview process continues after termination, in the minds of participants. Termination should be gradual, should involve adequate preparation, and should be followed by interview recording for a variety of purposes.

Chapter 7

~.~

Cross-Cultural
Interviewing

This chapter is concerned with the problems that frequently result from the separation between the worlds of the social work interviewer and interviewee. Class, color, age, and sex are some of the significant subcultural differences which might separate interviewer and interviewee, increasing social distance and limiting empathy and understanding (153). There is often doubt expressed that people can, in fact, bridge these gaps which separate them.

The problem is neatly delineated by a California study of services in the AFDC program, comparing characteristics of social workers and recipients. "Social workers were generally college trained, young, white and single; many recipients were older, of a minority group, had less than a high school education, had four or more children, had been on public assistance for two years or more and lived in an urban ghetto on an average income of $217 per month" (42, p. 4 of app. I).

The Middle-Class Interviewer—
the Lower-Class Interviewee

The social work interviewer is generally middle class in identification and orientation. The interviewee is frequently lower class. "Lower class" and any of the other identifying labels that have been employed—"low income," "working class," "the poor," "the disadvantaged"—are vague and ambiguous. They tend to include diverse subgroups which are distinguishable. There are differences between the well-organized poor and the disorganized, demoralized poor; between multiproblem families that are overwhelmed by their situation and more adequately functioning families with money problems.

As used here, the term "lower class" refers to that sector of the population that has lived under low-income conditions over a long period of time. Low income is not a temporary, atypical situation for them but a prime fact in their lives. Consequently, in defense and adaptation, they have developed a life style, a set of values, a configuration of attitudes, and a repertoire of behavior that is identifiable and characteristic (50, 139).

The poverty environment acts as a particular socializing matrix which influences and determines the ways people believe, think, and behave. Low-income life style, "the culture of poverty," is, of course, a convenient fiction, much as the middle-class life style is. It would be difficult to find any middle-class or low-income family that exactly mirrored the life-style configurations detailed in a sociology textbook. Still, there is sufficient empirical material to suggest that low-income people do have beliefs, attitudes, and patterns of behavior that are distinguishable from their middle-class counterparts.

For instance, scheduling, a relatively routine problem for the middle-class interviewee, is likely to be a special problem for the lower-class interviewee. There are persistently noted differences in time sense among the social classes. For a variety of reasons there is less concern with scheduling, with punctuality, with time-related regularity among lower-class interviewees. Consequently, while making the effort to schedule interviews, agencies offering service to lower-class clients might also consider an open-door arrangement. Such an arrangement permits the interviewee to come for an interview at unscheduled times with some assurance that an interviewer will be available. It might involve availability at the times most convenient for the lower-class male—evenings and weekends. Walk-in arrangements are, furthermore, in line with another facet of lower-class use of agencies. The motivation to use the agency is highest when the individual or family faces a crisis. Anticipating problems is a middle-class exercise; lower-class people are likely to respond to the problem when it is causing maximum discomfort. It is at this point that the client wants to see an interviewer and that one should be available if the opportunity for helping is not to be lost.

The open-door policy needs to be supplemented by a "revolving door" policy, making possible an easy return for later contacts. Lower-income interviewees are likely to have definite immediate goals for any contact. They are apt to want immediate alleviation of discomfort rather than to work toward any elaborate, long-range objectives. Consequently, once their limited goals are achieved, they may have little motivation for continuing the contact. At the time of the next crisis, however, they may want to return; agency policy should make them easily welcomed. Such a policy implies a willingness to be concerned with symptoms rather than with causes and a readiness to attempt to alleviate symptoms rather than extirpate causes. Each problem situation would be viewed as a distinct entity, and there would be acceptance of the probability that problems would recur.

Whenever the low-income interviewee is ready to come to an agency, physical inaccessibility is more of a deterrent than it is for the middle-class interviewee with a car. A woman has to count on long, inconvenient rides, the expenditure of badly needed money on carfare, arrangements for babysitters, etc. A man has to solicit his boss's permission to take time off and may lose pay. The physical accessibility of an agency which has offices in a low-income neighborhood is, therefore, an important prerequisite for effective service.

Coming to the agency at all, wherever it is, however flexible the schedule, may pose a problem. However brave the attempt at informality, an agency is still a place of middle-class strangers. The lower-class interviewee may be uneasy about her dress, language, and conduct, uncertain about acceptability, and anxious about doing the wrong thing. She may have doubts about whether she has the social skill required to initiate and maintain such a contact. With lower-class interviewees, therefore, the social worker should be more ready to consider a home interview. The interviewee is then on her own ground, in a milieu in which her dress, language, and conduct are appropriate.

Attitudes toward the agency prevalent in low-income neighborhoods also may reduce motivation to arrange for or accept an appointment. The agency may be viewed as an institution of social control, representing the Establishment, the oppressive, depriving society.

The interviewer and the interviewee bring different preconceptions into the interview. Lower-class clients are apt to come with a general cynicism which suggests that everyone is out for himself, everyone has an angle. Their whole life experience generally confirms such an assessment of human interaction. The exploitation, indifference, and rejection experienced by low-income people at the hands of members of the dominant culture exacerbate the difficulties in developing a relationship of trust and confidence between a middle-class interviewer and a lower-class interviewee.

A lower-class person is apt to be much more concerned with consequences of behavior than with explanations of causation. Where causation is considered, it is in terms of a single simplistic explanation rather than a complex, multiple one. "Why?" or "What explains . . ." is less likely to hold attention for discussion than "What has happened?" or "What will happen if. . . ." The client's orientation is more likely to be external and fatalistic. "Acts of fate" and "environmental pressures" are apt to be seen as causes for difficulty, in contrast to the psychological orientation to problem origin likely to characterize the worker's thinking. For the lower class, threats to sheer physical survival in the midst of pervasive physical deprivations take clear priority over concern with difficulties in personal relations. Lower-class clients are likely to discount intra- and inter-personal difficulties as explaining their situation because the pressures of deficiencies in their physical environment are so overwhelmingly obvious. At the very minimum, the interviewer has to be receptive to the idea that the interviewee's definition of the situation may be right. She must initially try to orient the interview to consider the solutions that the lower-class interviewee thinks are necessary.*

These differences in orientation help explain the unanimous conclusion of numerous studies which detail the reaction of lower-class clients to "talking cures" (casework included). The studies available show clearly that, when compared with middle-class clients, lower-class clients are offered psychotherapy less frequently, accept psychotherapy less frequently, drop out earlier and at a higher rate when they do accept it, and tend to benefit less from it (134, 202, 246).

The lower-class client's communication patterns pose problems for productive interviewing. Language generally is used within a limited group of people who share assumptions and interests that make elaboration unnecessary. Most people employ a restricted code for primary-group communication; they use shorthand speech which depends on considerable shared experience to fill in what is left unsaid but is mutually understood. People outside the group may find the speech difficult to understand because meanings are condensed and dislocated. A more elaborate, less particularistic communications code is generally used with outsiders in deference to their lack of understanding of the private language. The lower-class interviewee, however, is likely to use the restricted code even with outsiders, such as the interviewer, which hampers the inter-

* These brave statements simplify a complex problem. Agency workers often redefine the client's problems in their own terms not because they want to arbitrarily deny the lower-class client's definition of the situation but because, unless they redefine it, there isn't much they can offer the client. The agency may not be able to help the client in the way she wants to be helped. There isn't much it can do about solving the problems of poverty, lack of housing, lack of satisfying, self-actualizing, well-paying jobs, drugs in the streets, rats, falling ceilings, and plumbing that doesn't work. So the social workers try to help in the ways they think they can—mainly by exploration of feelings, attitudes, understanding. They often redefine the situation so that they can help in the only way they are equipped to help.

viewer's efforts to follow what she says and to understand her experiences.

One problem is simply a difference in word usage, as we have noted earlier on p. 29. But often the problems are complex and structural. A study of the contrast between middle-class and lower-class interviewees, all of whom had faced the same crisis experience (a tornado), revealed a number of significant differences (259, 260). Middle-class interviewees seemed to grasp what the interviewers wanted and presented reasonably well organized, coherent accounts of what had happened to them. They built structure into their stories and were responsive to relevant probes. There was a tendency to generalize from their experience. The lower-class interviewees had less tendency to take themselves as objects of introspective reflection. There was less inclination to empathize with the interviewer. Lower-class interviewees responded more to their own internal imagery than to the questions posed by the interviewer. The interviewees tended to personalize and concretize their experience. Their accounts of their experiences were apt to be rambling and unorganized, lacking a coherent focus. The interviewer had to be much more active and controlling if focus was to be maintained and the interview purpose accomplished.

The researchers concluded that these were differences in communicative styles that directly affect behavior in the interview. Other studies of lower-class speech support their conclusions. Such speech tends to "reflect a sender-centered, particularistic style of speech as against a more topic-centered style in the speech of the higher status speakers" (328, p. 97). Bernstein (17) notes significant discrepancies between the lower-class speech system and the communication code characteristic of the social work interview. The lower-class speech system puts less emphasis on a vocabulary of feelings. There is a preference for concrete rather than abstract propositions. Parenthetically, it might be noted that the lower class interviewee has less concern with confidentiality although he is not altogether insensitive to the invasion of privacy.

Cross-class interviewing difficulties do not originate exclusively from the interviewee's side of the desk. If the lower-class interviewee is uncomfortable with the middle-class interviewer, the reverse may also be true. The interviewer is understandably more uneasy in those situations in which interviewee's background is significantly different from her own. She cannot fall back on the fund of shared experience to understand what the client is talking about and to guide her judgments. For example, the interview opening may be somewhat more difficult. There is a smaller community of interest on which to base the social small talk which eases transition to the formal interview.

In contact with the unfamiliar, the interviewer is understandably more anxious. But anxiety is not the only feeling likely to be generated. Some of the feelings which may oppress the middle-class interviewer in contact with a lower-class interviewee are detailed by a member of a mental-health interviewing team assigned to a slum area.

We may experience feelings of guilt because of the realization that we are much better off than they and, in addition, are secretly glad that we are better off. Being faced with the living conditions of the poor and their lack of dignity may also stir up in us fears that "it could happen to me." On the other hand we cannot disregard a second feeling that may be aroused, i.e., the latent wish to be like them. We may envy them their freedom from responsibility, their leisure, and the fact that they are allowed free expression of their drives. We may secretly wish that we ourselves did not have to clean the house or go to work. Since in order to function as members of the middle-class we must reject these wishes, we may in the same way tend to reject the lower-class. (293, p. 328)

The interviewer may feel overwhelmed and depressed at the weight of environmental stresses and deprivation and feel hopeless about her capacity to be of any help.

The more activist-oriented social work interviewer may have another kind of difficulty. Such interviewers may face the overidentification reaction noted by McMahon in medical students who interviewed the poor as part of their training.

Because of the need to relieve the poor of responsibility and to blame society, they were unable to pay attention to the contribution of intrapsychic factors to their patients' situations. Because they tended to equate diagnosis for character and neurotic problems with criticisms of the poor, they had difficulty in observing and integrating psychological data with the rest of their patients' lives. (180, p. 565)

The caseworker may feel irritated by the lower-class client who does not afford him the opportunity to practice the more intensive brand of psychotherapy on which we still tend to place a high premium (311, p. 10). A psychiatrist attached to a public clinic expresses some of the disillusion which might be felt by some social workers in contact with lower-class clients.

> When I first came here I had high hopes of doing something about the neglected people who are sick—the Negroes, Mexicans, Puerto Ricans, the poor in general. But I've become sort of disillusioned. Most of them really can't be reached, because they live in cultures where "acting out" is habitual, where you don't talk much and practically never in intimate terms about yourself. So when I tried to discuss things with them, they just wouldn't discuss. "Look, Doc," they'd say, "forget the horseshit. I know all that. Just give me something to get through the day so I don't lose my temper so much." Well, what can you do? (244, p. 73)

The quotation reflects one of the principal findings of Hollingshead and Redlich's study of the social-class aspects of psychotherapy, namely, that middle-class psychotherapists frequently "dislike patients from a low socio-economic class, do not understand their values and often have difficulty in understanding them as persons. Reciprocally, lower class patients are less likely to understand what the psychotherapist is attempting to communicate even though they want relief from misery" (134, p. 397).

The fact that class affiliation is a significant factor in the social worker's assessment of the client is confirmed by Vail's research (320). Vail used case analogs to study workers' reactions to variations in client's race and class. The same case situation was presented to over 250 workers, except that the race and class identifications of the client were varied. Some workers were led to believe the client was a middle-class white; others were cued to believe the client was a lower-class black. Questions were asked about the worker's prognosis, the kind of treatment that should be offered, expectations for change. Socioeconomic class was found to have a "significant effect on such variables as the worker's assessment of the client, the general treatment plan—and the worker's expectation of the client in the treatment situation. . . . Class is a stronger influence than race in the worker's total assessment of the client" (302, p. 243; see also 34).

How can one reduce the gap between interviewer and client, to make the interview more effective? The following suggestions are supported by, and derive from, the writings of workers and researchers who have had experience with lower-class interviewees (15, 32, 51, 54, 86, 100, 171, 181, 193, 209, 222, 238, 290, 314, 339).

At the start of the interview, use of Mr. and Mrs. rather than just a surname or first names, shaking hands, and introducing oneself need to be observed with seriousness and sincerity. These rituals and forms are not empty gestures to people who have been persistently denied such elementary symbols of civility and courtesy. A clear statement of who the interviewer represents and the purpose of the contact is important. Low-income groups are currently being contacted by a wide variety of people representing a broad range of programs. They have been surfeited with promises. Justifiably cynical to begin with in response to their experience with missionaries from the dominant culture, they assume that everybody has a gimmick. Unless the social work interviewer can clearly communicate who she is, what she represents, and why the interview is being conducted, the interviewee will spend time and psychic energy trying to figure out the worker's gimmick.

The interviewer needs to be more active, take more of the initiative in these interviews than in interviews with middle-class clients. She needs to offer the interviewee a clearly defined and explicit structure; the purpose of the interview needs to be unambiguously stated; greater control and direction need to be exercised over interview interaction to maintain focus. The interviewer should communicate a definite statement of expectations to which she holds the interviewee with polite, kindly firmness. Rather than resenting this, lower-class interviewees may be receptive to direction from professionals whom they perceive as exercising a benign authority in their behalf. Without such direction and activity on the part of the interviewer, the interviewee is faced with responsibility for selecting, organizing, and focusing interview content. He has to have some appreciation and understanding of what material is relevant and the capacity to verbalize without blocking. All of this puts a great burden on the interviewee's skills—a burden that frequently may be beyond the capacity or level of sophistication of the lower-class interviewee.

The tempo of the interview needs to be slower with lower-class respondents. They need more time to accomodate to transitions, more repetition of questions and probes. Such an interview requires more frequent recapitulation and review.

Content selected for the interview and the questions formulated should concern concrete, specific, externally oriented considerations, as against a focus on abstract, symbolic, introspective matters. Concrete examples are better than abstract generalizations, concern with practical tasks preferred to "psychologizing." Questions should be framed in the context of the client's actual life situation.

> If the kids don't go to school what do you do? Who talks to them? What does he say? What do you do when Johnny hits the baby?
>
> Where did you go to look for a job? What did you say when he asked what you could do?

The mood that needs to be established is one of informal friendliness and non-patronizing understanding. Direct, frank, clear, critical statements are preferred over ambiguous subtleties and circumlocutions. The latter are characteristic of social work speech, but with lower-class clients the ambiguous and the indirect tend to be regarded as indicating weakness and also tend to cause confusion.

The class status difference reinforces the role status difference between interviewer and interviewee. The lower-class interviewee thus tends to feel more than ordinarily subordinate. The interviewer therefore has to make a deliberate effort to abandon some of her professional anonymity and come across as a human being. It is necessary to communicate an image of another fallible human being faced with similar problems. Because of the initial social distance, which makes the interviewer more of a stranger than she would be to middle-class people, lower-class interviewees have more of a need to know the interviewer as a person before they can trust her as an interviewer. There is more need for "self-sharing"—recipes, mutual problems in child rearing, helplessness in the face of defective appliances, etc.

It must be admitted that the core of traditional casework derives from theoretical conceptions which have limited applicability to many lower-class clients. Traditional casework is more applicable to the neurotic, introspective, articulate client whose problems are primarily intrapsychic. It suggests a psychotherapy which employs a supportive approach to encourage expressions of affect with the aim of producing change through the development of self-understanding and insight.

The traditional approach is less likely to be effective with clients with limited expressive capacity, who are not psychologically minded and for whom a major component of the problem situation is a highly deprived and constricting environment. Such clients require a modified approach. They require a casework which, in balancing the offer of psychotherapy (changing the client's capacity to cope with the situation) and sociotherapy (changing the situation so that it is easier to handle), includes a heavier emphasis on sociotherapeutic elements. Advice and the sharing of information by the interviewer are very much in line with the expectations of the lower-class interviewee. The working-class clients interviewed by Mayer and Timms on their reaction to their experience with caseworkers "welcomed the idea of receiving suggestions, advice and recommendations from the worker" (193, p. 88), even though they were not always ready and willing to act on them.

With middle-class interviewees the interviewer can assume a preference for "talk" as a mode of problem-solving, a readiness for introspection, and a readiness to talk about feelings. The middle-class interviewer in contact with the lower-class client has the more complex job of socializing the client to the normative demands of the interview as practiced in social agencies. The interviewer has to "teach" the client to focus on feelings, talk about feelings, label feelings. Words and talk are discounted by lower-class interviewees who have been talked into insensibility and cynical skepticism. In establishing a relationship of trust, the worker has to prove her utility to the interviewee on the basis of action. Demonstration of interest and concern by doing something takes clear precedence over verbal expressions of interest and concern.

Actually quieting a crying child, fixing a broken lamp cord, offering a ride when needed, or helping complete a difficult application form, is communicating in a different way what one might have said in the interview. Interview by demonstration is a very appropriate procedure with lower-class clients since they are action-oriented, emphasizing physical and visual communication as against oral communication. Their approach to problem-solving requires adaptations in interviewing technique. The approach is apt to be motoric rather than verbal. Words are used in relation to action. The interview should incorporate opportunities for the lower-class interviewee to act out his situation. Role-playing during some part of the interview may be appropriate (240).

Male, 32, Puerto Rican, lower class, probation interview.

WORKER: Like, you said you bought this transistor radio and it didn't work from the time you brought it home, and you are out the money but not sure you want to ask for a refund. Here, let's role-play this—I'll be the store owner, and let's say you're bringing the radio back.

MR. G.: You mean, play it like I was bringing it back?

WORKER: Yeah. Let's suppose it was happening, and you come into my store with the radio. Now what would you do? You go ahead. . . .

In family interviewing with low-income interviewees, games have been used to initiate the usual pattern of family interaction (174) and hypothetical problems have been proposed for family solutions, to get the family to interact—planning a purchase of furniture, or selection of a movie to see.

Many of these possibilities suggest the particular appropriateness of behavior-conditioning interview approaches with lower-class interviewees for those interviews which have a primarily therapeutic purpose. The emphasis in such an approach is on behavior rather than on symptoms, and on direct advice for particular kinds of behavioral problems.

White Interviewer–Black Interviewee;
Black Interviewer–White Interviewee

Racial difference between interviewer and interviewee is another subcultural impediment to an optimally effective interview. While "non-white" includes Mexican Americans, Indians, and blacks, the following material is almost exclusively concerned with black-white differences. Not only are blacks by far the largest single non-white minority, but also most of the descriptive, clinical, and experimental literature concerning race as an interview factor focuses on blacks.

The black interviewee often presents the interviewer with differences in socioeconomic background as well as differences in racial experience. Although the largest group of poor people in the United States is white, a disproportionate percentage of the black population is poor. The median income of the black family is substantially below the median income of the white family, and a large percentage of blacks live on incomes below the poverty level. The material on interviews with the poor is thus applicable to most black interviewees. But over and beyond the difference in socioeconomic background between the middle-class interviewer and the lower-class black is the racial factor—the differences that stem from the experiences of living white and living black. This is a factor affecting the interview with middle-class as well as lower-class black clients. Color is an additional problem (136).

If trust and confidence and openness between participants are necessary ingredients for a successful interview, how can they be achieved in the face of the long history between the races in this country in which trust was exploited, confidence betrayed, and openness violated? If blacks feel paranoid in their mistrust of whites, this is not pathology but a healthy reaction to the reality they have long experienced, it is asserted. Concealment and "putting the white man on" have been elaborated and institutionalized as a way of life, a necessary weapon contributing to survival, but one which is antithetical to the requirements of an effective interview.

If understanding and empathy are crucial, how can the white interviewer, it is asked, imagine what it is like to live day after day in a society that only grudgingly, half-heartedly, and belatedly (if at all) accords you the self-respect, dignity, and acceptance that is your right as a person? How can the white interviewer know what it is to live on intimate terms with early rejection, discrimination, harassment, and exploitation?

If a feeling of comfortable, untroubled interaction is required for a good interview, how, it is asked, can this be achieved in an atmosphere in which the black interviewee feels accusatory and hostile as the oppressed and the white interviewer feels uneasily anxious and guilty at his complicity with the oppressor? It is anticipated that the black interviewee in such a situation would tend to resort to concealment and disguise and respond with discretion or "accomodation" behavior (76). Often there is open refusal to share, as expressed in "Impasse" by the black poet Langston Hughes.*

> I could tell you,
> If I wanted to,
> What makes me
> What I am.
>
> But I don't
> Really want to—
> And you don't
> Give a damn.

The attitude toward permeability of the racial barrier for the social work interview has shifted over the last twenty years. In 1950, Brown (37), in a questionnaire to social agencies, attempted to assess the importance of race in the casework relationship. The response of 80% of the practitioners, assessing their experience,

* From Langston Hughes, *The Tiger and the Lash* (New York, Alfred Knopf, 1967), reprinted with permission of the publisher.

was that race intruded into the relationship but that it did not present much of a problem to the experienced worker with some sense of self-awareness.

In 1970, disillusionment with the integrationist stance and a greater accentuation by blacks of their special identity separate from the white culture, of the unique effects of their historical experience, has resulted in frequently repeated assertions that no white can understand what it means to be black. Consequently, it is said, an effective interview with a black interviewee requires a black interviewer. Many who have studied this problem, while not ready to go this far, concede that currently the racial barrier in the interview presents a much more difficult problem for rapport and understanding than had previously been imagined (12, 13, 26, 31, 40, 41, 49, 88, 103, 160, 204, 270, 278, 306–308, 338). A black mental health worker, retrospectively analyzing her personal experience, concludes that rapport is possible although not easy to achieve:

> In answering the question of whether a white middle-class psychiatrist can treat a black family, I cannot help but think back over my own experiences. When I first came to New York and decided to go into psychotherapy I had two main thoughts: 1) that my problems were culturally determined, and 2) that they were related to my Catholic upbringing. I had grown up in an environment in which the Catholic Church had tremendous influence. With these factors in mind, I began to think in terms of the kind of therapist I could best relate to. In addition to being warm and sensitive, he had to be black and Catholic. Needless to say, that was like looking for a needle in a haystack. But after inquiring around, I was finally referred to a black Catholic psychiatrist.
>
> Without going into too much detail, let me say that he turned out to be not so sensitive and not so warm. I terminated my treatment with him and began to see another therapist who was warm, friendly, sensitive, understanding, and very much involved with me. Interestingly enough, he was neither black nor Catholic. As a result of that personal experience, I have come to believe that it is not so much a question of whether the therapist

is black or white but whether he is competent, warm, and understanding. Feelings, after all, are neither black nor white. (255, pp. 210–11)

The fact that a cross-racial contact is inherently more difficult, however, may help to account for the higher attrition rate of black clients applying for many kinds of social services. This is true for black clients in family service and black applicants for adoption (85).

The question "Can cross-racial contact be established?" is more correctly redefined as "How can such contact be established?" (255). What can be done to ease the real difficulties inherent in the white interviewer–black interviewee interaction? On the most practical level, because the white worker may be initially regarded with suspicion, as a potential enemy until proven otherwise, it is necessary to observe with singular care all the formalities which are the overt indications of respect.

Discussion of racism has left every white with the uneasy suspicion that, as a child of his culture, he has imbibed prejudices in a thousand subtle ways in repeated small doses and that the symptoms of his racism, if masked to himself, are readily apparent to the black interviewee. It may be necessary to accept such uneasy suspicions as true. The worker needs to acknowledge frankly to himself the possibility of racist attitudes and the obligation to make the effort to change. This suggests a paraphrase of a Chinese maxim. The prospective white interviewer who says "Other white interviewers are fools for being prejudiced and when I am an interviewer I will not be such a fool" is already a fool.

A good interview requires some sense of security on the part of the interviewer that she knows her subject area. The white interviewer who is sensitive to the unfamiliarity of black experience and blackness certainly can make efforts to dispel her ignorance by reading about, and becoming familiar with, black history, black culture, black thinking and feeling. This is a professional responsibility. Here again, lack of knowledge about the interviewee's situation makes the interviewer appear "innocent." There is less respect for such an interviewer, she is more likely to be conned, and she is less likely to be a source of influence.

It may help for the white worker to be explicitly aware of her own reaction to racial difference in the interview. In making restitutions for felt or suspected racism, a white worker may be overindulgent. She may tend to simplify problems and attribute to race some behavior which she hesitates to ascribe to personal malfunctioning, although the difficulty objectively belongs there. Where color is exploited as a defensive rationalization, race is a weapon in the interview. The worker may be "too sympathetic to be of assistance; too guilty to be of help" (128, p. 375). Burns points out that black children "have learned how to manipulate the guilt feelings of their white workers for their own ends. They have also learned to exploit the conceptions most white workers have about the anger of black people" (40, p. 93).

Interview participants of different races are keenly aware of racial differences between them. Nevertheless, the racial factor is rarely discussed openly in interracial casework interviews (270). It is not clear whether race is not discussed because it is regarded as truly irrelevant to the work that needs to be done or because both participants conspire to ignore a potentially touchy issue. One study of racially mixed interviews found that "tape recorded interviews revealed almost no overt or veiled references to racial matters" (204, p. 19). However, race, like any other significant factor which intrudes to contaminate interview interaction, needs to be at least tentatively raised for explicit discussion. Being "color-blind" is denying the real differences which need to be accepted (26, p. 39).

Because the interviewer is less likely to have had the experience which permits empathic understanding of the black interviewee, she needs to be more ready to listen, less ready to come to conclusions, more open to guidance and correction of her presuppositions by the interviewee. The presumption of ignorance, needed in all interviews, is even more necessary here.

Although it is somewhat of a digression from the central focus of racial aspects of the interview, this may be the most appropriate point to discuss the problem of speaking the client's language. It is frequently asserted that lower-class and black interviewees lack the language fluency and facility required for a good interview. Yet studies of speech behavior in the black ghetto, of "rapping," "sounding," "jiving," suggest great imagination and skill in the use of language (162).

There is a good deal of speculation, but little empirical material, on the consequences of the worker's efforts to speak the language of the client as an expedient in reducing social distance. The general conclusion seems to be that unless the worker can speak the language, the jargon, the argot of the client naturally and easily, unless it is genuinely his own language, the attempt will come across as an insincere put-on. Assuming the language of the client in contrast to one's own is to risk "coming on too strong." Not only the phrasing used but also the style of delivery has to be natural to be accepted without ridicule by the interviewee. The "tone" is very difficult for an outsider to come by. The effort of a white, or even an educated, middle-class black, to talk like a lower-class black may sound forced and unnatural. It may appear patronizing and devious to the interviewee and generate contempt and suspiciousness at the interviewer's apparent attempts to con him.

Whyte, studying the social structure of an urban community as a participant observer, encountered this difficulty.

> I bumped into that problem one evening as I was walking down the street with the Nortons. Trying to enter into the spirit of the small talk, I cut loose with a string of obscenities and profanity. The walk came to a momentary halt as they all stopped to look at me in surprise. Doc shook his head and said: "Bill, you're not supposed to talk like that. That doesn't sound like you."
>
> I tried to explain that I was only using terms that were common on the street corner. Doc insisted, however, that I was different and that they wanted me to be that way.
>
> This lesson went far beyond the use of obscenity and profanity. I learned that people did not expect me to be just like them; in fact, they were interested and pleased to find me different, just so long as I took a friendly interest in them. Therefore, I abandoned my efforts at complete immersion. (325, p. 304)

Although the interviewer should refrain from speaking the language of the client when it is not native to her, she needs to be familiar with the language and indicate her understanding of it. If she is going to be working with black interviewees or lower-class interviewees, she should make an effort to learn something of the idioms and vocabulary of that group.

The agency may help by making an effort to hire black clerical and professional staff. Seeing people who are members of her group at the agency gives the black client a sense of greater assurance that she is likely to be accepted and understood.

Yet black interviewers working with black interviewees present problems as well (334). The fact that black social workers have achieved middle-class professional status suggests that they have accepted some of the principal mores of the dominant culture—achievement motivation, denial of immediate gratification, the work ethic, punctuality, self-denial, etc. To get to where they are, more than likely they have been educated in white schools, have read white literature and associated with white classmates, as they are now associating with white colleagues. The black middle-class social worker may feel estranged not only from whites but also from his own blackness. Establishing a clearly defined identification is more difficult for the "oreos"—those who are black on the outside but white on the inside because of their experiences in achieving middle-class status.

The black social worker returning to the ghetto after an absence for professional training may be viewed with suspicion (297). An "alien" returning from the outside world where he has been "worked over" by the educational enterprise to accept white assumptions, values, and language, he has, in the interim, supposedly lost contact with the fast-changing ghetto subculture. Whereas the black interviewee may see the white worker as representing the enemy, he may see the black social worker as a traitor to his race, a collaborator with the Establishment (255, p. 98). Barriers toward self-disclosure and openness may therefore be as great in the black interviewee–black interviewer combination as in the interracial combination.

The pervasiveness of the negative cultural definition of blackness also affects the black client. He may feel that being assigned to a black interviewer is less desirable, that a white interviewer may have more influence and be in a better position to help him. The black worker may be the target of displacement. The hostility felt by the black interviewee toward whites may be expressed toward the black worker simply because she presents a less dangerous target.

Recently some black social workers may have felt pressured into a greater militancy, a more vehement espousal of blackness, as against being Negro, than they genuinely feel. Such a stance is a defense against the implied accusation of having deserted their race and is an effort to retain their identification with their black brothers. In such a situation, the black interviewer may find it difficult to be relaxed and at ease in the interview. On the other hand, a militant black interviewer may have to suppress his fury at a docile black interviewee.

The black interviewee is a source of anxiety to the black interviewer in other ways as well. As one black psychiatrist says, "For the therapist who has fought his way out of the ghetto, the [black interviewee] may awaken memories and fears he would prefer to leave undisturbed" (255, p. 228). It is, therefore, not surprising that Brown found black social workers to be less sympathetic toward black interviewees than toward white clients (37). They were made anxious by failures on the part of black clients to live up to the standards of the dominant culture. They felt that such deviations reflected on the race as a whole, decreasing the acceptability of all blacks, including themselves. A black AFDC client talking about black social workers said:

Sometimes the ones that have had hard times don't make you feel good. They're always telling you how hard *they* had to work —making you feel low and bad because you haven't done what they done. (192, p. 153)

The danger of overidentification is greater in the black interviewer–black interviewee situation. In this context, overidentification is aptly defined by Calnek as "a felt bond with another black person who is seen as an extension of oneself because of a common racial experience" (43, p. 42).

One clear advantage, however, in the black interviewee–black interviewer situation is that the black professional makes possible the identification with a positive image. "A black counselor who has not rejected his own personal history may be most able to inspire a feeling of confidence and a sense of hope in his black client" (160, p. 888).

A situation where the interviewer is black and the interviewee white poses its own kinds of problems. The black interviewer in contact with a white interviewee has to control any hostility he feels toward whites generally so that it does not distort the interview. He is likely to be tense, fearing expressions of antipathy from the interviewee.

A white client who sees himself as lacking in prejudice may welcome assignment to a black worker. It gives him a chance to parade his atypically unprejudiced feelings. He may feel that he has been assigned to an unusually competent worker, since only an unusually accomplished black would have, in his view, achieved professional standing. Also, because whites who come to social agencies often feel inadequate and inferior, they may in some cases more easily establish a positive identification with the "exploited" and "oppressed" black worker (114).

Many white interviewees, however, may be reluctant to concede to the black interviewer a presumption of competence. They may wonder if the interviewer is as good as the agency's white workers and feel as though they had been assigned second best. The white interviewee, especially from the South, may be sensitive to the reversal in usual status positions. Where the interviewee brings a prejudicial attitude against blacks into the interview, he is less likely to regard the interviewer as a source of influence and, hence, less likely to respond to the interviewer's efforts to socialize him to the interview situation or guide him in the interview. A prejudiced interviewee in such a situation is less responsive to overt and covert conditioning cues communicated by the interviewer (279). This is only one aspect of a general resistance to submit to any kind of influence from a negatively perceived interviewer. Prejudice produces a functional deafness, reducing receptivity to communication from the interviewer.

Despite these difficulties, a study which tested the degree of distortion in responses to black and white psychiatrists by patients in a county psychiatric ward concludes that "the factor of race did not significantly affect the behavior of the subjects in the interview situation" (336, p. 690). The responses indicated that the patient perceived and responded to the professional status rather than to the racial factor.

A California study asked AFDC recipients to assess the help they received from their caseworkers. The study group was sufficiently large so that black and white caseworkers had had contact with both black and white recipients. The general conclusion was that the "race of the worker, per se, did not make a significant contribution to the amount of 'help' recipients received from the social service" (42, p. 10 of app. I).

In contrast, however, a recapitulation of findings from a dozen relevant studies indicates that, in almost every instance, there was some effect which derived from racial difference between interviewer and interviewee (258, pp. 149–151). In contact with white interviewers, blacks are more likely to make an acceptable "public response"; in contact with black interviewers, they offer a more "private" answer. Blacks are less ready to share their feelings about discrimination with white interviewers than with black interviewers (39), just as working-class respondents are less willing to share radical political beliefs with middle-class interviewers than with working-class interviewers (156).

Carkhuff and Pierce conducted experiments in which black and white interviewers from both middle- and lower-class backgrounds interviewed white and black interviewees from both class backgrounds. The variable tested was the "depth of self-exploration in interpersonal processes" as interviewers were exposed to the different interviewees. Both class background and race affected the readiness with which people shared intimate material. Interviewees were most open in contact with an interviewer of similar race and class.

If interview content is not concerned with matters that may call attention to race relations, there is likely to be less distortion in the interaction. While conscious of the racial difference between them, interviewer and interviewee can relate themselves to the neutral interview content. If, however, interview content does have racial significance, participants may become uneasy. The difficulty is that so much in the black interviewee's life today may be regarded as implicitly related to the racial problem. However, where the subject matter is meaningful and important to the interviewee, he may transcend any inclinations toward dissimulation and exploit a positive relationship to share honestly what he feels and thinks, whatever the race of the interviewer.

Just as the variables of class and race overlap to determine interview interaction, the variables of race and sex present a complex interrelationship. The black male interviewee may feel resentment toward the black female interviewer. The status relationship in the interview reflects problems deriving from the frequency of female-headed households in the black community. Perhaps the most problematic combination for a good interview is a white female worker and a black male client. This combination intensifies all of the threats to masculine pride involved in the subordinate position of interviewee and evokes all of the menacing mythology of interracial sex.

Male-Female

Men and women are members of different sexual subcultures. In many significant ways they differ in their orientations toward social relationships. The differences may result partly from differing socialization experiences. The research literature on public opinion interviewing confirms that the sex of the interviewer affects responses (137). The general conclusion is supported by studies on the sex of the examiner and responses to projective psychological tests (59).

Although the effect of sex of participants on the social work interview has not been studied, there has been some work on client preference for sex of counselor for vocational and personal problems (97, 164). Both male and female prospective clients expressed a preference for male counselors. Preference statements obtained after the counseling indicated that "clients who had preferred female counselors before counseling were more likely to change preference after counseling than were clients who preferred a male counselor" (97, p. 467). In general, studies tend to show that interviewees prefer older interviewers to younger interviewers and male to female interviewers. Apparently, the readily identifiable cues of age and sex suggest differences in expected capacity of the interviewer to be of help. The older male is perceived as more likely to be knowledgeable, understanding, and experienced (30).

Male dominance is manifested even when the male is the interviewee. In a study of joint interviews by female workers with husband and wife pairs, analysis of the interaction indicated that "husbands are less apt to follow the direction of workers or workers are more inclined to follow the lead of husbands. One may conjecture that the workers in the study felt more uncertain of themselves in interviewing the husbands than the wives, possibly because they had less experience with males than with female clients" (77, p. 572).

In general, females are more accepting of personal counseling interviews than males (117) and likely to be freer about expressing feelings in interviews, whether the interviewer is male or female (96, 147, 226). Men are more reticent generally, and especially about feelings; boys are less verbally accessible than girls (5).

Some interview content is more directly sex linked. It may be easier for women to talk of menstrual difficulties, birth experiences, clothing styles, and discrimination against women with a woman counselor. Men may feel freer to talk about sports, gambling, or "making out" with a male interviewer. The differences between "locker room" talk and "beauty parlor" talk reflect the possible barrier in interviews when participants are of opposite sexes (151). Despite difficulties, however, a good relationship can, and does, transcend sex differences (189).

Younger-Older

Most social workers are younger than many of their clients. Cultural aspects of age differences may operate as barriers to effective interviewing (78). The contact between younger and older people evokes reverberations of the parent-child relationship, but here the positions of helper and helped are reversed; the younger person is in control and directing, however lightly and permissively, the older interviewee. Both participants are apt to be somewhat edgy in response to this "unnatural" situation (46).

A generation gap is inevitable. The older client was socialized at a time when American problems, values, and mores were quite different. In effect he or she grew up in a different country. Another component of the subcultural age gap derives from the differences in physiology between youth and old age. The abatement of instinctual needs, the greater physical effort required for every activity, the slower tempo, the great susceptibility to physical insult and injury, the immediate awareness of the possibility, and inevitability, of death—in a thousand major and minor details, the world is a different place for the older person, beyond the easy imagining of a worker living in a 20- or 30-year-old body.

The social derogation of the aged, their foreshortened time perspective, the reversal from adult independence to greater dependency, the lack of a valued, useful social role, tend to differentiate further the aged client from the younger worker and introduce discontinuities in empathy and understanding. The aged are more susceptible to confusion in time periods, querulousness which stems from loneliness, and repetitive reminiscing, all of which create hazards for efficient, effective interviewing.

Older interviewees frequently tend to blur the focus of the interview by reminiscing. Rather than being random behavior of little purpose, reminiscing may contribute important functions in interview interaction. Pincus points out that reminiscing serves to reduce the age difference between the interviewee and interviewer. Reminiscing has the "effect of bringing the older person mentally back through time to the same age or situation as that of the younger [interviewer], thereby in effect erasing the existing age difference" (227, p. 51). If age difference is regarded as a threat to status, the older interviewee may meet the threat in this way. Reminiscences about past accomplishments also serve an expressive function. They reassure the interviewee that he was once more competent, more capable, than he is now.

Interviewing in the home rather than the office may frequently be necessary, sparing the client the physical insult of a long, tiring trip to the office, often up and down stairs that are difficult to negotiate. However, because an office interview requires the older person to mobilize himself to move out of his isolation into the world of other people, it may, on occasion, be the desirable choice.

Nonverbal information is of particular importance in interviewing the aged. The interviewer needs to be sensitive to the degree of physical and/or mental loss sustained by the interviewee as a result of aging. Hearing loss is frequent and may be indicated by the forward lean of the interviewee, a tendency to turn his ear toward the speaker or to gaze intently at his lips. It may be necessary for the interviewer to speak a little louder, slower, and more distinctly. The worker may need to watch for indications that the interview is making excessive demands on the interviewee's limited physical energy. The pace of the interview may need to be slower and the time allotted for the interview shorter. Studies of interviewing of aged respondents indicate, however, that such expectations are often erroneous and that large numbers of old people still are capable of engaging in prolonged interviews and do so with zest (340).

One of the advantages of aging is the freedom to ignore the social niceties. A person may be too old to be concerned with what others think. Such interviewees may be more outspoken, more insistent, more stubborn than the usual interviewee and consequently more difficult for the interviewer to take in stride; a greater measure of patience, understanding, and forbearance may be needed.

The interviewer may have special problems with his own feelings when working with aged interviewees. The problems encountered and the emotional reverberations initiated by contact with the older interviewee may create anxiety for the interviewer. The problems of illness and the constant reminder of the imminence of death haunt such interviews. The older client is everyone's parent, and the problem of the young adult in relation to an aging parent is one that many interviewers face in their own lives.

The social worker may feel a sense of futility and despair in response to what she regards as the limited resiliency and adaptability of the interviewee. Certainly there is less of a future available to such a client, and the interviewer may question the expenditure of effort in behalf of this age group. The interviewer may be discouraged by the slow pace of interaction and change exhibited, particularly when these may be compounded by the confusions of incipient senility. She may feel drained and exhausted by the demands made on her as a fellow human being by the interviewee. The world is "filling up with strangers" for many older clients. Faced with growing loneliness and isolation, older interviewees may rank the expressive, social functions of the interview interaction much higher than any possible instrumental rewards.

Interviewing Children

Interviewing children presents special problems (237). The child is still dependent on his parents and still has an intense affective tie with them. It colors his relationships with all adults and may present problems for the interviewer. The possibility of negative association of the adult interviewer with all hurtful, rejecting parental figures is apt to be most intense with disturbed children. Older children, and particularly adolescents are peer oriented and reticent about communicating with adults. If the interviewer is perceived as a parent surrogate, such resistance is likely to be a major barrier to an effective interview. If perceived more neutrally, however, the interviewer may be able to capitalize on the adolescent's ambivalence regarding adults and tap the component which makes them anxious to share with a friendly adult who has no authority over them. In general, then, the interviewer should clearly dissociate herself from the child's parents and teachers and present herself as a neutral, friendly adult.

A child's fears of collusion between parents and interviewer should be dispelled. Yet the general rules of confidentiality between adult interviewer and interviewee cannot be applied intact to interviews with dependent children. Since the child is dependent on his parents and since they are responsible for him, should all of the child's secrets shared with the interviewer be relayed to the parents? If not, what are the limits of what should be shared? There is currently no clear-cut answer to this difficult question.

When the interviewer meets the child, she can most often assume that he is willing to go with her. Consequently, it is better to say, "The interview room is ahead. Let me show you" than to ask "Do you want to come with me now?" Getting the child away from his mother to go with the stranger into the interview room, however, may present a problem. Moving easily, slowly, with some recognition of the child's anxiety in separating from his mother is a helpful approach.

Boy, 6, middle-class, child guidance clinic.

WORKER: [After introduction made by mother.] Hello, George. Let's go to the playroom together.

GEORGE: [Clings to mother, hides face, speaks in a whisper.] No, no, no.

WORKER: You don't know me, so you don't want to come with me. I can hardly blame you. [George looks shyly at interviewer.] Your mother will be waiting for you when you come back.

MOTHER: You go with the lady, George. I'll be waiting here for you.

WORKER: Yes, if you want to come with me to the playroom, you can look out and see your mother waiting for you.

It may be necessary to permit the parent to accompany the child to the interview room. If the interviewing room is far from the waiting room, the child cannot look out occasionally to see his parent. If it is too close, however, the child might be anxious about the parent hearing what he says.

As simple a gesture as shutting the door to the interview room to ensure privacy and quiet is more complicated in a child's interview. The child may feel frightened now that a way of escape is cut off. It might be well to leave the door open and let the child decide when to close it.

Nonverbal sources of communication provide rich data about mother and child. Their behavior in the agency waiting room is instructive. What seating arrangement have they selected—near each other, at a distance, the child on the mother's lap or standing pressed close against the seated mother? Is the mother reading to the child, talking to him, ignoring him? How does the mother handle the problem of outer clothing for the younger child as he prepares to leave the waiting room for the interview? Does she help with difficult boots and zippers? Does she help even when the child seems capable of managing on his own? What is her tone of voice—affectionate, querulous, guarded? What is the nature of the stream of comments addressed to the child—primarily directive ("Do this," Do that," "Watch this," "Sit here") or primarily reassuring ("Don't worry," "It will be all right," "I'll be here")? During the interview with the child, nonverbal communication provides a range of information—activity level, resistance to activity, freedom in initiating activity, and its focus, tics, thumb sucking, nail biting, hair stroking, genitalia rubbing, the smell emanating from the enuretic and the soiler.

Usually children do not initiate the contact for an interview. Children are not independent enough to do so, but, more important, the behavior which occasions the request for service is often a problem for others but not, frequently, for the child himself. Since the child almost always is referred and comes at the request or coercion of someone else—his parents, the school, the community —he may not know the reasons for the interview. The interviewer probably should start by asking if the child knows why the meeting was scheduled. Although the child may at least suspect the reason, he may deny having any difficulty. His parents certainly have told him something beforehand, which may only have increased his anxiety and resistance to the interview and interviewer. Clarification of the purpose of the meeting is of primary importance. We often forget that we owe the child an explanation.

Dr. —— asked us to see you because you seem to have a lot of accidents.

Your parents called and said they were worried about your work at school.

Your mother called and said there were constant fights between you and your brother.

The interviewer, recognizing that the appointment with the child was made by others, should indicate that he wants to hear the child's version of the situation.

Just as it is inadvisable for middle-class interviewers to use lower-class speech, or whites to use black ghetto language, the adult interviewer should not affect childish speech nor pat heads, tweak cheeks, or pull ear lobes in effusive intimacy. Some tend to speak in a loud voice, as though children were deaf, or to speak in an unnaturally sweet voice.

Because an interview requires some minimal language facility, there is a lower age limit for productive interviewing. Children younger than age 4 or 5 are in a preverbal stage, in terms of interview language requirements. The child's limited vocabulary requires that the interviewer choose his words carefully so that they are within the child's range. It might be helpful for anyone faced with interviewing children to review some of the studies of normal vocabulary attainments of children at different ages. The child's limited vocabulary also suggests that he may have difficulty in communicating complex feelings. He may not be able to discuss generalized behavior because he lacks the necessary abstract vocabulary.

Interviews with children require more structuring and guidance by the interviewer than do interviews with adults. The child's limited language development and limited conceptualizing capacities makes undesirable the funnel approach—initial general, open-ended questions, followed by progressively more limited specification of focus. It is best to start with specifics, although leaving the child considerable choice. Small, understandable questions eliciting a description of his actual behavior and actions are easier for a child to answer than questions asking him to explain his behavior.

What do you do that makes your mother mad?

What did you do yesterday that was fun?

How do you act when you're scared?

What do you and your brother fight about?

Because a child is highly suggestible, the interviewer has to be careful not to formulate questions so they telegraph an expected or desired answer.

Some aspects of childhood offer an advantage for the interviewer. Children have only begun to learn how to control and disguise their behavior and their speech. There is, consequently, a good deal of spontaneity in both, which is very revealing without their being aware of it. Children have less of a tendency to intellectualize and rationalize their situation simply because they have less capacity to do so and less practice in it. There is less concern with and awareness of logic and consistency and what is socially acceptable, hence a great likelihood to "tell it as it is."

Putting thoughts into words is a strain for children, who are new to language use; it is analogous to holding an interview in a foreign language for an adult. Hence children are apt to be tired within a shorter period of time. Since children's thought processes are slower, the interview tempo is slower.

The boundaries between fantasy and reality are more permeable in children, and the interviewer may be puzzled by communication in which the two have to be sorted out. A child's responses are apt to be garbled and redundant, lacking in organization. His sense of time, of past, present, and future events, is not so neatly ordered as with adults. The events that are remembered and are of significance are those which are important to children, not necessarily to adults. A common tendency to word repetition may try the patience of the interviewer. The interviewer faces an additional distraction, particularly with younger children, in poor articulation of words. Understanding a young child's speech may require constant, enervating attention.

The dictum that language often obscures rather than clarifies is even truer for a child than an adult. "What does he mean by that?" needs to be persistently asked in interviews with children. Ginott points to the need for translating the child's latent message. An intelligent child spells playroom "pleyroom" on the interviewing-room blackboard.

He turns to the therapist and says, "Is this the right spelling?" This is not a simple request for information. Johnny, with an IQ of 130, may or may not have known how to spell "playroom." But what he really wants to know is the therapist's attitude toward misspellers. Understanding this, the therapist does not rush to give the "right" spelling. He does not assume the conventional role of a teacher. Instead, he says, "In here you can spell any way you want to". . . .

Johnny learns a great deal from his spelling exercises. He learns that the clinic is a unique place, that the playroom is not a school, and that the therapist is not a teacher.

Next Johnny picks up a splintered plastic car and asks in a righteous tone, "Who broke the car?" What he really wants to know is what happened to the boy who broke the car. Understanding the question, the therapist gives a reassuring answer—"Sometimes toys get broken. It happens."

Johnny gets quite a bit of information with his car question. He learns that this grownup does not get angry easily, even when toys are broken, and that there is no need to be overcautious or to walk a tightrope in the playroom.

Finally Johnny says, "You have so many closets in here. What do you have in them?" The therapist answers, "You want to look and see?" Again Johnny obtains very pertinent information; it is all right to be curious in the playroom without being reminded that curiosity killed the cat. By responding to the hidden meanings of the questions, the therapist not only conveys deep understanding to the child but helps him to get a clearer picture of the therapist and the therapy situation. (102, p. 126)

Because children are not as able or as ready to consciously share their thinking and feeling directly with adults, interviews with children employ a variety of adjunctive procedures—doll play, toys and games, thematic apperception pictures that call for a story, picture drawing, puppet play, etc. These materials exploit the child's interest in play and fantasy and permit the active supplementation of limited verbal communication. They are more congruent with a child's usual activities than is the formal interview interaction. Doll play, clay modeling, drawing, and painting permit the child to express himself more freely and with fewer inhibitions than he can in words alone. Not only is the medium of com-

munication more familiar to the child, more in line with his
adequacies, but it may also permit him to share indirectly a socially unacceptable response. Absorbed in a game, playing with
toys, making up a story, or drawing a picture, he is apt to be less
self-conscious and to verbalize some of his related thinking and
feeling without being aware that he is doing it.

As the child plays, the interviewer asks questions: "Who is this
doll?" "What is he doing now?" "What makes him want to do
that?" "What do you think will happen if he does that?" The interview is a combination of nondirective play and interviewer intervention to encourage the child to verbalize about his activities.
The danger of which the interviewer needs to be aware is that fun
and games may become ends in themselves rather than a means for
more productive interviewing.

Most children are apt to be restless and full of energy. Probably
they will not sit quietly throughout an interview but will sometimes wander about the room while talking. The interviewer needs
a tolerance for such distractions and the ability to retain her composure despite constant squirming and fidgeting.

Children also have a limited attention span. Consequently they
find it hard to focus for any length of time on one topic. Interviewing a child is, therefore, apt to require more frequent transitions,
making such interviews appear erratic and unfocused. It is difficult
to adhere to any kind of interview schedule or outline. The interviewer has to be imaginative in using whatever the child offers, in
either his activity or verbalization, to tie in topics that need to be
discussed. Often questions have to be repeated, sometimes because
the child resists answering the question, sometimes because he was
distracted and did not listen to it, and sometimes because he did
not understand the question and it needs to be reworded.

The problems of restlessness, distractability, and limited attention span are likely to be greater in interviews with emotionally
disturbed children.

Because children have less practice in the social graces and feel
less constraint about observing the usual rules of interaction, they
can, and do, ignore questions, and feel less of an obligation to contribute to the interview. The sensitive interviewer needs to be

aware that children are likely to offend him but primarily because they don't realize they are being offensive.

Spontaneity and the more limited impulse control of children may require the imposition of behavioral limitations by the interviewer. Kicking, hitting, and biting the interviewer, destruction of toys and office equipment, need to be kindly but firmly stopped. This is done not only in response to concern for self-preservation and the agency budget, but also out of concern for the child. No limits are set on what the child can think, feel, or say, only on what he can do. This acts to protect him from himself. It may be advisable to raise the question of limits only when it appears that they will be transcended. As the danger becomes imminent, the interviewer might say firmly:

> I can't let you do that.
>
> No hurting people or destroying toys.
>
> You can shoot at the target but not at me.
>
> That's not permitted here.
>
> You can't make so much noise because it will disturb people in the next room.

The prohibition might include a statement of acceptable alternatives and a recognition of the child's feelings that prompted the behavior.

> You want to hit me because you're sore at me. Imagine the doll is me and hit him.

On the other hand, actions contraindicated in interviews with adults are sometimes necessary and acceptable with children. Comforting a child during stress by hugging or cradling is good if the child accepts it.

Matching Interviewer and Interviewee

The problems inherent in interviewing across the barriers of class, race, age, and sex lead inevitably to the question of matching. Would it not be desirable to select the interviewer so that she resembles the interviewee in terms of some crucial characteristics? Would this not reduce social distance, the resistance and constraints in interaction which derive from differences in group affiliation and related experiences and life style?

Homophily as a factor in human interaction is basic to some agency programs and some agency policies. Homophily suggests that members of some subcultural group prefer to associate with, and feel comfortable with, people of the same subcultural group. The denominational agencies and programs such as Alcoholics Anonymous, Synanon for drug addicts, and Recovery, Inc., for former mental hospital patients, are predicated in part on the factor of homophily. People who have shared the same significant experience are more likely to be "culturally at home" with each other.

In chapter 2 we noted the importance of the interviewer's empathic understanding as a condition for establishing a good relationship. Such responses indicate similarity and compatability between interview participants and reduce social distance. The worker's responses indicate that the client's life and feelings are not alien and remote. Such empathic understanding is most easily achieved by the interviewer who shares the interviewee's world.

The difficulties of empathic understanding across subcultural barriers can be exaggerated, however, and the disadvantages of matching the interviewer and interviewee can be as easily underestimated. The world's literature is testimony that one can understand and empathize with others despite having a life which is quite different from the life created for the fictional characters. For example, an American Christian, John Hersey, demonstrated empathic understanding of the feelings of the Polish Jew in his novel *The Wall*; a white American Jew, Elliot Liebow, demonstrates his understanding of blacks in the ghetto in *Tally's Corner*; a white

South African psychiatrist, Wulf Sachs, shows a sensitive under-standing of a Zulu in *Black Hamlet.*

Some of the social and psychological distance is reduced by pro-fessional training which enhances a person's ability to empathize with and understand different groups in the community and which provides the knowledge base for such understanding. The gap may be sufficiently reduced so that the interviewer is perceived as "within range," capable of understanding even though he or she is a product of a different life experience.

Waite points out that the interviewer can draw on analogous ex-periences in helping to bridge the cross-cultural gap. "Empathic resonance with the humiliation experienced by a Negro patient is based primarily upon the white therapist's earlier experiences of threats, insults, restrictions in opportunities and other narcissistic deprivations. . . . This helps fill in the . . . gaps between the ther-apist's own humiliations and those of his patient which are specific to living in a prejudicial society" (310, p. 432).

Although race, age, and sex differences between participants are unchangeable, they are mutable. That is, one can dress and behave to deemphasize rather than to accentuate them. The interviewer strives to act as an anonymous, social neuter, keeping the inevita-ble group identifications as inconspicuous as possible, thus reduc-ing, in some small measure, the barriers of social distance.

Not only is it possible to reduce the gap in social distance, but also the effects of matching interviewers and interviewees are not uniformly positive. Some shortcomings of this solution to the prob-lem of social and emotional distance have become more apparent as a result of experience with indigenous paraprofessionals in the human services. As a consequence of the efforts to find new careers for the poor, during the past few years many social agencies have hired people from the areas they serve as case aides of one kind or another. The case aides live alongside the client group in the same neighborhood, generally are of the same ethnic and racial back-ground as the client group, and often are struggling with similar problems. The case aides and the clients share values, life styles, problems, and deprivations. They therefore are in an excellent po-sition to empathize with, and understand, the problems of the poor and the blacks. Some of these expectations are, in fact, achieved, but the problems are also very real.

A study of evaluations of paraprofessional performance by agency executives and supervisors finds that such workers are given high ratings on their ability to establish relationship and rapport with clients. One agency administrator said:

In intake interviewing, paraprofessionals are very good at picking up clues and cues from the clients. They have a good ear for false leads and "put-ons." Their maturity and accumulated life experience, combined with first-hand knowledge of the client population, assists the agency in establishing communication with clients rapidly. . . . The new client is more comfortable with a paraprofessional because he or she is someone like himself. (112, pp. 5–6)

Another agency executive observed:

Clients may come in with suspicion based on experience with the white world in the ghetto, where they were dependent on this world for services. Now when they come to the agency, they see people like themselves in a different role, where they are not in a provider-beneficiary relationship, but are in a colleague/partner relationship, providing services to the ghetto or the community and to people like themselves. This serves to increase confidence in the agency. (112, pp. 6–7)

Despite these advantages, sympathy and understanding do not always automatically result from matching interviewer and interviewee in terms of background. Sobey notes this in a study of nonprofessionals in mental health agencies:

The assumption is often made that nonprofessional status per se ensures greater sympathy to the plight of the client group. However, this is not always so. . . . The fact that the nonprofessional has been hired will often immediately reinforce his social distance from the group being served, and may set off a feeling of superiority, annoyance, or impatience with those he is supposed to help. (281, pp. 119–120)

Goldberg (105) and Grosser (116) support this statement. Grosser adds that nonprofessional staff "often regard illegitimacy, unemployment, drinking, and even boisterous social behavior as evidence of moral turpitude" (116, p. 137). Riessman confirms these difficulties. Many paraprofessionals "see themselves as quite different from the other members of the poor community. . . . Moreover

. . . nearly all are greatly concerned about their new roles and their relationship to professionals" (239, p. 154). Too close a matching risks overidentification and activation, or reactivation, of problems faced by the interviewer which are very similar to those which concern the interviewee.

On the other side of the desk, the interviewee, feeling a deep rapport with the interviewer and anxious to maintain his friendship, might be prompted to give responses that he thinks the interviewer wants to hear or that would make him more acceptable to the interviewer (318). He does not want to hurt the interviewer's feelings and acts out of obligations of loyalty to the mutually satisfying interaction they have established. High rapport gives the interviewee an investment in the relationship which he would not like to risk by saying or doing anything which might alienate the interviewer.

If the effects of matching are not invariably positive, equally the effects of difference in cultural background between interviewer and interviewee are not always negative. An interviewer identified with one subculture (of sex, race, age, color, or class) and an interviewee affiliated with another represent one particular aspect of in-group—out-group relations generally. Because he is an outsider, the interviewer does not reflect in-group judgments. For the interviewee who has violated or disagrees with in-group values, this is an advantage. Currently, for instance, a middle-class, white-oriented, accommodative black might find it more difficult to talk to a black worker than to a white.

If the interviewee, in response to aspirations of upward mobility, is looking for sources of identification outside the group, contact with a non-matched interviewer is desirable. The lower-class client anxious to learn middle-class ways would seek such an interviewer.

The very fact that the outsider-interviewer may not initially understand the client may be helpful. In trying to make his situation clear to the interviewer, the interviewee may be forced to look at it more explicitly than before. In explaining it to an outsider, he may explain it better to himself.

In summary, it might be noted that too great a similarity between interview participants risk the danger of overidentification and loss of objectivity; too great a dissimilarity makes for greater difficulty in understanding and empathizing. It is not surprising, then, that the relevant research suggests that effective interviewing is not linearly related to rapport. The relationship appears to be curvilinear. Little rapport is undesirable but so is maximum rapport (132, 206). The best combination for the interview is moderate closeness between interviewer and interviewee. The need for some distance is one of the principal conclusions of Weiss's study of the validity of responses by a group of welfare mothers in a public-opinion interview (318–320). The answers given in the interview were checked for accuracy against voting records, school records, and welfare department records. In the study, the influence of interviewer-interviewee similarity and rapport were analyzed separately. Both factors operated in the same direction. Increasing the similarity between interviewer and interviewee increased the bias of the responses; increasing the level of rapport between participants also increased the bias. Socially desirable rather than valid responses were more likely to result under conditions of high similarity and high rapport. Weiss concludes that:

Both on factual and attitude items, high similarity between interviewer and respondent . . . particularly when coupled with high rapport, leads to a higher rate of socially desirable responses. On the factual questions, at least, such responses are known to be less valid. . . . The warm personal relationship which the interviewer rates as "confiding" may seem to the low income respondent to be "intrusive." Her reaction is to tell her friendly "confidante" an idealized version of the facts. (318, pp. 69–70)

Hyman, on the basis of his own research, also supports these conclusions.

Friendliness is important, but a certain degree of businesslike formality may be superior to maximum rapport. At some point on the continuum of increasing rapport, friendliness may pass over into intimacy. Then one is no longer a stranger and the respondent [interviewee] may prefer not to hurt the interviewer's feelings or may be eager to defer to the interviewer's opinion. (138, p. 214)

Further support comes from Dohrenwend, who summarizes her research by stating that "interviewer effects is a curvilinear function of social distance with minimal effects at intermediate social distance" (72, p. 122).

The research on client preference does not uniformly support the contention that the client would invariably select a professional from his own group. Dubey (74), a social work researcher, offers empirical support for the contention that blacks do not indicate an overwhelming preference for black workers. He developed an interview questionnaire with the help of black ghetto residents. Employing black interviewers, he asked some 500 residents of the ghetto area such questions as "Would you rather talk with a Negro social worker or with a white social worker?" "Would you rather go to an agency where the director is Negro or to one where the director is white?" Some 77–79% of the respondents said it made no difference to them. Only 10–11% said they strongly preferred a Negro worker or a Negro agency director.

In another study, however, where respondents viewed racially different counselors in operation, via videotapes of a standard interview based on a script, blacks selected blacks as the preferred counselor and whites selected whites. Clearly the respondents "indicated a desire to be counseled by one of their own kind" (289, p. 43).

A third relevant study showed that preference was dependent on certain conditions. Students at a school of social work in Chicago interviewed residents of a black ghetto in 1968 and elicited their racial preferences regarding service personnel (36). They asked, "If both were equally good, would you prefer that the [doctor, caseworker, teacher, lawyer, parents' group leader] be Negro [black, colored] or white?" Interviewers were both white and black. One relevant result demonstrated the important effects of similarity or dissimilarity in the race of interviewer-interviewee pairs. The white interviewer had a statistically significant, larger percentage of respondents saying that they had "no preference" as compared with black interviewers, to whom respondents confessed they preferred a black (doctor, caseworker, teacher, etc.). However, of the black respondents interviewed by black interviewers, only 55% indicated they would prefer a black caseworker, 45% having either no preference or a preference for a white caseworker.

The basis for preferring a black caseworker, all other things being equal, was that such an interviewer was more likely to be interested in the problems of the black interviewee, was less likely to talk down to people, was less likely to make people feel that they didn't amount to much, would give them more of a feeling of hope, and would be more likely to know the meaning of poverty.

A second question introduced competence as a factor. The question asked for a statement of preference regarding a white or black worker if the white worker was better qualified. A large percentage of those who preferred "equally good" black caseworkers preferred a white caseworker with better qualifications. Competence, then, proved to be more important than race in determining caseworker preference of this group of black respondents.*

In conclusion, then, while cross-cultural interviewing presents some very real problems, they can be resolved by the sensitive interviewer who takes the time and the trouble to try to understand the interviewee who is different from herself. This is a comforting conclusion, when one considers the administrative nightmare that would follow from a well-validated conclusion that only those who shared the experience of the interviewees could effectively act as their interviewers.

One source of difficulty is that the interviewee does not have a free choice of interviewer in coming to a social agency. The client may select his doctor or his lawyer to meet his preferences for race, sex, or age. At the social agency he is assigned an interviewer. Perhaps agencies can offer the interviewee a greater measure of choice if he feels strongly that considerations of matching have considerable importance for him. Experience suggests, however, that these differences are relatively less important in determining the course of the interview than are the psychological cli-

---

* Two additional studies, which came to my attention after this chapter was completed, should be cited. Both empirically support the conclusions that effective counseling of black clients by white workers is possible and that black clients do not uniformly prefer a black worker. Franklin T. Barrett and Felice Perlmutter, "Black Clients and White Workers: A Report from the Field," *Child Welfare* 51 (1972), 19–24; Burton Backner, "Counseling Black Students: Any Place for Whitey?" *Journal of Higher Education* 40 (1970), 630–37.

mate established by the interviewer and technical proficiency in conducting the interview. At best, the considerations described in this chapter are general guidelines which might be helpful if flexibly applied, with a listening ear and an understanding heart attuned to detect individual differences.

Chapter 8

~.

Nonverbal
Communication

We have observed that verbal content is only one
of the channels utilized by interview participants to communicate
their messages. In this chapter we are concerned with the other
channels. "I *see* what you mean" is the nonverbal supplement to "I
hear you talking".

Despite social workers' great interest in nonverbal communication and the frequent exhortations to be conscious of its importance, relatively little systematic attention has been devoted to it
in social work contexts. A survey of three leading journals—*Social
Work, Social Casework,* and *Social Service Review*—between 1958
and 1968 indicated that although 69% of the articles dealt with
casework with individuals, only 3.5% of this group of articles included discussion on any aspect of nonverbal communication
(231).

The neglect in social work is paralleled by neglect in allied disciplines. Freud rarely commented on nonverbal communication despite his observation that "he that has eyes to see and ears to hear may convince himself that no mortal can keep a secret. If his lips are silent he chatters with his fingertips; betrayal oozes out of him at every pore" (94). Deutsch (63) in psychiatry and Allport (3) in psychology devoted attention to this topic some time ago, but development of systematic study was hampered by lack of technology that would permit "capture" of nonverbal communication for analysis.

The tape recorder, movie camera, and video tape have made possible the preservation of the interview almost intact and the replaying each moment for repetitive examination by different observers. Technology also permits the electronic analysis of the characteristics of vocal communication—its exact pitch, volume, "roughness," quavering, etc. (220, 250). As a result, the last decade has witnessed the rapid development of interest and research in nonverbal communication of all kinds. The earlier observational analysis by gifted clinicians is currently being examined more rigorously in studies by Birdwhistell (23, 24), Dittman (67), Eckman (79, 80), Eckman and Friesen (81), Eckman, Sorenson, and Friesen (82), Exline, Gray, and Schuette (83), Exline and Messick (84), Hall (122, 123), Mahl (182–184), Mahl and Kasl (185), Mehrabian (196–199), Mehrabian and Friar (200), Scheflen (261, 262), and Wachtel (309). The relevant literature includes specialized studies of specific nonverbal variables—proxemics (distance and body orientation between speakers), kinesics (body motion), and paralinguistics (acoustical accompaniments of words).

Nonverbal communication can be a very expressive channel for those who have a rich gestural vocabulary. Deaf-mutes communicate exclusively and adequately through the language of gestures. The prize fight is a good example of an "interview" in which all the messages are sent through changes in positioning of arms, legs, body, and head, each fighter carefully watching the other "telegraph" his intentions via body language. A gifted mime, such as Marcel Marceau, can communicate most of what he wants to say without resorting to words.

Indian sign language and the sign language of the deaf, which is derived from the communication systems used in monastic orders pledged to silence, indicate the rich possibilities of the powerful language of nonverbal communications. It is important to note, however, that the gestural language of the deaf, like Indian sign language, has a clearly established, standard, consensually accepted lexicon. There is, in effect, a dictionary of definitions of such gestures. This is not true for much of the nonverbal communication that the interviewer will want to decode.

Channels of Information

We can dispose rather readily of some information channels that are rarely used by the interviewer. The olfactory channel, a source of considerable communication for lower animals, is rarely, if ever, investigated or discussed as a useful source of communication. Subtle changes in body odor might well signal changes in emotional states. However, the cultural emphasis on cleanliness tends to mask all natural body odors. Also, our noses are not educated to detect changes in body odor, and such messages are rapidly attenuated over even the short distances which separate interview participants. Even if we did detect changes, we would not be able to make psychological sense out of them, because we have not studied them. We are aware of the heavily perfumed or the odoriferous interviewee, the smells of liquor and bad breath, and we draw some general conclusions from such data. In general, however, we do not use our noses as instruments for information gathering in the interview.

Similarly, tactile sensory communications are rarely employed. This is particularly true for the dyadic interview. There is currently a great burst of interest in tactile communications in group interviewing. The book *Joy* (265) details the "experiences" developed by sensitivity groups, as at Esalen, in the use of tactile communication as a way in which group members get to know each other. These exercises have been adopted and employed by some social workers who deal with group therapy. Galper's procedures include (a) exploration of space: "Sit on the floor in a circle fairly close to each other with your eyes closed. Feel the space around you," and (b) pass the person: "Stand in a circle comfortably close to each other. Take turns going into the center, close your eyes, lean back as much as you can and let the group pass you around the circle" (99, p. 75).

Occasionally, in moments of great stress, the interviewer will reach over and briefly touch the interviewee in a gesture of comfort and sympathy. Aside from this and the attempts to translate the meaning of a firm or flabby handshake, tactile communication in the dyadic interview is almost nonexistent (207).

The visual channel, however, is a source of a great deal of information in the interview. Whether she explicitly recognizes it or not, the interviewer is constantly observing the great variety of motions the interviewee makes with various parts of her body. As Hamilton says, one can observe without interviewing but one cannot interview without observing (126). Yogi Berra, the ballplayer, often said, "It's amazing how much you can observe by just looking." Good interviewing requires that you be a good "watcher" as well as a good "listener."

Visual sensations, like auditory ones, can be received over longer distances than olfactory or tactile sensations, although here, too, there are limits. Changes in the size of the pupils, tensing of neck muscles, contraction of the pelvic muscles, slight changes in skin coloration (blanching, blushing), and changes in respiration rate all require keen eyesight and are easily lost. At distances of eight or nine feet, distances which sometimes separate interview participants, these messages may not be perceived. Being close to the interviewee may permit detection of subtle movements, but we then may not be able to detect the grosser, more general changes simply because we lose perspective.

What are the sources of visual nonverbal communication? One, of particular interest in home visits, is the language of objects (251). People tend to express their interests and taste in the objects they buy and display. In one home the book collection is prominent; in another home the hi-fi and the record collection are given high visibility; in a third home many kinds of plants are everywhere. The type of art on the walls, the magazines on the table, and the style of furniture communicate something about the people. Is the house open or closed to the outside world? Are curtains and shades drawn, or are the windows uncovered so that people can look out and in? Is the decor formal and stiff or loose and familiar, cluttered or uncluttered, bright or dull colored? Is the furniture arranged so that it encourages comfortable conversation? Are there beds enough for everybody, a place for privacy if needed, enough chairs to seat the whole family at one time, a table big enough for a family meal?

The language of objects includes personal adornments—clothes, hair style, makeup, jewelry. These, like the home, are expressive extensions of self that will be discussed in greater detail below.

The body itself is an object of significant nonverbal communication. The importance of bodily communications is shown by the frequency with which expressions referring to the body are used metaphorically. Schutz has collected a list of terms in common use that describe behavior and feelings in bodily terms (265, pp. 25–26). Included are the following: chin up, grit your teeth, pain in the neck, sink your teeth into, get off my back, tight-fisted, knuckle under, elbow your way, choke up, shrug it off, itching to do it. We talk of being tight-lipped to indicate secrecy; a stiff upper lip suggests fortitude; and we associate dejection with being down in the mouth. We scan the body for indications of age—wrinkles, sagging, changes in skin color, graying hair, dentures —and for scars, tattoos, tobacco stains, occupational stigmata.

Posture is whole-body communication. It might be the stiff and rigid posture of the military, the bent posture of the book-addicted scholar, the loose, casual, relaxed posture of the hippie. The posture may be open or closed—open, allowing access to the body; closed, denying access. Arms held crossed across the chest or legs crossed high up, knee placed on knee, are posturally closed conditions.

The body as an object of observation takes on particular importance at the present time, when drugs are a matter of concern. Needle marks on the arms and "tracks" (discoloration along the course of veins in the arms) accompanied by sniffling, flushing, drowsiness, and very contracted pupils may indicate the heroin ad-

dict. Shakiness, itching, tension states, profuse perspiration, and
body odor all suggest the use of amphetamines (speed). Use of
marihuana is not likely to be observable, since the effects wear off
quickly and leave no evident signs. If seen very shortly after inha-
lation of a strong dose, the person may show reddening of the eyes
and a cough due to the irritating effects of the smoke on the lungs.
If the interviewer knows the characteristic odor of marihuana
smoke, he might detect it.

Most of the body is not ordinarily open to observation, being
masked by clothes. What we have then as a source for nonverbal
communication is, in effect, an extension of the body that offers us
a source of artifactual communication, similar to home furnishings.
Clothing identifies sex, age, socioeconomic status, and nationality.
We expect people of different groups to dress differently. At the
extremes, the dress of the Bowery drifter and the socialite permit
clear identification. In the middle range, drawing inferences may
be difficult. It takes a keen eye to distinguish the upper-lower-class
sales clerk from the upper-middle-class minor executive.

We tend to associate certain dress with certain occupations;
upon seeing it, we draw inferences about the person. The most obvious examples are, of course, in clothing designated as a uniform,
as for the soldier, the policeman, the postman. The priest's collar,
the nun's habit, the hospital uniforms of orderlies, interns, and doctors, registered, practical, and student nurses, require a more practiced eye for accurate identification. But there is, further, a uniform
implied in the designations "white collar worker" and "blue collar
worker," and in the stereotype of the tweed-wearing, pipe-smoking
professor.

There are uniforms of group identification—the long hair, beard,
and headband of the hippie; the studded leather jacket and boots
of the Hells Angels motorcyclist; and the afro haircut and dashiki
of the militant black.

Clothing is an extension of the body and is closely related to
body image. It is therefore an expression of self but also conditions
our self-image (90). Choice of clothing designed to make a short
man look tall, a tall woman look short, loose-fitting clothing to disguise corpulence, and tight clothing to accentuate voluptuousness

tell us something about the interviewee's body image and response to this image.

Shakespeare correctly notes in *Hamlet* that "the apparel oft proclaims the man." The problem lies in accurately deciphering the proclamation. In general, the studies available do not permit attribution of personality characteristics from observation of clothing style, choice of colors, etc. The correlation between clothing and tested personality attributes is not generally much greater than chance (253).

High interest in dress does seem to suggest some dependence on others for stimulation and approval and more anxiety directed toward the environment of other people. Lower levels of interest in dress indicate less dependence on the environment for stimulation and support. Since one motive that determines clothing choice is a desire to make a good impression on others, to ensure their acceptance and enhance our self-esteem, a careless disregard for dress suggests a disregard for the reactions of others. If this is not the result of rebelliousness against conventional society and the triviality of concern with dress, it may suggest a depressive withdrawal. Psychiatrists often chart improvements of previously psychotic patients in part by their gradually increased concern with their appearance.

Clothing is worn for protection in addition to the fact that it serves the cause of modesty and permits self-expression and pleasure in decorative self-adornment. The social worker in protective service, investigating cases of neglect, observes the child's clothing to determine if it is adequate protection against cold and snow, and rain.

The interviewee also observes the clothing worn by the interviewer. If it is at variance with what is generally expected of a middle-class social worker, the worker communicates a disconcerting message. Of relevance is a study in which manual and white-collar workers were told of a man who was consulting a lawyer for the first time. "The man arrived at the lawyer's office and was surprised to find him casually dressed in a faded sport shirt that hung over an unpressed pair of slacks. They [were asked to indicate] what they would have done in the man's place" (253, p. 66). About two-thirds of the respondents indicated a negative evaluation of dress, and a sizable percentage expressed reluctance to use the lawyer's services.

Jewelry is another unit of artifactual communication. Jewels as artifacts of conspicuous consumption tell something about socio-economic status. Elks pins, Phi Beta Kappa keys, peace-symbol jewelry, and slogan buttons indicate the subgroups with which the interviewee and interviewer are affiliated and feel identified. Wedding rings and engagement rings, of course, communicate marital status.

The principal channel of communication and information in the interview is, expectedly, the auditory channel, the transmission and reception of "noises" the participants make. There is much more to auditory interaction than the words themselves. A spoken word can be modified in meaning by the accompanying pitch, intensity, speed, stress, intonation, inflection, articulation, and gesture. Pitch refers to differences in frequency from low bass to high soprano. The velocity of speech refers to movement of the words as they issue from the mouth. Does one word follow another slowly or rapidly? Is the movement jerky or smooth and fluent? Is articulation precise to the point of being pedantic or slurred and mumbled? Intensity refers to volume of speech—so loud that it beats at you, so soft that you wonder if the person wants to be heard? Stress refers to the pattern of increase and decrease in loudness within clauses or as applied to different syllables within words.

The same verbal communication can carry different messages, depending on the acoustical accompaniment. Vocal nonverbal communication tells us how the person says what he says. These are the oral language sounds which accompany the words but are not a property of the words themselves. The vocal nonverbal accompaniments, the meta-communications, the para-linguistics, are like aerial punctuation marks.

The Meaning of
Nonverbal Communication

In general, the study of nonverbal communication is much farther along in description and codification of behavior than in establishing its "meanings." Further, we can be more confident in inferring feelings than in inferring personality or character traits. It is not appropriate here to detail the clinical and experimental procedures through which investigators have established, at some level, the validity of meanings inferred from the observation of specific nonverbal behaviors. The studies cited in the bibliography are the best source of this information. What follows is a summary of some results, of interest to interviewers, from studies concerned with the meaning of nonverbal communication.

A voice can be emotional, so that it breaks, trembles, chokes, is full of sighs, and reflects deep or rapid respiration. It can be flat, neutral, unexpressive, and controlled. A voice can be full of energy or it can be thin. Smooth fluent speech may indicate a lack of conflict or anxiety; it may also indicate a rehearsed speech, designed to deceive.

Anger tends to be expressed by a relatively fast rate of speech that is more than normally loud, by short durations and short pauses. Grief or sadness is indicated by a high ratio of pauses and by slowness of speech, which are characteristic of contempt as well, although the tone of voice differs; fear is shown by a relatively high pitch. A quavery voice may indicate anxiety; a squeezed voice, depression. Dibner confirmed that repeating words and phrases, leaving sentences unfinished, frequent changes in thought, shifts in volume of voice, and stuttering are related to level of felt anxiety (65). Rate of speech and productivity increase with anxiety, and the silence quotient is low. Conversely, depression is characterized by a low speech rate and a high silence quotient (230).

Studies attempting to associate personal characteristics and emotions with speech properties have been reviewed by Kramer (168) and Starkweather (285). They suggest that vocal communication tells us something, but exactly what it tells us is not always clear. The length of silent periods, the length of a pause before a response, the length of utterances before a person permits his partner to speak, the frequency and forcefulness with which he interrupts his partner, unnecessary repetitions, the frequency of incomplete sentences, the omission of parts of words, the frequency of "ahs" and "ums" are characteristic speech patterns whose meanings we grasp only in general terms.

The interviewee may speed up his speech and increase the volume in response to a perception that the interviewer wishes to interrupt. Speed and amplitude change are designed to ensure continued control. The interviewee may increase speed when talking about something embarrassing in order to get it over with as fast as possible. He may decrease volume at the same time, as if to hide the words.

Just as there are postural sterotypes associated with certain occupations—a military bearing, a scholar's stoop—there are occupational voice stereotypes—a clergyman's voice, a teacher's voice, a top-sergeant's voice.

Vocabulary choice is sometimes regarded as a para-linguistic cue (315). The interviewee may choose to say any one of the following: "I should take care of my family," "I must take care of my family," "I need to take care of my family," and "They want me to take care of my family." He may preface any one of these variants by "I think," "I feel," or "I believe." Every variation in use of "think," "feel," or "believe" in combination with "should," "must," "need," or "they want" makes a sentence with distinctively different meaning. Subtle variations in word choice may be cues to differences in underlying attitudes. It may have some significance that the interviewer says "my mother and father" rather than "my father and mother" or "my parents."

"Distancing" in speech indicates an attitude toward the subject of communication. "Those people need help," "These people need help," "Our people need help," and "Our people need our help" suggest a progressively more intimate, less distant attitude. Similarly, an interviewee discussing a previous interview might choose to say "in the interview," "in your interview," "in our interview," or "in my interview." The last phrasing indicates the most intimate acceptance of involvement.

Analysis of speech disturbance, body movements, and interview content through movies and tape recordings of interviews leads Boomer to conclude that increases in speech disturbance as well as nonpurposive body movement were related to anxiety and conflict in the interview (29). He notes that "when the drift of a patient's communication is toward conflictful and difficult areas, his caution increases and there is a greater necessity to choose words carefully. The tension involved in encountering and coping with increasingly frequent and critical syntactic choices is accompanied by rising skeletal muscular tonus" (29, p. 265). His conclusions are supported by Sainsbury's research:

Gestural movements were measured every half minute in 16 interviews. The interviews were divided into periods in which stressful and unstressful topics were discussed, and it was found that significantly more movements occurred in the stressful periods.

The topics which were most affectively disturbing to the patient [by prediction from the case history and from the ratings independently given to the utterances composing the topics] were accompanied by significantly more movement. Resentment was the affect associated with most gesture. (256, p. 469)

Similar kinds of studies indicate the association between vascular disturbances, such as sweating and face flushing, and anxiety and tension (232).

People who like each other tend to reduce physical distance between them; people who dislike each other tend to put more distance between them. Psychological distance also is maintained by avoidance of eye contact. Leaning toward the interviewee, smiling, and looking directly at him are associated with interviewer warmth (93, 196, 199). Conversely, "looking away, leaning away, not smiling and intermittently drumming the fingers on the table is interpreted by the interviewee as interviewer 'coldness'" (234). The interviewee's leaning forward and back is a significant positive indication of a good relationship, the movements indicating also his more active involvement.

An open position which permits access to the speaker's body (arms are not crossed, legs are not crossed) is more generally used when in communication with a liked partner. Interview rapport is associated with the greater likelihood that interviewer and interviewee would mirror congruent postures—that is, if one has his chin in his hand, or is sitting sideways, soon the other will mimic the position without realizing that he is doing so. Postural shifts may relate to the intensity of emotions associated with various topics, as described above by Sainsbury. Also, "postural shifts involving movement away from others often seem to indicate completion of a unit of interaction and temporary disengagement" (261, p. 324).

The status difference between participants in the interview determines some of the nonverbal behavior. For example, an interviewer relaxes his posture most with a lower-status interviewee and least with a higher-status interviewee. The behavior of the higher-status person has a greater effect on the lower-status person than is true for the reverse. Head nodding and speech patterns of the high status interviewer will determine the speech behavior of the lower-status interviewee.

The part of the body which offers the interviewer the greatest number and variety of gestural cues is the face. The face is naked and so is open to observation. "You should have seen the look on his face" is testimonial to the expressiveness of facial gesturing. Courtesy and custom dictate that we look at a person's face while he talks, so it is legitimate to scrutinize the face for messages. The face can be hidden behind the hands, as when we shield our eyes or our mouth with our hands. It can also be hidden behind sunglasses, which may block the eyes and part of the face, making them inaccessible. Removing his sunglasses may indicate that the person is ready to make himself more available. In other instances, when a person wears corrective glasses, the gesture of removing them temporarily may indicate withdrawal. Since he sees less with the glasses off, the world is masked from him.

The face is very mobile and capable of making rapid gestural changes. The forehead wrinkles and furrows, the eyebrows arch and contract, the eyes shift and widen or narrow, eyelids close slowly or flutter rapidly, nostrils flare, the lips curve, curl, tremble, turn up, turn down, open, close, and are moistened and patted by the tongue, jaws clamp, and teeth grind. The head can nod or bob or shake, be raised or lowered; the chin can be thrust forward or drawn in. Anger is expressed by a frown, tensed lips pushed forward, head and chin thrust forward, glowing eyes; pleasant surprise by a broad smile and lifting of the eyebrows.

The facial features are capable of very considerable modulation of gesturing. There is a whole range of possibilities between eyes closed to mere slits and wide-open eyes; between the slight smile and the loud laugh.

Eye contact is an important aspect of interview participants' interaction. It affects the nature of the relationship and indicates how the participants feel about each other. We "hold" people with our eyes and turn away from them by merely shifting our gaze, without moving our body. Interviewees tend to have more eye contact with an interviewer with whom they have a positive relationship.

Women seek to maintain eye contact more consistently than men, an aspect of their greater orientation toward affectionate and inclusive relationships with others (83). A person will attempt eye contact more frequently when listening than when speaking. Physical distance between participants also affects the consistency of eye contacts. At closer interaction distances, people spend less time in eye contact.

Looking directly at an interviewee throughout is a strain and may be embarrassing. Constant efforts to maintain eye contact often end in a power struggle as to who will flinch first. Constant eye contact suggests too great a desire for intimacy and not enough respect for the other person's privacy. Too little contact may suggest disinterest, deception, or dishonesty. An interviewee aware of this frequent interpretation of lack of eye contact may look the interviewer squarely in the eye to suggest a candor he does not feel.

Actual avoidance of eye contact, sometimes by hiding the eyes with a hand or with dark glasses, is apt to be more frequent during a discussion of embarrassing material. Avoidance may indicate shame or a desire to maintain a psychological distance during this time when composure is threatened by the nature of the material being shared. It may also indicate a desire to reduce distraction from introspection, a wish to avoid being threatened by seeing the other person's reaction to the revelations, or a resentful withdrawal from the person who asks personal questions.

Eye contact, like other kinds of nonverbal communication, has a regulatory as well as an expressive function. It marks the initiation and termination of the contribution of one participant or the other (159). For example, we tend to look directly at the other person as we finish asking a question, as though we were saying, "Over to you."

The hands, like the face, are also naked but are easier to hide. By putting one's hands in pockets or by sitting on them, one can withhold them from view. They can be placed in the lap if the lower part of the body is behind a desk or table.

The fingers can make a fist or be extended, palm upward. An open palm, upward, and extended toward the interviewer, suggests supplication. The fingers of both hands can be interlaced tightly or loosely or fingertips can meet to make a "cathedral." Hands held tightly locked suggest inhibited aggression.

The fingers can be used to scratch or to pull earlobes, or to rub one's nose, knuckle the eyes, adjust one's clothes, nervously arrange and rearrange ash trays and pencils on the desk, or to pull apart paper clips. A hand touched to the nose may suggest disdain, contempt, or disgust. Scratching may suggest inhibited hostility turned inward. Finger play around the lips may suggest oral gratification. Picking, smoothing, and cleaning gestures may imply obsessive compulsive traits.

The hands can be used to pound the table, rub the desk or arms of the chair, or squeeze a handkerchief. They can be rubbed, clapped, or wrung together, draped over the back of the chair or clasped around the knees. They can rub the temples, slap the thigh or forehead, pat the hair or pass through the hair in a combing motion, or snap a pencil during a stressful moment. When agitated, women make a rapid hand-to-neck movement, disguised as a hair-grooming gesture; men in similar situations may make an open, palm-down sweep of the hair. A palm placed on the back of the neck is associated with a feeling of defensiveness. We pat the stomach to indicate hunger and press our hands to our heart to indicate sincerity. The arms can be crossed at the waist or akimbo at the chest, or be used to swing in an arc.

The feet and legs are less valuable sources of nonverbal communication. Generally the lower part of the body is obscured from view by a desk or table. The feet are hidden in shoes, so that toes curling or the instep arching is difficult to detect. Even if the feet were open to view, it is generally not considered polite to gaze directly at them, particularly if the interviewer is a man and the interviewee a woman.

Feet and legs have a relatively limited repertoire of motions and the rearrangements can not be rapidly executed. People can tap their feet; they can shuffle them, sliding them back and forth; they can cross their legs in a variety of ways. Women more frequently cross their legs with one knee over the other; men more frequently adopt an "open leg cross," the ankle of one leg over the knee of the other. Women can extend or cross their legs for flirtatious exposure or squeeze them together erotically. Legs can be swung in a circular motion or kicked back and forth.

Seating arrangements involve proxemics—the organization of space relationships between people. Each person has what has been variously termed "personal space," "dynamic space," and the "body buffer zone." Haase and DiMattia (118) studied counselor and client preferences for interview seating arrangement by using four pictures of a male-female dyad talking to each other. In one photograph, the participants' chairs were placed side by side at a 45-degree angle; in the second, the chairs were opposite each other but on the same side of a desk; in the third, the chairs were placed opposite each other with a desk between them; and in the fourth, the chairs were placed at a 45-degree angle with only a corner of the desk between them. A semantic differential scale was used in obtaining a statement of preference. The most preferred position, as indicated by both counselor and client, was the one in which the participants interact over the corner of the desk. Although the counselors also showed a high preference for two chairs facing each other with no desk between them, clients were decidedly more negative toward this arrangement. Apparently the client does not feel sufficiently protected by the open position that might be preferred by counselors because it does encourage openness of interaction. The researchers note that talking over the corner of a desk, as preferred by clients, is somewhat open yet provides a partial barrier. "Conceivably such an arrangement might be preferred by the individual who enters counseling with trepidation about the experience, who is hopeful of help yet threatened by the therapeutic encounter. The 'protected sociopetal space' might serve the purpose of inviting a limited negotiation toward interaction yet offer the necessary security and safety required by most humans in a new and ambiguous situation" (118, p. 324).

The arrangement least preferred by both counselor and client was two chairs with a desk directly between. This format suggests that the participants are opposed to each other. A face-to-face, opposite position also forces each participant to look directly at the other or deliberately turn her face away, a gesture that hints at rudeness. An arrangement which puts the interviewer sideways to the desk or table and the interviewee at the end of the desk or table permits the participants to let their gaze wander without seeming to avoid eye contact.

Nonverbal behavior at the start and end of the interview is likely to be especially significant. The interviewee's actions communicate her attitude toward the interview, the interviewer, and the agency. Does the interviewee enter aggressively, with quiet confidence, or with apologetic diffidence; does she knock timidly before she enters or does she knock with assurance, asserting her right to the scheduled time; does she interrupt a preceding interview that has run past the time allotted or wait self-effacingly until called; does she keep her coat on after she enters, protecting her withdrawal route, or does she indicate that she is ready to remain? The family therapist is cautioned to observe carefully the manner in which the family enters the room and the seating arrangements they choose—who sits next to whom.

Within the interview itself there is a progression of changes in nonverbal communication. If the interview is going well, the interviewee most likely will feel more relaxed, and the stiff beginning posture should start to loosen, precise diction give way to some slurring, formal speech change to more colloquial speech, the clenched fist open. The interviewee will probably turn more directly toward the interviewer and lean more frequently in his direction. If rapport has developed, one would expect the interviewee to take more initiative in terminating silences (324).

At the end of the interview, the participants' behavior again tends to show their attitudes towards each other and towards the interaction. Does the interviewer (or interviewee) keep looking at the clock? Does the interviewee leave hesitantly, trying to prolong the interview by a variety of actions—refusing to rise, put on his coat, move to the door—or does he leave hastily, as though in flight?

Problems in Inferring Meanings

A detailed and precise observation of nonverbal behavior is important. It is only a first step, however. The interviewer still has to infer some valid meaning from the gesture. Accurate observation is a necessary but insufficient requisite to understanding the psychological relevance of the gesture. While the richness and importance of nonverbal communication is unquestioned, its usefulness to the interviewer needs to be established. Attention to, and concern with, nonverbal behavior would be important only if it reliably told the interviewer something he could not learn by listening to the interviewee's words. The significance would be in translating behavior into useful meanings regarding the interviewee's emotional state, his personality, his defenses, his unconscious desires, or some additional, valid information regarding the verbal communication.

The problem is the validity of the inferences we draw from our observations. Is it true that the uncluttered, neat, clean home implies rigidity and anality? Are most women who use heavier than average makeup narcissistic and flirtatious? In how many cases does erect posture imply rigidity? What valid conclusion can we infer from fluttering eyelids? What exactly is a "long-suffering look," "a mocking smile," "a conspirational glance"? Closing or screwing up the eyes *may* represent an effort to blot out the world; wrinkling up of the nose *may* represent disgust; a kicking foot *may* represent aggression. But how often is this actually the case? What nonverbal manifestations differentiate between the slow, hesitant speech of the timid and the slow, hesitant speech of the uninterested and indifferent? Extreme and frequently encountered emotions are easier to "read"—depression, joy, and anger. But it is difficult to distinguish between anger and impatience or disgust, shame and embarrassment, hate and envy, fear and timidity.

We need, and do not have, a dictionary of nonverbal behavior that reliably and validly translates its meanings. The lack of a standard nonverbal vocabulary might be easily tested by the reader. What gestures would one use to communicate a moderate level of disgust, an intense feeling of suspicion, a low level of guilt, a moderate level of concern? It might be easier to convey an intense feeling of sadness or of hate but even here there may be differences in what people regard as the appropriate gestural manifestations of such emotional states.

Some gestures, of course, have a commonly accepted meaning for all Americans. There is a general consensus about the meaning of a handshake, a shrug of the shoulders, a fist pounding the table, the "yes" or "no" shake of the head, or the wink of intimacy. These gestures are similar to sign language "vocabulary" that has universal understanding—the extended thumb of the hitchhiker, the thumb forming a circle with the forefinger, and the circle then extended, to mean "okay," the wavy, two-handed gesture meaning a curvaceous woman, the waving hand meaning "good-bye," the hand-to-forehead salute of the military, the clenched-fist salute of the militant revolutionary. It is also easier to interpret nonverbal behavior that is uniform cross-culturally and might be innate—crying in pain, weeping in sorrow, trembling in fear, laughing in joy (82).

Scheflen (261) rightly warns that attempts to ascribe meaning to nonverbal events should consider the context in which the events occur and the verbal accompaniments. Any interpretation that ignores or slights these considerations is on hazardous ground. He notes, in analogy, that "a letter of the alphabet does not carry meaning until it is part of a word which is part of a sentence which is part of a discourse and a situation" (261, p. 324). The context gives meaning to the nonverbal communication. But, further, in interpreting the meaning it is necessary not only that we know how to translate the nonverbal communication, but also that we know the ethnic, race, and class setting in which the interviewee learned the gesture. The same nonverbal communication may be differently expressed by a white and a black person, differently expressed by a lower-class Scandinavian and a middle-class Italian. Different "speech communities" assign greater or lesser importance to nonverbal aspects of communication and differ as well on the meaning assigned to specific gestures.

In addition, we have to assess the persistence and repetitiveness of the behavior. A single, fleeting instance in which a father, during a family therapy session, turns his back on the rest of the family is quite different from frequent instances in which the father turns away and maintains this position for some time. It makes a difference, too, if he does this in a furtive, jerky, hesitant manner or if he does it in a deliberate, open manner. The quality of the gesture needs to be taken into consideration.

Interpreting gestures requires the recognition that they have both expressive and communicative functions. The interviewee engages in them because they satisfy some need, not because he consciously or unconsciously wants to communicate a message in every instance. The interviewee is supplying information which he had no intention of communicating, which he is usually unaware of having given.

The interviewer faces yet another problem which is spared us in writing or reading a chapter on nonverbal communication. He has the difficult task of receiving, sorting, understanding, and responding to the great number of messages being transmitted simultaneously and continuously on a variety of channels. And he has to do all of this rapidly, while being bombarded by a continuous stream of these multi-channel messages.

In all of this we infer meanings, with least risk, on the basis of deviation. "There is no information in a steady state," so that only by establishing some base line of the way the client talks, moves, etc., can we be aware that at this moment his gesture and/or speech are different. The fact of difference suggests that something is being communicated. Departures from a norm are most significant. If increase in the frequency of motions suggests anxiety, we need to know how much the interviewee tends to move around when at ease. If we say that anger tends to be expressed in a relatively fast rate of speech, we need to know how fast the interviewee tends to speak ordinarily. When he deviates from this base line and speaks at more rapid pace, one might pay close attention to determine whether he is, in fact, responding angrily. Even the base line, however, may have significance. A person whose speech and movements are habitually rapid and jerky—more than the social worker would expect from her acquaintance with a large number of people—may be in a chronic state of nervous tension. Such an inference, should, of course, be checked against the person's response to the content of the interview.

We have learned the nonverbal language as we have learned speech—as a consequence of daily practice, without explicit awareness of how we learned it or what we have learned. Since there is no standard lexicon of nonverbal language, it is not learned as systematically as is speech; responses are apt to be highly individualized. Mahl and Kasl (185) found that some people uttered more "ahs" as they moved into anxiety-provoking content. Others, however, became more studied in their speech.

The risks in deriving valid inferences from nonverbal communication are to be expected. If, after so many years of talking together, we are still novices in the art of verbal communication, what permits us to presume a facility in the more difficult art of nonverbal communication? In spite of all these necessary qualifications, one must concede the validity of Edward Sapir's cogent summation. In spite of difficulties of conscious analysis, "we respond to gestures with an extreme alertness and, one might almost say, in accordance with an elaborate code that is written nowhere, known by none, and understood by all" (quoted in 24, p. 182).

Nonverbal Communication
by the Interviewer

All the visible attributes of the interviewer evoke some kind of response from the client. They may evoke a positive response; they may, however, arouse dislike, anxiety, or hostility. Since we do not know what reactions our visible identifications will call up in the interviewee, it might be well to limit the marks of such identifications. The more neutral the image projected, the fewer the complications likely to arise for interview interaction. Thus, although it might seem to be demeaning and politically timid to remove peace pins and necklaces, what effect do such symbols have on the interview with a pro-Vietnam hardhat? At the very least, we need to be aware that such artifacts do have their effects. Similarly, dress which accentuates and broadcasts the upper-middle-class affiliation of the interviewer increases social distance and interview difficulty in contact with clients receiving public assistance.

The interviewee will scan the interviewer to discern what kind of person he is. In this she is aided by the age, sex, and color of interviewer and also by dress, grooming, diction, accent, word usage, and identifying marks such as wedding rings or lodge pins. The office arrangement and decor also suggest the kind of person one is. Pictures of the family, classical or modern art, a cluttered desk or a clean top, reveal much incidental information.

The interviewer is communicating nonverbal information as actively as the interviewee. The interviewer's behavior often is deliberate and consciously designed to enable some kind of interviewee response. Head-nodding, smiles, body movements toward and away from the interviewee, etc., offer encouragement and support, emphasizing the verbal message "go on" or "yes, I understand."

The interviewer, like the interviewee, having less conscious awareness of and control over his nonverbal communication than over his words, runs the risk of "saying" what might best be left unsaid.

*A 32-year-old mother on public assistance is talking about
her children's vaccinations.*

MRS. Y.: And I said, "Bill, when you were little, they put them in
your butt."

WORKER: Mm-mmm.

The worker comments:

> There was more to this last "mm-mmm" than can be seen in the
> typescript. I have always had an aversion to the word "butt" and
> my distaste came out loud and clear in my inflection in this little
> "mm-mmm." It was clear that Mrs. Y. caught my attitude. A lit-
> tle later I noticed she used the word "thigh" rather than "butt"
> as we continued the discussion.

The behind-the-couch position of the traditional psychoanalyst,
and the church confessional box not only protect the interviewer
from the interviewee, but also prevent the interviewer from communicating what he does not want to share. The telephone is a
source of immunity as well. In talking to people over the telephone, we indulge ourselves in gestures we ordinarily censor when
we can be seen. Our gestures may perhaps express a real dislike
for the person with whom we are speaking. We often forget, however, that we can be seen when we accept a call while in the presence of a client, whose interview the call interrupted. He then can
see us in our deceptive, behind-the-scenes behavior.

Significance for Interviewing

What importance does nonverbal communication have for the interview? It tells us something about the nature of the relationship
between the participants. Body movements toward or away from
each other, changes in frequency of eye contact, changes in positioning with reference to each other are indicative of the state of
the relationship. The nonverbal messages received by the eye help

to confirm the validity of the spoken messages received by the ear. Are the participants comfortable with each other, is there a sense of intimacy and understanding? Body language speaks to these considerations.

Nonverbal information helps to regulate communication. It provides some of the feedback which lets us know if the other person is listening, is anxious to say something, is getting ready to interrupt, is getting bored and restive. It helps us evaluate the emotional response to what is being said. Is the message being received with satisfaction or resentment, with hostility or indifference?

Nonverbal behavior may communicate what the interviewee cannot bring himself to say. The interviewee may not be able to put highly charged material into words, or he may not have sufficient verbal ability to express how he feels. Crying may communicate inexpressible grief; the shame the client may feel but not want to admit may be communicated by hiding her eyes. Emotional expression by nonverbal response was the earliest means of communication available to us as children. In moments of stress we tend to revert to such "language." It substitutes for a verbal message and provides information unavailable otherwise. As Ruesch and Kees say, "There are certain things which cannot be said; they must be done" (251).

Nonverbal communication provides information about feelings and attitudes of which the interviewee has only dim awareness or of which he is unconscious. Nonverbal behavior "is less susceptible than verbal behavior to either conscious deception or unconscious censoring. . . . [Although people can hear what they are saying], most people do not know what they are doing with their bodies when they are talking and nobody tells them" (81, p. 181). Without such feedback, it is difficult to train oneself to control the body so as to transmit the message one would prefer to transmit. Nonverbal behavior tends then to evade and frustrate any efforts of self-censorship. A good deal of it is not only enacted below the level of conscious awareness, but may not be readily available to conscious control. Blushing, twitching, or facial grimaces may "erupt" before the person can gain control.

Since people are more aware of their verbal behavior, they tend to monitor it more carefully and more persistently; they tend to be less guarded and more spontaneous in their nonverbal communications. People also take advantage of their lesser control over nonverbal messages. We tend to accept responsibility and are held accountable for what we say; we take somewhat less responsibility for gestures. Whereas we might never presume to express hostility verbally, we might employ nonverbal channels to do so. Nonverbal messages which contradict the verbal message express ambivalence and permit denial of responsibility. While the person is saying one thing, his nonverbal behavior communicates, in effect, "You know I don't mean it."

Nonverbal communication may amplify the verbal message, emphasize it, contradict it, accent part of it, or anticipate it. In all these ways the interpretation and understanding of the actual verbal message are aided.

AMPLIFICATION:

She wants me to help with the shopping and watch the kids and clean the house. Hell, I worked hard enough on the job. I don't want any part of that crap. [He gestured with his right forearm, palm out, from his body outward, as though he were pushing it away.]

EMPHASIS:

Good, good, that's fine [nodding head vigorously in a yes motion while smiling].

And every god-damn time she [wife]came to visit, you think she would stay with me? No, [bangs desk] not her! She had to see this doctor, or that damn doctor [bangs desk] or some damn social worker [bangs desk].

ANTICIPATING:

When Mrs. B. was speaking of her symptoms, with practically no mention of her husband, she slid her wedding ring back and forth on her finger. Soon she started to talk about her marital problems which were associatively lined to her symptoms. Her wedding-ring play anticipated her verbalizations. (184, p. 322)

ACCENTING:

> You just can't make it on welfare. You're always behind. For God's sake, how the hell would you like to live in this dump? [As she said "you" she pointed a finger at the social worker; when she said "this dump," she swept her arm wide to include the room, at the same time turning her head in half a circle, following her moving arm.]

CONTRADICTION:

> "I'm not stupid, you know. I know it's wrong. Don't think I don't know that. I am not proud of it, you know." [Corners of mouth turned up in what seemed a self-satisfied smirk.]

> The interviewee, a bench hand and machinist's helper, deftly manipulated a pencil through a motley of maneuvers extended over most of his interviews. His skill failed him at only one point when he was defensively claiming that his work efficiency was 100%. He lost control over his pencil and dropped it on the floor. (184, p. 320)

The contradiction can be between the verbal content and any single channel of nonverbal communication. Mehrabian (197) defines sarcasm as a message in which the information transmitted vocally contradicts the message transmitted verbally. One nonverbal message can contradict another. The body posture may be relaxed, but the drumming motion of the fingers on the table indicates tension.

Although the interviewer is admonished to make a conscientious effort to observe nonverbal communication, it might be noted, in conclusion, that the usual rules of etiquette require that we sometimes avoid noticing such gestures. We "turn away" from ear and nose picking and crotch scratching, much as we pretend not to hear stomach rumblings, belching, and farting. However, here, as is similarly true for the verbal channel of communication, the courageous interviewer may act on the supposition that the conventional rules of communication etiquette are suspended in the social work interview. Just as the interviewer might "confront" the interviewee with something he has implicitly said but is reluctant to acknowledge, the interviewer might call attention, for instance, to persistent crotch scratching and introduce explicit discussion of the gesture.

Summary

Much of the interview is conducted through nonverbal channels. Artifacts, clothing, and the body itself are rich sources of communication, as are speech sounds accompanying the spoken word. Research has established, to a limited extent, the meaning of facial, arm, leg, and body gestures and the changes in speech sounds. Seating arrangements selected have communicative significance. In the absence of a well-established lexicon of meanings, it is difficult to interpret nonverbal messages with confidence. Nonverbal communication has significance for the interview in that it provides additional content regarding the relationship, helps regulate interview communication, permits the interviewee to communicate content about which he is reticent or unaware, and amplifies, emphasizes, accents, or contradicts verbal messages.

Chapter 9

~~~~~~

The Group Interview

Social workers developed a great deal of interest and enthusiasm for group interviewing during the 1960s. The group interview was seen not as a replacement for the individual interview but as a useful supplementary procedure on some occasions and as a preferred alternative in other instances. The two kinds of interviews were seen as serving differing purposes and meeting different needs, each more or less appropriate in particular situations.

By convention, a group is generally defined as more than two people. The upper limit of group size is set at a level that still enables each person in the group to have access to everybody else so as to permit direct communication.

The statistics regarding social workers' perceptions of their activity support the contention that there has been a strong trend in the direction of group interviewing. A national study of a random sample of members of the National Association of Social Workers, conducted in 1969, obtained information on job functions. Although casework was still by far the primary job function of most respondents, "a surprisingly large number of the respondents—16%" checked group work as a secondary job function (*Personnel Information*, May, 1969).

While there is evidence indicating a trend, the actual extent of group-interview activity can easily be exaggerated. Statistics made available by the Family Service Association of America recapitulating the experience of family service agencies throughout the country in 1968 indicate that only eighteen percent of all family service contacts with clients involved joint interviewing of husbands and wives and only five percent of such contacts involved family or multiple interviews (*Family Service Statistics*, Nov., 1969).

In 1965 the Child Welfare League of America conducted a nationwide survey of the practice of agencies offering foster family care or institutional child care. Both public and voluntary agencies were included in the survey. The research notes that the agencies report an almost exclusive dependence on casework and the one-to-one relationship in foster care practice, use of group-work methods being reported by "few respondents" (288, p. 27).

Whatever the actual level of activity, there is currently a greater emphasis on viewing the individual interviewee in the context of his family and social group situation rather than in isolation. The fact that social work is concerned primarily with the socius—the social group—suggests that such an orientation is congenial for the profession. The interest in family therapy is both a confirmation and exemplification of this change in the orientation toward the client. Rather than seeing the disturbed child, for instance, as an isolated entity requiring treatment, the supposition is that a disturbed child implies a disturbed family, and that help for the child requires help for the family. The child is what he is because the family is what it is, and since the child does not get sick alone, he will not get well alone. The very act of assembling the family members and having them participate together in the discussion is symbolic confirmation and reinforcement of the idea that the problem belongs to the family as a unit and not to any one member.

Our principal aim in this chapter is to delineate the similarities and differences between interviewing an individual and interviewing a group. The objective is to help the interviewer make the transition as she attempts to move from the familiar context of the dyad to the less familiar group situation. Much that she already knows about interviewing individuals can be readily adapted, with some shift in focus, to the group setting. There are, however, some special problems and novel elements that need to be brought to attention.

Similarities between the Individual Interview and the Group Interview

GENERAL

Content regarding beginnings, range, depth, transition, handling of silence, maintaining focus, and moving toward termination, discussed in the individual interview context, is applicable with modifications to the group situation (287). The same problems are encountered.

The interviewer finds himself engaged in many of the same activities that occupied him in the individual interview—teaching the ground rules of interview interaction and seeing that they are followed, asking questions, soliciting and supporting the expression of ideas, attitudes, and feelings, encouraging and assisting communication, requesting amplification, clarifying ideas and feelings, confronting, giving information and advice, interpreting, helping to make overt what is covert, and summarizing.

As in the individual interview, the group interviewer must seek to establish and maintain an emotional atmosphere that will foster the achievement of goals. He seeks to establish a climate that will enable people to learn freely, to consider freely all alternatives to a decision, to risk themselves in change, to communicate freely and openly. The kinds of relationship between interviewer and interviewee which are helpful in the dyadic situation are similarly helpful in the group interview. The responses of the group interviewer demonstrate to group members a model of tolerance, acceptance, and good patterns of communication.

The group interview also moves through a sequential, identifiable process. It moves through a phase of preparation and beginning, a stage of interaction around the common purpose, and a stage of ending. In its problem-solving aspects it moves sequentially from data gathering to data assessment to use of data in effecting change—specific remedial measures, derived from understanding based on the facts of the situation.

Both dyadic and group interviews require some designation of the interviewer-leader, who is ultimately responsible for the proceedings. There is, in both situations, a differentiation of role between interviewee and interviewer, between group leader and group members. In either situation the interviewer may choose to share his leadership function. As in the individual interview, the group interviewer faces the dilemma of how to structure without appearing to structure, lead without leading, direct without directing, suggest without suggesting, impose without imposing. Actually, for all our brave words and gracious intentions, it is no more possible here than in the individual interview. We have to settle for offering minimal structure, lead, direction.

As in the dyad, the worker cannot divest himself of his status as agency representative. His position gives him some authority in the social system of the group. His authority is reinforced by his special professional education, giving him some special knowledge and skills which he is responsible for using on behalf of the group. Special knowledge is of utmost importance. The interviewer needs to know not only about the processes of individual human development and behavior but also about group development and behavior if he expects to understand what is happening. And he needs to know how to translate such knowledge so as to direct group interaction to achieve the purposes of the interview.

PURPOSE

A group interview, like a dyadic interview, must have a purpose. Just as purpose distinguishes a dyadic interview from a conversation, purpose distinguishes a group interview from a bull session or a coffee klach.

The group social work interview, like the individual interview, is conducted to achieve the general purposes of restoring, maintaining, or enhancing social functioning. The interview can be focused on a variety of specific purposes. The purpose can be purely educational. Family-life education groups meet to help parents acquire useful knowledge about skills of parenthood. Groups meet under social agency auspices to learn about budgeting, meal planning, etc. Or a group may be designed to come to a decision and plan social action about some particular problem—a rent strike, or a demonstration for more adequate assistance grants. It may be designed to help participants cope more adequately with a problematic social situation—rearing of handicapped children, living on a ward in a mental hospital, unmarried motherhood, release from prison, retirement, or living on assistance. A group might be designed to achieve a general psychosocial therapeutic purpose like better communication within a family or resocialization of neglectful and/or abusive parents.

As in the individual interview, members may have their own private purposes in addition to those they share with the group. The hidden personal agenda is as much a fact in group interaction as in the individual interview.

A shared purpose, however, is basic. All participants must know, and accept, a purpose for the group's existence. Shared concern and shared purpose lead to psychosocial interaction of members of the group. This interaction, fostered by the shared purpose, leads to the development of group feeling, group cohesion. The group becomes an entity different from the sum of all individual members.

The difficulties around clearly defining a purpose, noted as a problem for workers conducting individual interviews, are repeated for the group interview. A study of joint interviews of husbands and wives noted that "despite repeated emphasis in the literature on the importance of defining the focus of treatment in joint interviews, there was no attempt to do so in 80 percent of the cases. . . . In some instances no effort was made to identify specific problems in the marriage or to ascertain whether the pair had a mutual goal in seeking the agency's help" (77, p. 570).

The group interviewer has the responsibility of helping the

group achieve its purposes—orchestrating the activities of all the individuals. This is the instrumental function of leadership. The interviewer also has the responsibility of keeping the system in operation until the purpose is achieved—the expressive function of leadership. In both group and individual interviews, the interviewer has the obligation of consciously using herself to help achieve the purposes of the meeting, to do all the things which serve the purpose, and to make an honest effort to refrain from doing anything which might impede the achievement of the purpose. As in the individual contact, the group interviewer seeks to enhance the attractiveness of the encounter for group members by increasing the likelihood that they will get what they want from the contact and by decreasing the cost, the anxieties, they must experience in order to do so.

Interviewees are likely to continue with the group if the gains derived from the contact exceed the cost to them, if they get something from it that they want at a price they are prepared to pay. The results the group interviewee is likely to be looking for are similar to those sought by the individual interviewee—a reduction in discomfort in his social situation, less tension and anxiety and greater satisfaction in his marriage, in relationships with children, on the job, in relating to illness or some other problem. The price that he has to pay is anxiety concerning his ability to meet the demands of an unfamiliar situation, anxiety at self-disclosure, anxiety about what changes he might experience if he lets himself become involved, shame and guilt at the open admission of difficulties in functioning, symbolized by his being at the agency.

If the group does not fulfill any needs, a member may remain in the system physically but drop out socially and emotionally. This is done even more readily and more easily in the group situation than in the individual interview. Since two is an irreducible minimum for an interview, emotional and social withdrawal by a reluctant interviewee effectively kills the dyad. In a group situation, however, one member can absent himself physically, socially, or emotionally without challenging continuation.

Groups, like individuals, resist the difficult, unpleasant, uncomfortable tasks which often need to be engaged in if the purposes of the interview are to be achieved. Groups, too, manifest ambivalence and resistance by irrelevant degressions that are an escape from the tasks, by unproductive silences, by fruitless arguing, by separate conversations among a subgroup. The interviewer faces the responsibility of holding the group to its purpose, of focusing on, encouraging, rewarding, stimulating the kind of group interaction that will lead optimally to the goals. As in the individual interview, the longest way around may be the shortest way there. Digressions may be useful at times, fallow silences may be necessary, a breakdown of group interaction may be a necessary prelude to a productive reintegration.

The interview's purpose is an important determinant of its structure and the differential allocation of group roles. The group formed for a specific educational or action purpose is likely to have a specific agenda, to be task oriented, to be less concerned with personal interaction in the group interview. The group formed for a therapeutic purpose is likely to have less structure and a more open-ended agenda and to be much more concerned with personal interaction. An action group will require different kinds of contributions from its members than will a family therapy group or a meeting of adoptive applicants.

SIGNIFICANCE OF PHYSICAL ARRANGEMENT
AND NONVERBAL COMMUNICATION

A group, as distinguished from a collection of individuals in close physical proximity, involves interaction and conscious, differentiated recognition of each other. The physical arrangements need to be such as to encourage such interaction. A circle of chairs in a room of moderate size for the size of the group is perhaps the most generally desirable arrangement. Too large a room would make the group feel insignificant and lost; too small a room may elicit a cramped feeling and may require too great a closeness and intimacy between members. A circular arrangement permits each person to look at, and talk to, everybody else, and it does not permit the reluctant or resistant member to withdraw easily from the interaction by selecting a seat apart from the group. A circle also has no identifiable status position, no front of the group, and the interviewer can melt in by taking his place unobtrusively in the circle.

A circle of chairs without tables permits all group members and the leader to observe each other to a maximum extent. Yet maximum exposure may be a disadvantage, and tables might be provided, behind which members could take partial refuge. Tables also provide a place for leaning, a place to put papers, handbags, ash trays, and cigarettes—all the usual accessories for a group session.

The selection of seating position is significant. People sitting side by side are more apt to interact. There is a tendency to select a seat close to a person with whom one feels comfortable and with whom one might want to develop a relationship. Sitting next to the leader solicits his support; sitting opposite the leader may suggest a desire to be competitive.

While sight and sound are the principal avenues of communication in both group and individual interviews, the balance is different. There is more nonverbal behavior in the group interview—while one person is talking, many are silent but keeping up a stream of behavioral communication. They grimace, shift in their chairs, move their arms, stretch, twist, flex their legs. They listen to some group members and ignore others; they talk to some and ignore others. Some group members only ask questions; others only answer them. Some people are always interrupting; others are always interrupted; some are selective in whom they choose to interrupt. Some people are included by the group; others are excluded.

SOCIALIZATION TO NORMS

The behavioral norms of the group interview are somewhat different from the norms of usual social group interaction, just as the norms of the individual interview are distinguished from those of a conversation. The interviewer, again, has the responsibility of educating the group to the special norms of this different social system. Productive group interviewing requires members' adherence to such norms as the following:

1. To allow everyone to have his say without undue interruption.

2. To listen carefully and attentively to what others are saying.

3. To respond to what others have said.

4. To keep one's contribution and response reasonably relevant to the focus of what is being discussed.

5. To share, for discussion, meaningful and significant material without regard to the usual social taboos. In fact, the more likely it is to be off limits for ordinary social interaction, the greater the obligation to share this material in the group interview.

6. To be willing to forego the usual social norms of self-defense and accept open discussion and group criticism of one's own problems and feelings.

7. To accept limitations on verbal and nonverbal acting out which might seriously threaten to break up the group.

8. To encourage emotional expressiveness. As in the individual interview, the rules regulate the flow of communication and are designed to let participants know who speaks, how he speaks, to whom, about what, for how long, under what conditions. And, parenthetically, a good many of the prescriptions are equally applicable to the individual interview situation. The rules provide the basis for order in the social system temporarily established when interviewer meets interviewee.

Participant Composition

The problem of group composition parallels the problem of social distance in the individual interview. If group members are too different from one another, they may find it difficult to identify with each other. Since we tend to compare ourselves with those who are similar in some crucial ways, we would resist seeing the group as a reference point for our own behavior if we perceived others in the group as much different from ourselves. Consequently, the best group composition may be of people sufficiently similar to feel comfortable with each other but different enough that the variety is stimulating. Once again the relationship is curvilinear—the extremes of likeness and dissimilarity both being undesirable. In discussing group composition, Northern confirms this curvilinear relationship:

Perhaps the most generally accepted principle is what Redl calls "the law of optimum distance": groups should be homogeneous in enough ways to insure their stability and heterogeneous in enough ways to insure their vitality. This principle is based on the premise that the major dynamics in a group are mutuality of support and mutuality of stimulation among the members. (215, p. 95)

The value of heterogeneity is expressed in the folk saying, "When two people agree on everything, one of them is unnecessary."

If participants are widely different in background, they may be able to share solutions which had not previously occurred to the others. However, the social distance among participants may be so great that they find it difficult to learn from each other.

High group rapport, like high rapport in the individual interview, has its disadvantages. If members derive considerable satisfaction from pleasure in each other's company, they may fear to risk endangering the relationship. They may hesitate to challenge, to raise embarrassing questions, to do the unpleasant but necessary work required if group purposes are to be achieved. Group maintenance then takes priority over achievement of group purposes, and may become an end in itself. Optimum rapport is again part of a curve—high enough that the group can function without undue conflict, but not so high that maintenance of rapport takes precedence over all other considerations.

Advantages of Group Interviews

What reasons specifically and explicitly justify the desirability of a group interview instead of, or in addition to, meeting with each member individually? In what ways are the two kinds of interviews significantly different? The worker needs to answer these questions for herself before deciding to see interviewees in group rather than individual interviews.

A study of the experience by family service agency workers with group approaches suggests some of the advantages (57). Meeting with the family as a whole, rather than individually, permits the worker to obtain more quickly an accurate and relevant diagnostic understanding of the family. Rather than being told about family interaction, she can observe the patterns *in vivo*—leadership, control, role allocation, the pattern of intra-family communication, the nature of conflict, the operations and effectiveness of mutual defenses, the nature of family alliances and rejections, extent and nature of existing family strengths. Intrapersonal problems can be observed as they become manifest in interpersonal encounters.

One family member blurts out what another is anxious to hide. Different attitudes toward joint problems are clearly revealed. Family members correct each other, contradict each other, aggravate and pick on each other. All of this is available for workers' observation and as material that furthers understanding. The whole family is truly greater than the sum of all its parts.

As far as treatment is concerned, through the family interview "the worker and all participating family members are directly and mutually exposed to each other's impact, with the result that the worker is placed in an especially strategic position for intervening directly in the system" (57, p. 280). The worker can directly encourage expression of feelings previously withheld. At the same time she can provide a safe context for the expression of such feelings and offer protection to the family member against whom negative feelings might be expressed. She can demonstrate for family observation, consideration, and possible emulation, new ways of relating to each other. In the presence of the whole family, the worker "legitimizes new norms and expands members' perception of the range of permissible and worthwhile behavior, thus stimulating all [family members] simultaneously to modify basic norms controlling their family interaction" (57, p. 284).

The group situation provides an opportunity for reality testing which is not available in the individual interview. Any changes in attitude that take place as a result of individual therapy ultimately needs to be translated into actual behavioral changes in contact with other members of the family or other social groups. The parent who is more accepting of his child as a result of counseling in a child guidance clinic needs to implement the more accepting attitude at home. Family therapy gives the parent the opportunity of actually practicing such behavior. Such sessions are the laboratory in which a person can experiment with changed behavior under the direction and guidance of the worker. Group reaction helps to inform the member as to how other people are likely to respond. Peer group support for the first tentative efforts in the enactment of new behavior can help the group member feel comfortable with it.

Group sessions may be a preferable kind of contact for those interviewees who need a more diluted and diffuse relationship with the interviewer or who are made anxious by the dependency which might be encouraged in a one-to-one relationship.

That the group interview provides the opportunity for live social interaction, for acting out behaviorally (within limits), for doing rather than only talking, makes it a valuable resource for working with less verbally oriented client groups.

Suggestions for changes may be more easily accepted in the group situation than in the individual interview. Criticism which might not ordinarily be accepted without resentment from a social worker may be accepted from a fellow group member. Identification with the group makes the behavioral norms of the group a reference point for determining individual behavior.

Anxiety is reduced as a group member encounters others who have the same problem or similar ones. The reassurance which derives from universalization of problems has a greater impact through living contact with others similarly troubled.

The repertoire of possible responses to psychosocial problems that is available to group members is increased as they share their variety of experiences.

The group situation permits each person to give as well as receive aid—to be a helper as well as a helpee. Each participant can help other members of the group by offering support, proposing solutions for common problems, encouraging communication, being accepting and receptive. This experience in giving assistance, in contributing to what is therapeutic for others, is, in itself, therapeutically reassuring to the client.

The group interview permits a greater specialization of function than does the dyadic interview. More people are available to perform the variety of functions required for effectively maintaining and implementing the purpose of the interview. Simultaneous support and stimulation, acceptance and expectation are characteristic of the process by which people are helped to change in both kinds of interviews. But whereas in the individual interview the interviewer has sole responsibility for both support and stimulation, acceptance and expectation, the group permits a division of responsibilities. While the worker is supportive, some member of the group may stimulate; while the worker offers acceptance, a member may communicate expectations. While one member is offering a reassuring comment to some person in the group, another member may confront this person with an inconsistency in behavior.

The fact that both instrumental and expressive functions are performed by the same person—the interviewer—in the individual interview may create problems. The instrumental demands may be antithetical, at some points, to the expressive needs. To insist that expectations be met, to confront in order to get the work done, conflicts with the need to support, to comfort, to reassure. The interviewer needs to be simultaneously the "good" and the "bad" parent. The group situation, in allowing for delegation of antithetical functions to different people, simplifies the tasks of the interviewer. He can let the group members carry the instrumental functions—to confront, expect, demand, raise uncomfortable questions—while he devotes himself more or less exclusively to supportive interventions. Or, depending on the composition of the group, he can do the needling, counting on the group to do the supporting.

Providing information and answering repetitive questions once to a group rather than many times in a series of interviews is an administrative advantage. Group intake in foster care and adoption, for example, is frequently used because it provides this advantage of greater efficiency.

Disadvantages of Group Interviewing

Some aspects of group interviewing are simultaneously advantageous and disadvantageous. Some aspects of the group interview are simpler and others are more complex than the individual interview.

The group interview is at one and the same time easier in some respects and more difficult in other respects for the interviewee. The group interview provides more alternative sources of satisfaction than does the individual interview. If the interviewee feels uncomfortable with the interviewer, the dyadic interview is likely to be a failure. If the group member feels uncomfortable with the interviewer, he may find a fellow member to whom he can relate with greater satisfaction. This alternative relationship may keep him working within the group. But this same factor may be a hazard to another member, who derives considerable satisfaction from his relationship with the social worker. In the individual interview he would have exclusive access to the worker. In the group situation he has to share the worker's attention with other people. The situation encourages the development of a sibling rivalry problem and the difficulties which this implies.

While other members of the group may provide support and so make the work of the interviewer easier, they may also be the source of stress and attack on some individual group member. In the individual interview, the interviewer has to be concerned with herself as a source of unproductive stress impinging on the interviewee. In the group situation the interviewee has to be protected from unproductive stress imposed by any other group member or members.

The threat from sharing embarrassing material may be greater in the group since the disclosure is communicated to a larger number of people. However, sharing is made easier by the recognition that others are troubled by the same concerns. Universalities stated by the interviewer in the dyad—"many parents have difficulties with their children," "all married couples fight on occasion"—are actually encountered in the group, as one member after another admits to some problem. Thus, depending on the circumstances, the group may inhibit or promote free expression of private, intimate material.

Since an interviewee is not the sole participant, he can at times withdraw from the interaction without being conspicuous and without threatening the continuity of the interview. However, with more people listening and responding, there is a greater likelihood that an inconsistency or falsehood will be spotted. Some threatening aspects of the situation, which might be missed by the interviewer, may be picked up by members of the group, attuned to what the interviewee may hope to conceal even from himself. By the same token, there are more sources of support than in the individual interview.

From the preceding discussion it is clear that there are some specific advantages in group interviewing. However, the worker also needs to be aware that there are special hazards to be faced when deciding in favor of a group interview.

A caseworker, in particular, must be aware that in moving to a group interview she needs to reorient her focus. The caseworker habitually focuses on the individual as the center of interest. Facing a group, she needs to see the group entity as the center of concern. The worker has to shift her focus from individual behavior to group behavior, individual mentality to group mentality, individual identity to the group image. Her behavior must exemplify for the group a shift from individually centered concerns to those which are of mutual interest. That caseworkers can successfully make the transition is confirmed in a study by Ehrenkranz (77).

Such refocusing may be difficult. In the group situation the caseworker may continue to deal not with the group but with the individual members—to engage in an interview with an individual in the presence of others. There is, of course, a need to focus simultaneously on both the individual and the group; each member is concerned with his own problems as well as group problems and may, in fact, be working on his individual problem by working on group problems. The worker has to travel the narrow path between aiding the group at the expense of any one member and aiding one member at the expense of the group. But the group is first among equals in priority for the interviewer's attention.

The situation for the interviewer is inevitably more difficult as a consequence of a need for a dual focus. The worker has to develop and maintain a relationship and a productive pattern of communication between himself and each interviewee. In addition, he has to develop and maintain relationships and communication patterns between each group member and all the others.

Achieving a common purpose is likely to be more difficult in the group interview. The purposes of a number of people need to be expressed and reconciled. The greater the initial diversity, the greater the difficulty in achieving some working consensus. Purpose, once clarified and accepted, may be easier to stick with in the individual interview. In the group interview the private and competing needs of many people may keep distorting the stated purpose, even after there is some agreement on what the interview is all about. In the individual interview, difficult as it often is, the social worker has the responsibility of motivating only one interviewee to a concern for participation, to a commitment to the purposes of the interview. In a group interview one has to obtain a relatively equal level of commitment from all the members, even though some may see themselves as less involved, less concerned, and less "responsible" for the problem.

Silence in the group is a shared responsibility. The interviewer may thus feel less uncomfortable about a continuing silence, since every member of the group has some obligation to break it. On the other hand, an interviewer may feel that because a number of people are discomforted by the silence, his obligation to do something about it is greater. The pressure of expectation from many may be more keenly felt than the pressure of expectation from one.

Since the interviewer does not have to take sole responsibility for keeping the interview moving or for maintaining the social system, she has more time to sit back and observe and absorb. This advantage is offset by the greater complexity of interaction; there are many more cues to observe and absorb in the group interview.

The influence potential of the worker in the group interview is, in a sense, diluted. She competes with others in the group in affecting the responses of any one member. Indirectly, however, her influence may be magnified. Other members of the group can reinforce her efforts to influence the responses of any one member.

The worker needs to relate himself simultaneously in different ways to different members of the group, yet most communication has to be addressed to all in general and to no one in particular. Communication within a group interview risks a higher probability of failure than in the dyadic interview. In the dyad the communicator can select his ideas and choose his words with regard for what may be specially required to ensure accurate reception by his one partner. In facing a group of people, each of whom requires a somewhat different approach to the idea, a somewhat different vocabulary for best understanding, the interviewer must compromise. He must select his message and his words so that they can be received with reasonable accuracy by all, but they may fail to meet the particular needs of any one.

An intervention that meets the needs of one person may, at the same time, create a problem for someone else. For example, responding supportively to a wife's statement of feeling lonely and isolated may sound accusatory to the husband. And support for the husband's statement of difficulties in providing adequately for the family may trigger anxiety in the wife about her handling of the family budget. This problem of conflicting consequences from the same statement is spared the worker in the individual interview.

The pacing of the group interview is again a compromise between the varying rates that are best for the different members of the group. "Too fast" for one may be "too slow" for another. The possibility of individualization is much less than in the dyad.

The complexity of interaction increases geometrically although the number of people the interviewer faces increases arithmetically. Four times as many people results in a sixteenfold rise in the complexity of interaction. The interviewer has to monitor, receive, understand, and respond to so much more than in the relatively limited dyadic situation. There are not only more people but different kinds of people to which the interviewer must respond. For instance, the family therapy interview requires a capacity for simultaneous empathy with different sexes and different age groups.

In any group there are, concurrently, interactions between individual group members, individual group members and the interviewer, the group as a whole and individual members, the group as a whole and the interviewer, subgroups and the interviewer, and subgroups and individual members. There is simultaneous communication from one to the many, from the many to the one, and from the many to the many.

Being outnumbered, having to react to a number of people, all pulling in somewhat different directions, is likely to be overwhelming and frightening to the group interviewer. The individual interview seems to be much more manageable, much less hectic, and it is. In self-defense the tendency might be to attempt to persevere with a familiar focus—to center on individuals by separating them, in perception, from the group, rather than focusing on the group, on group patterns, on group behavior.

In the dyadic interview the interviewer relates to a verbal recital of the action. In the group situation the interviewer is faced with responding to the action itself, to people behaving, reacting, dealing with each other. The interaction may be primarily on a verbal level but nevertheless this is a living, ongoing, social situation. Members of the group try to manipulate the interviewer into supporting them in conflicts with others, into serving as a weapon against others. In family therapy an effort often is made to draw the interviewer into the family and make him party to the family conflicts. The demands are great and the effort to remain uninvolved needs to be commensurately great.

Both the individual interviewer and the group interviewer have to have faith in the interviewee's ability to play his role competently. In each instance the interviewer tries to maximize the interviewee's participation in and responsibility for the interview. The group interview, however, requires greater personal security on the part of the social work interviewer. The worker needs a willingness to share interview responsibility without feeling threatened. As Schwartz says, the movement from the individual interview to the group interview is from "helping people to help themselves" to "helping people to help others" (266). In the group interview, members at one time or another actually engage in roles usually reserved for the professional. They offer support to other members, they clarify the thinking and feeling of fellow members, they offer interpretations or understanding. The professional is not so directly challenged in a takeover of his usual responsibilities in the individual interview.

Further, the interviewer takes a greater risk of actually losing control of the proceedings in the group situation. Encouraging participation and according the group a larger measure of responsibility for the interaction is an act of control by the interviewer. He is "letting" the group do what needs to be done. But the group may decide to do some things that the worker does not want done. The worker may suddenly find that the group has taken the play out of his hands. In the individual interview, when this happens the interviewer can without great difficulty reassert control. In the group situation, he is outnumbered. Faced with the solidarity of a group in opposition to him, the interviewer may find it very difficult to regain control of the situation.

The larger number of participants in the group interview, permitting the advantage of diversification of roles, has as one of its consequences the appearance of problematic roles. Either by assignment or assumption, different group members may perform such roles as scapegoat, monopolizer, or the silent one. The scapegoat is the target for the displaced hostility and aggression in the group; the monopolizer attempts to usurp all the time available for his own point of view and concerns; and the silent one is a source of disquiet because no one knows what he is thinking and feeling. The interviewer must respond to these members if the group is to operate effectively. She must protect the scapegoat, discourage the monopolizer and encourage others to speak, and tease the silent one out of his fortress—if the group does not anticipate her by dealing with the situation itself. She may initiate group action by asking what prompts their allowing the monopolizer to control the floor, permitting the silent one to withhold himself, or their ganging up on the scapegoat. She might be more directive, suggesting to the monopolizer that he has had his say and perhaps the group might want to hear from others, by intervening as the monopolizer pauses momentarily and asking others what they think, by directly addressing the silent one and asking for her reaction, or by responding to the slightest nonverbal indication of a desire to participate with "Yes, you seemed about to say something?"

Safeguarding confidentiality is more difficult in the group interview situation. The greater the number of people involved, the greater the possibility that there might be violations of confidences. Even if members of the group scrupulously avoid sharing with nonmembers what is discussed, the very fact that group members are party to "secrets" about each other poses a problem. Members may meet each other outside the group—this is a certainty for family groups or groups in institutions. How then should members relate to each other outside the group after sharing confidential information inside it? This problem is less frequently encountered in the dyadic interview.

The individual interview has no prehistory. The particular interviewee-interviewer dyad never existed before the two came together for the interview. In contrast, the group interview situation has frequently existed prior to the interview. Family groups and marital pairs have existed and evolved habitual patterns of interaction for long periods of time before they meet to interact in the presence of the social work interviewer. The presence of the interviewer is, it is true, a new factor. But much in the nature of previous patterns of group interaction is brought into the new situation.

The family, as a natural group, comes to the interview with a structure, an established pattern of interaction, a previous allocation of roles. And it is this as a "given" with which the interviewer is confronted as he meets the family.

If anxiety interferes with achieving the purposes of the interview, then there are more possible sources of interference in the group interview. Each member has to find his position in a more complex social system; he has to find out how he can relate to and obtain acceptance from a number of different "others"; he is trying to determine his relative status with reference to all of them.

There is intra-group pressure to maintain the group. It operates to mitigate conflict and discourage the introduction of divisive content. Participants may have more difficulty in expressing divergent content in the group interview than in an individual interview. Whereas in the individual interview the interviewee strives to be consistent with himself, in the group interview there is pressure toward consistency and conformity with others. The interviewer has to work harder to make certain that the atypical thought, the atypical emotional reaction, is encouraged and permitted expression.

Summary

The current focus on the family unit as a center of therapeutic interest has increased concern with the group interview. The group interview and the dyadic interview are similar in the problems of range, depth, and transition encountered by the interviewer, in the instrumental and expressive activities which the interviewer is called on to perform, in concern with purpose, in the significance of nonverbal channels of communication, in problems of participant composition and socialization to the norms of the interview.

The group interview has diagnostic, therapeutic, strategic and administrative advantages which make it preferable to an individual interview in some circumstances.

Such an interview, however, requires a change of primary worker focus from the individual to the group; a readiness and ability to share interview control with participants; a greater complexity of reactions and a greater heterogeneity of participants to which the interviewer has to respond; greater hazards to confidentiality and to the establishment and achievement of a common purpose; the necessity of dealing with participants who assume problematic roles.

Bibliography

1. Adams, Walter. "The Negro Patient in Psychiatric Treatment," *American Journal of Orthopsychiatry* 20 (1950), 305–310.

2. Allen, Thomas W. "Effectiveness of Counselor Trainees as a Function of Psychological Openness," *Journal of Counseling Psychiatry* 14 (1967), 35–40.

3. Allport, Gordon W. *Studies in Expressive Movement,* New York, Macmillan Co., 1933.

4. Alves, Joseph T. *Confidentiality in Social Work,* Washington, D.C., Catholic University of America Press, 1959.

5. Appelberg, Esther. "Verbal Accessibility of Adolescents," *Child Welfare* 43 (1964), 86–90.

6. Arbuckle, Dugald. "Client Perception of Counselor Personality," *Journal of Counseling Psychology* 3 (1956), 93–96.

7. Aronson, H., and Overall, Betty. "Treatment Expectations of Patients in Two Social Classes," *Social Work* 11, no. 1 (1966), 35–49.

8. Athey, K. R., Coleman, J. E., Reitman, A. P., and Tang, J. "Two Experiments Showing the Effect of the Interviewer's Racial Background on Responses to Questionnaires Concerning Racial Issues," *Journal of Applied Psychology* 44 (1960), 244–46.

9. Axelrod, Morris, and Cannel, Charles F. "A Research Note on an Attempt to Predict Interviewer Effectiveness," *Public Opinion Quarterly* 23 (1959), 571–76.

10. Bandura, Albert. "Psychotherapists' Anxiety Level, Self-Insight and

Psychotherapeutic Competence," *Journal of Abnormal and Social Psychology* 53 (1956), 333–37.

11. Bandura, Albert, Lipsher, David, and Miller, Paula. "Psychotherapists' Approach: Avoidance Reactions to Patient's Expression of Hostility," *Journal of Consulting Psychology* 24 (1960), 1–8.

12. Banks, George P. "The Effects of Race on One-to-One Helping Interviews," *Social Science Review* 45 (1971), 137–146.

13. Banks, George, Berenson, Bernard, Carkhuff, Robert. "The Effects of Counselor Race and Training Upon Counseling Process with Negro Clients in Initial Interviews," *Journal of Clinical Psychology* 23 (1967), 70–72.

14. Barbara, Dominick. *The Art of Listening*, Springfield, Ill., Charles C Thomas, 1966.

15. Baum, Eugene, and Felzer, Stanton R. "Activity in Initial Interviews with Lower Class Patients," *Archives of General Psychiatry* 10 (1964), 345–53.

16. Behrens, Marjorie, and Ackerman, Nathan. "The Home Visit as an Aid in Family Diagnosis and Therapy," *Social Casework* 37 (1956), 11–19.

17. Bernstein, Basil. "Social Class, Speech Systems and Psychotherapy," *British Journal of Sociology* 15 (1964), 54–64.

18. Bernstein, Saul. "Self-Determination: King or Citizen in the Realm of Values?" *Social Work* 5, no. 1 (1960), 3–8.

19. Biestek, Felix P. *The Principle of Client Self-Determination in Social Casework*, Washington, D.C., Catholic University of America Press, 1951.

20. Biestek, Felix P. "The Non-Judgmental Attitude," *Social Casework* 34 (1953), 235–39.

21. Biestek, Felix P. *The Casework Relationship*, Chicago, Loyola University Press, 1957.

22. Billingsly, Andrew. *The Role of the Social Worker in a Child Protective Agency—A Comparative Analysis*, Boston, Massachusetts Society for the Prevention of Cruelty to Children, 1964.

23. Birdwhistell, Ray L. *Introduction to Kinesics*, Louisville, Ky., University of Louisville Press, 1952.

24. Birdwhistell, Ray L. *Kenesics and Context: Essays on Body Motion Communication*, Philadelphia, University of Pennsylvania Press, 1970.

25. Blau, Peter. "Patterns of Choice in Interpersonal Relations," *American Sociological Review* 27 (1962), 41–55.

26. Bloch, Julia. "The White Worker and the Negro Client in Psychotherapy," *Social Work* 13, no. 2 (1968), 36–42.

27. Boehm, Werner. *Objectives of the Social Work Curriculum of the Future*, New York, Council on Social Work Education, 1959.

28. Bogdanoff, Earl, and Glass, Arnold. *The Sociology of the Public Assistance Case Worker in an Urban Area*, Master's thesis, University of Chicago, 1954.

29. Boomer, D.C. "Speech Disturbances and Body Movement in Interviews," *Journal of Nervous and Mental Disease* 136 (1963), 263–66.

30. Boulware, Donald W., and Holmes, David S. "Preferences for Therapists and Related Expectancies," *Journal of Consulting and Clinical Psychology* 35 (1970), 269–77.

31. Bowles, Dorcas. "Making Casework Relevant to Black People: Approaches, Techniques, Theoretical Implications," *Child Welfare* 48 (1969), 468–75.

32. Brager, George A., and Barr, Sherman. "Perceptions and Reality: The Poor Man's View of Social Services," in *Community Action Against Poverty*, George A. Brager and Frank P. Purcell, eds., New Haven, Conn., College and University Press, 1969.

33. Braginsky, B. M., and Braginsky, D. D. "Schizophrenic Patients in the Psychiatric Interview—An Experimental Study of Their Effectiveness at Manipulation," *Journal of Consulting Psychology* 31 (1967), 543–47.

34. Briar, Scott. "Use of Theory in Studying Effects of Social Class on Students' Judgments," *Social Work* 6 (1961), 91–97.

35. Briar, Scott. "Welfare from Below: The Recipient's View of the Public Welfare System," *California Law Review* 54 (1966), 370–85.

36. Brieland, Donald. "Black Identity and the Helping Person," *Children* 16 (1969), 170–76.

37. Brown, Luna B. "Race as a Factor in Establishing a Casework Relationship," *Social Casework* 31 (1950), 91–97.

38. Bruck, Max. "The Relationship Between Student Anxiety, Self-Awareness and Self-Concept and Student Competence in Casework," *Social Casework* 44 (1963), 125–31.

39. Bryant, Eugene C., Gardner, Isaac, and Goldman, Morton. "References on Racial Attitudes as Affected by Interviewers of Different Ethnic Groups," *Journal of Social Psychology* 70 (1966), 95–100.

40. Burns, Crawford E. "White Staff, Black Children: Is There a Problem?" *Child Welfare* 50 (1971), 90–96.

41. Calia, V. F. "The Culturally Deprived Client: A Reformulation of the Counselor's Role," *Journal of Counseling Psychology* 13 (1966), 100–105.

42. California Legislature. *California Welfare: A Legislative Program for Reform*, Sacramento, California Legislature, Assembly Office of Research, 1969.

43. Calnek, Maynard. "Racial Factors in the Counter-Transference: The Black Therapist and the Black Client," *American Journal of Orthopsychiatry* 40 (1970), 39–46.

44. Cannell, Charles F., Fowler, Floyd J., and Marquis, Kent H. *The Influence of Interviewer and Respondent: Psychological and Behavioral Variables on the Reporting in Household Interviews*, Public Health Service Publication, series 2, no. 26, Washington, D.C., U.S. Government Printing Office, 1968.

45. Carkhuff, Robert R., and Berenson, Bernard G. *Beyond Counseling and Therapy*, New York, Holt, Rinehart, and Winston, 1967.

46. Carkhuff, Robert R., Feldman, Marvin J., and Truax, Charles. "Age and Role Reversal in Therapy," *Journal of Clinical Psychology* 20 (1964), 398–402.

47. Carkhuff, Robert R., and Pierce, Richard. "Differential Effects of Therapist Race and Social Class upon Patient Depth of Self-Exploration in the Initial Clinical Interview," *Journal of Consulting Psychology* 31 (1967), 632–34.

48. Chance, Erika, and Arnold, J. "Effect of Professional Training, Experience and Preferences for a Theoretical System Upon Clinical Case Description," *Human Relations* 13 (1960), 195–214.

49. Chethik, Morton, et al. "A Quest for Identity: Treatment of Disturbed Negro Children in a Predominantly White Treatment Center," *American Journal of Orthopsychiatry* 37 (1967), 71–77.

50. Chilman, Catherine S. "Social Work Practice with Very Poor Families: Some Implications Suggested by the Available Research," *Welfare in Review* 4 (1966), 13–22.

51. Chilman, Catherine. "Poor Families and Their Patterns of Child Care: Some Implications for Service Programs," in *Early Child Care: The New Perspectives*, Laura Dittman, ed., New York, Atherton Press, 1968.

52. Chwast, Jacob. "The Delinquent's View of the Therapist," *Federal Probation* 23, no. 3 (1959), 25–31.

53. Clemes, S. R. "Patients' Anxiety as a Function of Expectation and Degree of Initial Interview Anxiety," *Journal of Consulting Psychology* 29 (1965), 397–401.

54. Cohen, Jerome. "Social Work and the Culture of Poverty," *Social Work* 9, no. 1 (1964), 3–11.

55. Cook, J. J. "Silence in Psychotherapy," *Journal of Counseling Psychology* 11 (1964), 42–46.

56. Cotler, Sheldon, and Shoemaker, Donald J. "The Accuracy of Mothers' Reports," *Journal of Genetic Psychology* 114 (1969), 97–107.

57. Couch, Elsbeth H. *Joint and Family interviews in the Treatment of Marital Problems*, New York, Family Service Association of America, 1969.

58. Curry, Andrew D. "Negro Worker and White Client: A Commentary on the Treatment Relationship," *Social Casework* 45 (1964), 131–36.

59. Curtis, H. S., and Wolf, B. "The Influence of the Sex of the Examiner on the Production of Sex Responses on the Rorschach," *American Psychologist* 6 (1951), 345–346.

60. David, John D. *The Interview as Arena*, Stanford, Calif., Stanford University Press, 1971.

61. Davitz, J. R. *The Communication of Emotional Meaning*, New York, McGraw-Hill Book Co., 1964.

62. Denham, William W., and Shatz, Eunice O. "Impact of the Indigenous Non-Professional on the Professional's Role," in *Human Services and Social Work Responsibility*, Willard C. Richan, ed., New York, National Association of Social Workers, 1969.

63. Deutsch, Felix. "Analytic Posturology," *Psychoanalytic Quarterly*, 21 (1952), 196–214.

64. Dexter, Lewis A. *Elite and Specialized Interviewing*, Evanston, Ill., Northwestern University Press, 1970.

65. Dibner, Andrew. "Cue Counting: A Measure of Anxiety in Interviews," *Journal of Consulting Psychology* 20 (1956), 475–78.

66. Ditman, K. S., and Crawford, G. C. "The Use of Court Probation: The Management of the Alcohol Addict," *American Journal of Psychiatry* 122 (1966), 757–62.

67. Dittman, A. T. "Relationship Between Body Movements and Moods in Interviews," *Journal of Consulting Psychology* 26 (1962), 480–86.

68. Dohrenwend, Barbara S. "Some Effects of Open and Closed Questions," *Human Organization* 24 (1965), 175–84.

69. Dohrenwend, Barbara S. "An Experimental Study of Directive Interviewing," *Public Opinion Quarterly* 34 (1970), 117–25.

70. Dohrenwend, Barbara S., Colombotos, J., and Dohrenwend, B. P. "Social Distance and Interviewer Effects," *Public Opinion Quarterly* 32 (1968), 410–22.

71. Dohrenwend, Barbara S., and Richardson, Stephen A. "Directiveness in Research Interviewing: A Reformulation of the Problem," *Psychological Bulletin* 60 (1963), 475–85.

72. Dohrenwend, Barbara S., Williams, J. A., and Weiss, C. H. "Interviewer Biasing Effects: Toward a Reconciliation of Findings," *Public Opinion Quarterly* 33 (1969), 121–29.

73. Donnan, H. H., Harlan, G. E., and Thompson, S. A. "Counselor Personality and Level of Functioning as Perceived by Counselees," *Journal of Counseling Psychology* 16 (1969), 482–85.

74. Dubey, Sumati. "Blacks' Preference for Black Professionals, Businessmen and Religious Leaders," *Public Opinion Quarterly* 34 (1970), 113–16.

75. Duncan, S. "Non-Verbal Communication," *Psychological Bulletin* 72 (1969), 118–37.

76. Duvinage, Thelma. "Accommodation Attitudes of Negroes to White Caseworkers and Their Influence on Casework," *Smith College Studies in Social Work* 9 (1939), 264–302.

77. Ehrenkranz, Shirley M. "A Study of Joint Interviewing in the Treatment of Marital Problems: Parts I and II," *Social Casework* 48 (1967), 498–502; 570–574.

78. Ehrlich, June. "Age and Authority in the Interview," *Public Opinion Quarterly* 25 (1961), 39–56.

79. Ekman, Paul. "Body Position, Facial Expressions, and Verbal Behavior During Interviews," *Journal of Abnormal and Social Psychology* 68 (1964), 295–301.

80. Ekman, Paul. "Non-Verbal Leakage and Clues to Deception," *Psychiatry* 32 (1969), 88–106.

81. Ekman, Paul, and Friesen, Wallace V. "Non-Verbal Behavior in Psychotherapy Research," in *Research in Psychotherapy: Proceedings of the Third Conference*, John M. Shlien, ed., Washington, D.C., American Psychological Association, 1968.

82. Ekman, Paul, Sorenson, E. R., and Friesen, W. V. "Pancultural Elements in Facial Displays of Emotion," *Science* 164 (1969), 86–88.

83. Exline, Ralph V., Gray, David, and Schuette, Dorothy. "Visual Behavior in a Dyad as Affected by Interview Content and Sex of Respondent," *Journal of Personality and Social Psychology* I (1965), 201–209.

84. Exline, Ralph V., and Messick, David. "The Effects of Dependency and Social Reinforcement Upon Visual Behavior During an Interview," *British Journal of Social and Clinical Psychology* 6 (1967), 256–66.

85. Family Service Association of America. "Non-White Families are Frequent Applicants for Family Service," *Family Service Highlights* 25 (1964), 140–44.

86. Fantle, Berta. "The Work of Berta Fantle," *Smith College Studies in Social Work* 34, no. 3 (1964).

87. Faucett, Emily. "A Re-evaluation of the Home Visit in Casework Practice," *Social Casework* 42 (1961), 439–45.

88. Fibush, Esther. "The White Worker and Negro Client," *Social Casework* 46 (1965), 271–77.

89. Fliess, R. "Silence and Verbalization," *International Journal of Psychoanalysis* 30 (1949), 21–30.

90. Flugel, J. C. *The Psychology of Clothes*, London, Hogarth Press, 1950.

91. Foran, Robert, and Bailey, Royston. *Authority in Social Casework*, London, Pergamon Press, 1968.

92. Foulds, Melvin. "Self-Actualization and Level of Counselor Interpersonal Functioning," *Journal of Humanistic Psychology* 9 (1969), 87–92.

93. Fretz, Bruce R. "Postural Movements in Counseling Dyad," *Journal of Counseling Psychology* 13 (1966), 335–43.

94. Freud, Sigmund. "On the Beginnings of Treatment," in *Complete Works*, vol. 12, J. Strachy, ed., London, Hogarth Press, 1958.

95. Frings, John. "Experimental Systems of Recording," *Social Casework* 38 (1957), 55–63.

96. Fuller, Frances. "Influence of Sex of Counselor and of Client on Client Expressions of Feeling," Journal of Counseling Psychology 10 (1963), 34–40.

97. Fuller, Frances. "Preferences for Male and Female Counselors," *Personnel and Guidance Journal* 42 (1964), 463–67.

98. Gallant, D. M., et al. "Enforced Clinic Treatment of Paroled Criminal Alcoholics," *Quarterly Journal of Studies in Alcoholism* 29 (1968), 77–83.

316   Bibliography

99. Galper, Jeffrey. "Non-Verbal Communication Exercises in Groups," *Social Work* 15, no. 3 (1970), 71–78.

100. Geismar, Ludwig L., and La Sorte, Michael A. "Research Interviewing with Low-Income Families," *Social Work* 8, no. 2 (1963), 10–13.

101. Gill, Merton, Newman, Richard, and Redlich, Frederick. *The Initial Interview in Psychiatric Practice*, New York, International Universities Press, 1954.

102. Ginott, Haim G. *Group Psychotherapy with Children: The Theory and Practice of Play Therapy*, New York, McGraw-Hill Book Co., 1961.

103. Gochros, Jean. "Recognition and Use of Anger in Negro Clients," *Social Work* 11, no. 1 (1966), 28–38.

104. Golan, Naomi. "How Caseworkers Decide: A Study of the Association of Selected Applicant Factors with Workers' Decisions in Admission Services," *Social Service Review* 43 (1969), 286–96.

105. Goldberg, Gertrude. "Non-Professionals in Human Services," in *Non-Professionals in the Human Services*, Charles Grosser, William Henry, and James Kelly, eds., San Francisco, Jossey-Bass, 1969.

106. Goldberg, Gordon. "Visual Behavior and Face to Face Distance During Interaction," *Sociometry* 32 (1969), 43–53.

107. Goldenberg, G. M., and Auld, Frank. "Equivalence of Silence to Resistance," *Journal of Consulting Psychology* 28 (1964), 476–79.

108. Goldman-Eisler, Frieda. "Individual Differences Between Interviewers and Their Effect on Interviewees' Conversational Behavior," *Journal of Mental Science* 98 (1952), 660–71.

109. Goldman-Eisler, Frieda. "A Study of Individual Differences and of Interaction in the Behavior of Some Aspect of Language in Interviews," *Journal of Mental Science* 100 (1954), 177–97.

110. Goldsmith, Avel. "The Therapist's View of the Delinquent," *Federal Probation* 23, no. 3 (1959), 20–25.

111. Gordon, Raymond L. *Interviewing—Strategy, Techniques, and Tactics*, Homewood, Ill., Dorsey Press, 1969.

112. Gould, Karolyn. *Where Do We Go from Here: A Study of the Roads and Roadblocks to Career Mobility for Paraprofessionals Working in Human Service Agencies*, New York, National Committee on Employment of Youth, 1969.

113. Grater, Harry A. "Client Preferences for Affective or Cognitive Counselor Characteristics and First Interview Behavior," *Journal of Counseling Psychology* 11 (1964), 248–50.

114. Grier, William. "When the Therapist is Negro: Some Effects on the Treatment Process," *American Journal of Psychiatry* 123 (1967), 1587–92.

115. Grosser, Charles. "Class Orientations of the Indigenous Staff." In *Community Action Against Poverty*, George A. Brager and Frances P. Purcell, eds., New Haven, Conn., College and University Press, 1967.

116. Grosser, Charles. "Manpower Development Programs," in *Non-Professionals in the Human Services*, Charles Grosser, William Henry, and James Kelly, eds., San Francisco, Jossey-Bass, 1969.

117. Gurin, Gerald, Veroff, Joseph, and Feld, Sheila. *Americans View Their Mental Health*, New York, Basic Books, 1960.

118. Haase, Richard F., and DiMattia, Dominic J. "Proxemic Behavior: Counselor, Administrator, and Client Preference for Seating Arrangement in Dyadic Interaction," *Journal of Counseling Psychology* 17 (1970), 319–25.

119. Hackney, Harold L., Ivey, Allen E., and Oetting, Eugene R. "Attending Island and Hiatus Behavior: A Process Conception of Counselor and Client Interaction," *Journal of Counseling Psychology* 17 (1970), 342–436.

120. Haggard, Ernest, Brekstad, Arne, and Skard, Ase G. "On the Reliability of the Anamnestic Interview," *Journal of Abnormal and Social Psychology* 61 (1960), 311–18.

121. Hahn, Irving. *The Case of Ricky*, American Academy of Psychotherapists Tape Library, Vol. 19. Camden, N.J., American Academy of Psychotherapists, n.d.

122. Hall, Edward T. *The Silent Language*, Garden City, N.Y., Doubleday & Co., 1959.

123. Hall, Edward T. *The Hidden Dimension*, Garden City, N.Y., Doubleday & Co., 1969.

124. Halleck, Seymour L. "The Impact of Professional Dishonesty on Behavior of Disturbed Adolescents," *Social Work* 8, no. 2 (1963), 48–56.

125. Halmos, Paul. *The Faith of the Counsellors*, New York, Schocken Books, 1966.

126. Hamilton, Gordon. *Principles of Social Case Recording*, New York, Columbia University Press, 1946.

127. Handler, Joel, and Hollingsworth, Ellen J. "The Administration of Social Services and the Structure of Dependency: The Views of AFDC Recipients," *Social Service Review* 43 (1969), 406–410.

128. Heine, R. W. "The Negro Patient in Psychotherapy," *Journal of Clinical Psychology* 6 (1950), 373–76.

129. Heller, K., Davis, J. D., and Myers, R. A. "The Effects of Interviewer Style in a Standardized Interview," *Journal of Consulting Psychology* 30 (1966), 501–508.

130. Heller, Kenneth, Meyers, Roger A., and Kline, Linda Vikan. "Interviewer Behavior as a Function of Standardized Client Roles," *Journal of Consulting Psychology* 27 (1963), 117–22.

131. Henry, Charlotte S. "Motivation in Non-Voluntary Clients," *Social Casework* 39 (1958), 130–36.

132. Hill, Richard, and Hall, Nason. "A Note on Rapport and the Quality of Interview Data," *The Southwestern Social Science Quarterly* 44 (1963), 247–55.

133. Hilles, Linda. "On the Reliability of Anamnestic Data," *Bulletin of the Menninger Clinic* 31 (1967), 219–28.

134. Hollingshead, A., and Redlich, F. *Social Class and Mental Illness*, New York, John Wiley & Sons, 1956.

135. Houts, Peter, MacIntosh, Shirley, and Moose, Rudolf. "Patient-Therapist Interdependence: Cognitive and Behavioral," *Journal of Counseling and Clinical Psychology* 33 (1969), 40–45.

136. Houwink, Eda. "Color is an Additional Problem," *Mental Hygiene* 32 (1948), 596–604.

137. Hyman, Herbert H. "Interviewing as a Scientific Procedure," in *The Policy Sciences*, D. Lerner and H. D. Lasswell, eds., Stanford, Calif., Stanford University Press, 1951.

138. Hyman, Herbert H. *Interviewing in Social Research*, Chicago, University of Chicago Press, 1954.

139. Irelan, Lola. *Low Income Life Styles*, U.S. Department of Health, Education and Welfare, Welfare Administration, Division of Research, U.S. Government Printing Office, Washington, D.C., 1966.

140. Isaac, Jean R. *Adopting a Child Today*, New York, Harper & Row Publishers, 1965.

141. Jacobs, Jerry. "Symbolic Bureaucracy: A Case Study of a Social Welfare Agency," *Social Forces* 47 (1969), 413–22.

142. Jarrett, F. J. "Silence in Psychiatric Interviews," *British Journal of Medical Psychology* 39 (1966), 357–62.

143. Johnston, Norman. "Sources of Distortion and Deception in Prison Interviewing," *Federal Probation* 20, no. 1, (1956), 43–48.

144. Jourard, Sidney. *Disclosing Man to Himself,* Princeton, N.J., D. Van Nostrand Co., 1968.

145. Jourard, Sidney M., and Jaffe, Peggy E. "Influence of an Interviewer's Disclosure on the Self-Disclosing Behavior of Interviewees," *Journal of Counseling Psychology* 17 (1970), 252–57.

146. Jourard, Sidney M., and Landsman, M. "Cognition Cathexis and the 'Dyadic Effect' in Men's Self-Disclosing Behavior," *Merrill-Palmer Quarterly* 6 (1960), 178–86.

147. Jourard, Sidney M., and Lasakow, P. "Some Factors in Self-Disclosure," *Journal of Abnormal and Social Psychology* 56 (1958), 91–98.

148. Jourard, Sidney M., and Richman, P. "Disclosure Output and Input in College Students," *Merrill-Palmer Quarterly* 9 (1963), 141–48.

149. Kadushin, Alfred. "The Effects of Interview Observation on the Interviewer," *Journal of Counseling Psychology* 3 (1956), 130–35.

150. Kadushin, Alfred. "The Effects of Interview Observation on the Client," *Social Service Review* 31 (1957), 22–38.

151. Kadushin, Alfred. "Social Sex Roles and the Initial Casework Interview," *Mental Hygiene* 42 (1958), 354–61.

152. Kadushin, Alfred. "An Experience in Tape Recording Interviews: Report of an Adoptive Follow-up Study." *Journal of Jewish Communal Services* 43 (1967), 327–33.

153. Kadushin, Charles. "Social Distance between Client and Professional," *American Journal of Sociology* 67 (1962), 517–31.

154. Kahn, Alfred J., et al. *Neighborhood Information Centers: A Study and Some Proposals,* New York, Columbia University School of Social Work, 1966.

155. Kanfer, F. H. "Implications of Conditioning Techniques for Interview Therapy," *Journal of Counseling Psychology* 13 (1966), 171–77.

156. Katz, D. "Do Interviewers Bias Poll Results?" *Public Opinion Quarterly* 6 (1942), 248–68.

157. Keith-Lucas, Alan. "A Critique of the Principle of Client Self-Determination," *Social Work* 8, no. 3 (1963), 66–78.

158. Kemp, C. G. "Influence of Dogmatism on the Training of Counselors," *Journal of Counseling Psychology* 9 (1962), 155–57.

159. Kendon, A. "Some Functions of Gaze Direction in Social Interaction," *Acta Psychologica* 26 (1967), 22–63.

160. Kincaid, Marylou. "Identity and Therapy in the Black Community," *Personnel and Guidance Journal* 47 (1969), 884–90.

161. Kinsey, Alfred, Pomeroy, Wardell, and Martin, Clyde. *Sexual Behavior in the Human Male*, Philadelphia, W. B. Saunders Co., 1948.

162. Kochman, Thomas. "Rapping in the Black Ghetto," *Transaction* 6, no. 4 (1969), 26–34.

163. Kogan, Leonard S. "A Two-Year Study of Case Record Uses," *Social Casework* 35 (1954), 252–57.

164. Koile, E. A., and Bird, Dorothy J. "Preferences for Counselor Help on Freshman Problems," *Journal of Counseling Psychology* 3 (1956), 97–106.

165. Komarovsky, Mirra. *Blue Collar Marriage*, New York, Random House, Vintage Books, 1967.

166. Koos, Earl L. *Families in Trouble*, New York, King's Crown Press, 1946.

167. Korsch, Barbara M., Gozzi, Ethel K., and Frances, Vida. "Gaps in Doctor-Patient Communication," *Pediatrics* 42 (1968), 855–71.

168. Kramer, Ernest. "Judgment of Personal Characteristics and Emotions from Non-Verbal Properties of Speech," *Psychological Bulletin* 60 (1963), 408–420.

169. Krumboltz, J. D. "Changing the Behavior of Behavior Changers," *Counselor Education and Supervision*, Special Publication, Spring, 1967.

170. Lakin, Martin, and Lebovits, Benjamin. "Bias in Psychotherapists of Different Orientations: An Exploratory Study," *American Journal of Psychotherapy* 12 (1958), 79–86.

171. Lansing, John B., et al. *Working Papers on Survey Research in Poverty Areas*, Ann Arbor, University of Michigan Institute for Social Research Survey Research Center, 1971.

172. Leighton, Neil. "The Myth of Self-Determination," *New Society*, no. 230, February 1967, pp. 275–76.

173. Lennard, Henry L., and Bernstein, Arnold. *The Anatomy of Psychotherapy: Systems of Communication and Expectation*, New York, Columbia University Press, 1960.

174. Levine, Rachel. "Treatment in the Home: An Experiment with Low Income Multi-Problem Families," in *Mental Health of the Poor*, Frank Riessman, Jerome Cohen, and Arthur Pearl, eds., Glencoe, Ill., Free Press, 1964, pp. 329–35.

175. Lindsey, Inabel B. "Race as a Factor in the Caseworker's Role," *Journal of Social Casework* 28, no. 3 (1947), 101–7.

176. Loewenstein, R. M. et al. "Symposium on the Silent Patient," *Journal of the American Psychoanalysis Association* 9 (1961), 2–90.

177. Maccoby, Eleanor, and Maccoby, Nathan. "The Interview: A Tool of Social Science," in *Handbook of Social Psychology*, Gardner Lindzey, ed., Cambridge, Mass., Addison-Wesley Publishing Co., 1954.

178. McCord, Joan, and McCord, William. "Cultural Stereotypes and the Validity of Interviews in Child Development," *Child Development* 32 (1961), 171–85.

179. McIsaac, Hugh, and Wilkinson, Harold. "Clients Talk About Their Caseworkers," *Public Welfare* 23 (1965), 147–54.

180. McMahon, Arthur W., and Shore, Miles F. "Some Psychological Reactions to Working with the Poor," *Archives of General Psychiatry* 18 (1968), 562–68.

181. McMahon, James T. "The Working Class Psychiatric Patient: A Clinical View," in *Mental Health of the Poor*, Frank Riessman, Jerome Cohen, and Arthur Pearl, eds., Glencoe, Ill., Free Press, 1964,

182. Mahl, George F. "Disturbances and Silences in the Patient's Speech in Psychotherapy," *Journal of Abnormal and Social Psychology* 53 (1956), 1–15.

183. Mahl, George F. "Measuring the Patient's Anxiety During Interviews from Expressive Aspects of His Speech," *Transactions of the New York Academy of Sciences* 21 (1959), 249–57.

184. Mahl, George F. "Gestures and Body Movements in Interviews," in *Research in Psychotherapy: Proceedings of the Third Conference*, John M. Shlien, ed., Washington, D.C., American Psychological Association, 1968.

185. Mahl, George F., and Kasl, S. V. "The Relationship of Disturbances and Hesitations in Spontaneous Speech to Anxiety," *Journal of Personality and Social Psychology* 1 (1965), 425–33.

186. Margolis, Marvin, Krystal, Henry, and Siegel, S. "Psychotherapy with Alcoholic Offenders," *Quarterly Journal of Studies on Alcoholism* 25, (1964), 85–99.

187. Mattarazzo, Joseph D., Weilman, Morris, and Saslow, George. "Interview Content and Interviewee Speech Durations," *Journal of Clinical Psychology* 19 (1963), 463–72.

188. Mattarazzo, Joseph D., Weins, Arthur, Mattarazzo, Ruth, and Saslow, Ruth. "Speech and Silence Behavior in Clinical Psychology and Its Laboratory Correlates," in *Research in Psychotherapy: Proceedings of the Third Conference,* John M. Schlien, ed., Washington, D.C., American Psychological Association, 1968.

189. Mattson, Ake. "The Male Therapist and The Female Adolescent Patient," *Journal of the American Academy of Child Psychiatry* 9 (1970), 707–21.

190. Mayer, John E., and Rosenblatt, Aaron. "The Client's Social Context: Its Effect on Continuance in Treatment," *Social Casework* 45 (1964), 511–18.

191. Mayer, John E., and Rosenblatt, Aaron. "Client Disengagement and Alternative Treatment Resources," *Social Casework* 47 (1966), 3–12.

192. Mayer, John E., and Timms, Noel. "Clash in Perspective Between Worker and Client," *Social Casework* 50 (1969), 32–40.

193. Mayer, John E., and Timms, Noel. *The Client Speaks: Working Class Impressions of Casework,* London, Routledge and Kegan Paul, 1970.

194. Mayfield, E. C. "The Selection Interview: A Reevaluation of Published Research," *Personnel Psychology* 17 (1964), 239–60.

195. Mednick, Sarnoff, and Shaffer, John. "Mothers' Retrospective Reports in Child Rearing Research," *American Journal of Orthopsychiatry* 32 (1963), 457–61.

196. Mehrabian, Albert. "Orientation Behavior and Non-Verbal Attitude Communication," *Journal of Communication* 17 (1967), 324–32.

197. Mehrabian, Albert. "Communication Without Words," *Psychology Today* 2, no. 4 (1968), 53–55.

198. Mehrabian, Albert. "Methods and Design: Some Referents and Measures of Non-Verbal Behavior," *Behavioral Research Method and Instruction* 1 (1969), 203–7.

199. Mehrabian, Albert. "Significance of Posture and Position in the Communication of Attitude and Status Relationships," *Psychological Bulletin* 71 (1969), 359–72.

200. Mehrabian, Albert, and Friar, John T. "Encoding of Attitude by a Seated Communicator Via Posture and Position Cues," *Journal of Consulting and Clinical Psychology* 33 (1969), 330–66.

201. Merton, Robert K., Fiske, Marjorie, and Kendall, Patricia. *The Focused Interview,* Glencoe, Ill., Free Press, 1956.

202. Meyers, Jerome K., and Roberts, Bertram H. *Family and Class Dynamics in Mental Illness*, New York, John Wiley & Sons, 1959.

203. Miles, Arthur. "The Utility of Case Recording in Probation and Parole," *The Journal of Criminal Law, Criminology and Police Science* 56 (1965), 285–93.

204. Miller, Roger. "Student Research Perspectives on Race," *Smith College Studies in Social Work* 41 (1970), 1–23.

205. Miller, Ronald, and Podell, Lawrence. *Role Conflict in Public Social Services*, New York, New York State Office for Community Affairs, Division of Research and Innovation, 1971.

206. Miller, S. M. "The Participant-Observer and 'Over-Rapport,'" *American Sociological Review* 17 (1952), 97–99.

207. Mintz, E. E. "On the Rationale of Touch in Psychotherapy," *Psychotherapy: Theory, Research and Practice* 6 (1969), 232–34.

208. Mintz, N. L. "Effects of Esthetic Surroundings: Prolonged and Repeated Experience in a Beautiful and Ugly Room," *Journal of Psychology* 41 (1956), 459–66.

209. Minuchin, Salvador, et al. *Families of the Slums*, New York, Basic Books, 1967.

210. Moos, R. H. and Clemes, S. R. "A Multivariate Study of the Patient-Therapist System," *Journal of Consulting Psychology* 31 (1967), 119–30.

211. Mullen, Edward S. "Differences in Worker Style in Casework," *Social Casework* 50 (1969), 347–53.

212. National Association of Social Workers, "Model Statute Social Workers' Licensing Act," *N.A.S.W. News*, 1967.

213. Neisse, Marianne. "Judgments and the Non-Judgmental Attitude in Therapeutic Relationships," *Social Casework* 41 (1965), 278–82.

214. Nichols, Ralph, and Steven, Leonard. *Are You Listening?* New York, McGraw-Hill Book Co., 1957.

215. Northen, Helen. *Social Work with Groups*, New York, Columbia University Press, 1969.

216. Oldfield, R. C. *The Psychology of the Interview*, London, Methuen and Co., 1951.

217. Orlinsky, David E., and Howard, Kenneth I. "The Good Therapy Hour: Experimental Correlates of Patients' and Therapists' Evaluation of Therapy Session," *Archives of General Psychology* 16 (1967), 621–32.

218. Ornston, Patricia S., Cicchetti, Domenic, Levine, Jacob, and Fierman, Louis B. "Some Parameters of Verbal Behavior that Reliably Differentiate Novice from Experienced Psychotherapists," *Journal of Abnormal Psychology* 73 (1968), 240–44.

219. Ornston, Patricia S., Cicchetti, Domenic, and Towbin, Alan P. "Reliable Changes in Psychotherapy Behavior Among First-Year Psychiatric Residents," *Journal of Abnormal Psychology* 75 (1970), 7–11.

220. Ostwald, Peter. *Soundmaking: The Acoustic Communication of Emotion*, Springfield, Ill., Charles C Thomas, 1963.

221. Overton, Alice. *Clients' Observations of Social Work*, Mimeographed. St. Paul, Minn., Greater St. Paul Community Chest and Councils, Inc., Family Centered Project, 1959, p. 12.

222. Overton, Alice, and Tinker, Katherine. *Casework Notebook*, Mimeographed. St. Paul, Minn., Greater St. Paul Community Chest and Councils, Inc., Family Centered Project, 1959.

223. Perlman, Helen H. *Social Casework: A Problem Solving Process*, Chicago, University of Chicago Press, 1957.

224. Perlman, Helen H. "Self-Determination: Reality or Illusion," *Social Service Review* 39 (1965), 410–21.

225. Pfouts, Jane H., and Rader, Gordon E. "The Influence of Interviewer Characteristics on the Initial Interview," *Social Casework* 43 (1962), 548–52.

226. Phillips, D. L., and Segal, B. E. "Sexual Status and Psychiatric Symptoms," *American Sociological Review* 34 (1969), 58–72.

227. Pincus, Allen. "Reminiscence in Aging and Its Implications for Social Work Practice," *Social Work* 15, no. 3 (1970), 47–53.

228. Pohlman, Edward, and Robinson, Francis. "Client Reaction to Some Aspects of the Counseling Situation," *Personnel and Guidance Journal* 38 (1960), 546–51.

229. Polansky, Norman, and Kounin, Jacob. "Clients' Reactions to Initial Interviews," *Human Relations* 9 (1956), 237–62.

230. Pope, Benjamin, Blass, Thomas, Siegman, Aaron W., and Raher, Jack. "Anxiety and Depression in Speech," *Journal of Consulting and Clinical Psychology* 35 (1970), 128–33.

231. Quota, Andrew. *The Importance and Significance of Non-Verbal Communication in Social Casework with Individuals*, Master's thesis, Worden School of Social Service, May, 1969.

232. Raskin, Allen. "Observable Signs of Anxiety or Distress During Psychotherapy," *Journal of Consulting Psychology* 26 (1962), 389.

233. Redl, Fritz, "Strategy and Techniques of the Life Space Interview," *American Journal of Orthopsychiatry* 29 (1959), 721–36.

234. Reece, M. M., and Whitman, R. N. "Expressive Movements, Warmth and Verbal Reinforcements," *Journal of Abnormal and Social Psychology* 64 (1962), 234–36.

235. Reid, William, and Shyne, Ann W. *Brief and Extended Casework.* New York, Columbia University Press, 1969.

236. Rice, Laura N., and Wagstaff, Alice K. "Client Voice Quality and Expressive Style as Indexes of Productive Psychotherapy," *Journal of Consulting Psychology* 31 (1967), 557–63.

237. Rich, John. *Interviewing Children and Adolescents,* London, Macmillan & Co., 1968.

238. Riessman, Frank. *New Approaches to Mental Health Treatment for Labor and Low Income Groups,* Department of Psychology, Columbia University, and National Institute of Labor Education, 1964.

239. Riessman, Frank. "Strategies and Suggestions for Training Non-Professionals," in *Psychotherapeutic Agents: New Roles for Nonprofessionals, Parents and Teachers,* Bernard Guerney, ed., New York, Holt, Rinehart, and Winston, 1969.

240. Riessman, Frank, and Goldfarb, Jean. "Role Playing and the Poor," in *Mental Health of the Poor,* Frank Riessman, Jerome Cohen, and Arthur Pearl, eds., Glencoe, Ill., Free Press, 1964.

241. Robbins, Lillian. "The Accuracy of Parental Recall of Aspects of Child Development and Child Rearing Practices," *Journal of Abnormal and Social Psychology* 66 (1963), 261–70.

242. Robinson, Francis, and Tindall, Ralph. "The Use of Silence as a Technique in Counseling," *Journal of Clinical Psychology* 3 (1947), 136–41.

243. Rogers, Carl R., ed. *The Therapeutic Relationship and Its Impact,* Madison, Wis., University of Wisconsin Press, 1967.

244. Rogow, Arnold A. *The Psychiatrists,* New York, G. P. Putnam's Sons, 1970.

245. Rosen, Albert. "Client Preferences: An Overview of the Literature," *Personnel and Guidance Journal* 45 (1967), 785–89.

246. Rosenthal, D., and Frank, J. D. "The Fate of Psychiatric Clinic Outpatients Assigned to Psychotherapy," *Journal of Nervous and Mental Disease* 127 (1958), 330–43.

247. Rosenthal, Robert. *Experimenter Effects in Behavioral Research,* New York, Appleton-Century-Crofts, 1966.

248. Ross, M. and Mendelsohn, F. "Homosexuality in College," *Archives of Neurology and Psychiatry* 80 (1958), 253–63.

249. Rubenstein, Eli. "A Comparison of Terminators and Remainders in Outpatient Psychotherapy," *Journal of Clinical Psychology* 12 (1956), 345–49.

250. Rubenstein, Leonard, and Cameron, D. Ewen. "Electronic Analysis of Non-Verbal Communication," *Comprehensive Psychiatry* 9 (1968), 200–208.

251. Ruesch, Jurgen, and Kees, Weldon. *Non-Verbal Communication: Notes on the Visual Perception of Human Relations*, Berkeley, Calif., University of California Press, 1956.

252. Russo, J. R., Kelz, J. W., and Hudson, G. R. "Are Good Counselors Open-Minded?" *Counselor Education and Supervision* 3 (1964), 74–77.

253. Ryan, Mary S. *Clothing: A Study in Human Behavior*, New York, Holt, Rinehart, and Winston, 1966.

254. Ryan, William, and Morris, Laura B. *Child Welfare Problems and Potentials: A Study of Intake of Child Welfare Agencies in Metropolitan Boston*, Boston, Massachusetts Committee on Children and Youth, 1967.

255. Sager, Clifford J., Brayboy, Thomas L., and Waxenberg, Barbara R. *Black Ghetto Family in Therapy: A Laboratory Experience*, New York, Grove Press, 1970.

256. Sainsbury, P. "Gestural Movement During Psychiatric Interviews," *Psychosomatic Medicine* 17 (1955), 458–69.

257. Sandifer, Myron G., Jr., Hordern, Anthony, and Green, Linda M. "The Psychiatric Interview: The Impact of the First Three Minutes," *American Journal of Psychiatry* 126 (1970), 968–73.

258. Sattler, Jerome A. "Racial 'Experimenter Effects' in Experimentation, Testing, Interviewing and Psychotherapy," *Psychological Bulletin* 73 (1970), 137–60.

259. Schatzman, Leonard, and Strauss, Anselm. "Social Class and Mode of Communication," *American Journal of Sociology* 60 (1955), 329–38.

260. Schatzman, Leonard, and Strauss, Anselm. "Cross Class Interviewing: An Analysis of Interaction and Communicative Styles," *Human Organization* 14, no. 2 (1955), 28–31.

261. Scheflen, A. E. "The Significance of Posture in Communication Systems," *Psychiatry* 27 (1964), 316–31.

262. Scheflen, A. E. "Quasi-Courtship Behavior in Psychotherapy," *Psychiatry* 28 (1965), 245–47.

263. Schmidt, Julianna. "The Use of Purpose in Casework Practice," *Social Work* 14, no. 1 (1969), 77–84.

264. Schuman, Howard, and Converse, Jean M. "The Effects of Black and White Interviewers on Black Responses in 1968," *Public Opinion Quarterly* 35 (1971), 44–68.

265. Schutz, William C. *Joy*, New York, Grove Press, 1967.

266. Schwartz, William. "Group Work in Public Welfare," *Public Welfare* 26 (1968), 322–69.

267. Seaberg, James R. "Case Recording by Code," *Social Work* 10, no. 4 (1965), 92–98.

268. Seaberg, James R. "Systematized Recording: A Follow-up," *Social Work* 15, no. 3 (1970), 32–41.

269. Sears, Robert R. "Comparison of Interviews with Questionnaires for Measuring Mothers' Attitudes Toward Sex and Aggression," *Journal of Personality and Social Psychology* 2 (1965), 37–44.

270. Seligman, Michele. "The Interracial Casework Relationship," *Smith College Studies in Social Work* 39 (1968), 84.

271. Shapiro, Jeffrey G., Krauss, Herbert H., and Truax, Charles B. "Therapeutic Conditions and Disclosure Beyond the Therapeutic Encounter," *Journal of Counseling Psychology* 16 (1969), 290–94.

272. Sheatsley, P. B. "An Analysis of Interviewer Characteristics and Their Relationship to Performance," *International Journal of Opinion and Attitude Research* 4 (1950), 473–98; 5 (1951), 79–84.

273. Shepard, Martin, and Lee, Margerie. *Games Analysts Play*, New York, G. P. Putman's Sons, 1970.

274. Shulman, Rena. "Treatment of the Disturbed Child in Placement," *Jewish Social Service Quarterly* 30 (1954) 315–22.

275. Shyne, Ann. "What Research Tells Us About Short Term Cases in Family Agencies," *Social Casework* 38 (1957), 223–31.

276. Siegel, Nathaniel, and Fink, Max. "Motivation for Psychotherapy," *Comprehensive Psychiatry* 3 (1962), 170–73.

277. Silverman, Phyllis R. "A Re-examination of the Intake Procedure," *Social Casework* 51 (1970), 625–34.

278. Simmons, Leonard. " 'Crow Jim': Implications for Social Work," *Social Work* 8, no. 3 (1963), 24–30.

279. Smith, Edward W., and Dixon, Theodore R. "Verbal Conditioning as a Function of Race of the Experimenter and Prejudice of the

Subject," *Journal of Experimental Social Psychology* 4 (1968), 285–301.

280. Smith, Henrietta T. "A Comparison of Interview and Observation Measures of Mother Behavior," *Journal of Abnormal and Social Psychology* 57 (1958), 278–82.

281. Sobey, Francine. *The Non-Professional Revolution in Mental Health*, New York, Columbia University Press, 1970.

282. Sommer, Gerhart, and Mazo, Bernard. "An Empirical Investigation of Therapeutic 'Listening,'" *Journal of Clinical Psychology* 11 (1955), 132–36.

283. Sommer, R. *Personal Space: The Behavioral Basis of Design*, New York, Prentice-Hall, 1969.

284. Sonne, T. R., and Goldman, L. "Preferences of Authoritarian and Equalitarian Personalities for Client-Centered and Eclectic Counseling," *Journal of Counseling Psychology* 4 (1957), 129–35.

285. Starkweather, J. A. "Vocal Communication of Personality and Human Feelings," *Journal of Communication* 11, (1961), 63–72.

286. Steffre, B., King, P., and Leafgren, F. "Characteristics of Counselors Judged Effective by Their Peers," *Journal of Counseling Psychology* 9 (1962), 335–40.

287. Sternbach, Jack. *Group Interviewing*, Madison, Wis., University of Wisconsin School of Social Work, 1965.

288. Stone, Helen D. *Reflections on Foster Care*, New York, Child Welfare League of America, 1969.

289. Stranges, Richard J., and Riccio, Anthony C. "Counselee Preferences for Counselors: Some Implications for Counselor Education," *Counselor Education and Supervision* 10, no. 3 (1970), 39–45.

290. Strean, Herbert S. "Some Reactions of Caseworkers to the War on Poverty," *Journal of Contemporary Psychotherapy* 1 (1968), 43–48.

291. Strupp, Hans H., Fox, Ronald, and Lessler, Ken. *Patients View Their Psychotherapy*, Baltimore, Johns Hopkins Press, 1969.

292. Sullivan, Harry Stack. *The Psychiatric Interview*, New York, W. W. Norton & Co., 1954.

293. Taylor, James B., Levy, Phyllis, and Filippi, Ronald. "Psychological Problems in Low Income Families: A Research Project," *Bulletin of the Menninger Clinic* 29 (1965), 312–39.

294. Timms, Noel. *Social Casework Principles and Practice*, London, Routledge and Kegan Paul, 1964.

295. Tobin, Dorsey. "Diagnostic Use of the Home Visit in Child Guidance," *Smith College Studies in Social Work* 38 (1968), 203–213.

296. Tosi, Donald J., and Carlson, William A. "Client Dogmatism and Perceived Counselor Attitudes," *Personnel and Guidance Journal* 48 (1970), 657–60.

297. Townsend, Orville. "Vocational Rehabilitation and the Black Counselor: The Conventional Training Situation and the Battleground Across Town," *Journal of Rehabilitation* 36 (1970), 16–18.

298. Truax, Charles B., and Carkhuff, Robert R. *Toward Effective Counseling and Psychotherapy: Training and Practice,* Chicago, Aldine Publishing Co., 1967.

299. Ulrich, L., and Trumbo, D. "The Selection Interview Since 1949," *Psychological Bulletin* 63 (1965), 100–116.

300. United Nations, Department of Economic and Social Affairs. *1963 Report on the World Social Situation,* New York, United Nations, 1963.

301. U. S. Department of Health, Education and Welfare, Office of the Undersecretary. *Closing the Gap in Social Work Manpower,* Washington, D.C., U.S. Government Printing Office, 1965.

302. Vail, Susan. "The Effects of Socio-Economic Class, Race and Level of Experience in Social Workers' Judgments of Clients," *Smith College Studies in Social Work* 40, no. 3 (1970).

303. Van der Veen, Ferdinand. "Effects of the Therapist and Patient on Each Other's Therapeutic Behavior," *Journal of Consulting Psychology* 29 (1965), 19–26.

304. Vernick, Joel. "The Use of the Life Space Interview on a Medical Ward," *Social Casework* 49 (1963), 465–69.

305. Volsky, T., et al. *The Outcomes of Counseling and Psychotherapy,* Minneapolis, University of Minnesota Press, 1965.

306. Vontross, Clemmont. "Cultural Barriers in Counseling Relationships," *Personnel and Guidance Journal* 48 (1969), 11–16.

307. Vontross, Clemmont. "Counseling Blacks," *Personnel and Guidance Journal* 48 (1970), 713–19.

308. Vontross, Clemmont. "Racial Differences," *Journal of Counseling Psychology* 18 (1971), 7–13.

309. Wachtel, P. L. "An Approach to Body Language in Psychotherapy," *Psychotherapy* 4 (1967), 97–100.

310. Waite, Richard R. "The Negro Patient and Clinical Therapy," *Journal of Consulting and Clinical Psychology* 32 (1968), 427–33.

311. Warren, Effie. "Social Class Dimensions in Family Casework," *Smith College Studies in Social Work* 33 (1962), 1–18.

312. Wasserman, Harry. "Early Careers of Professional Social Workers in a Public Child Welfare Agency," *Social Work* 15, no. 3 (1970), 93–101.

313. Webb, Allen P., and Riley, Patrick V. "Effectiveness of Casework with Young Female Probationers," *Social Casework* 51 (1970), 566–72.

314. Weinandy, Janet E. "Techniques of Service," in *Mental Health of the Poor*, Frank Reissman, Jerome Cohen, and Arthur Pearl, eds., Glencoe, Ill., Free Press, 1964.

315. Weiner, Morton, and Mehrabian, Albert. *Language Within Language: Immediacy, A Channel in Verbal Communication*, New York, Appleton-Century-Crofts, 1968.

316. Weingarten, Viola. *Life at the Bottom*, New York, Citizens Committee for Children of New York.

317. Weisman, Avery. "Silence and Psychotherapy," *Psychiatry* 18 (1955), 241–60.

318. Weiss, Carol H. "Interviewing Low-Income Respondents: A Preliminary View," *Welfare in Review* 4, no. 8 (1960), 1–9.

319. Weiss, Carol H. *Validity of Interview Responses of Welfare Mothers: Final Report*, Bureau of Applied Social Research, Columbia University, 1968.

320. Weiss, Carol. "Validity of Welfare Mothers' Interview Responses," *Public Opinion Quarterly* 32 (1968–69), 622–34.

321. Weller, Leonard, and Luchterhand, Elmer. "Interviewer-Respondent Interaction in Negro and White Family Life Research," *Human Organization* 27 (1968), 50–55.

322. Weller, Leonard, and Luchterhand, Elmer. "Comparing Interviews and Observations on Family Functioning," *Journal of Marriage and the Family* 31 (1969), 115–22.

323. Wenar, Charles. "The Reliability of Mothers' Histories," *Child Development* 32 (1961), 491–500.

324. White, A. M., Fichtenbaum, L., and Dollard, J. "Evaluation of Silence in Initial Interviews with Psychiatric Clinic Patients," *Journal of Nervous and Mental Disease* 139 (1964), 550–57.

325. Whyte, William F. *Street Corner Society*, rev. ed., Chicago, University of Chicago Press, 1955.

326. Wilkie, H. Charlotte. "A Study of Distortions in Recorded Interviews," *Social Work* 8, no. 3 (1963), 32–36.

327. Williams, Frederick, ed. *Language and Poverty: Perspectives on a Theme*, Chicago, Markham Publishing Co., 1970.

328. Williams, Frederick, and Naremore, Rita C. "On the Functional Analysis of Social Class Differences in Modes of Speech," *Speech Monographs* 36 (1969), 78–102.

329. Williams, J. Allen, Jr. "Interviewer-Respondent Interaction: A Study of Bias in the Information Interview," *Sociometry* 27 (1964), 338–52.

330. Williams, Juanita. "Conditioning of Verbalization: A Review," *Psychological Bulletin* 62 (1964), 383–93.

331. Williams, Robert I., and Blanton, Richard L. "Verbal Conditioning in Psychotherapeutic Situations" *Behavior Research and Therapy* 6 (1968), 97–103.

332. Wilson, G. T., Hannon, Alma, and Evans, W. I. M. "Behavior Therapy and the Therapist Patient Relationship," *Journal of Consulting and Clinical Psychology* 32 (1968), 103–109.

333. Wineman, David. "The Life Space Interview," *Social Work* 4, no. 1 (1959), 3–17.

334. Witbeck, G. B. "The Attitude of Negro Clients Toward Negro Caseworkers," *Smith College Studies in Social Work* 17 (1946), 150–51.

335. Wolberg, Lewis. *Techniques of Psychotherapy*, New York, Grune & Stratton, 1954.

336. Womack, William M. "Negro Interviewers and White Patients: The Question of Confidentiality and Trust," *Archives of General Psychiatry* 16 (1967), 685–92.

337. Yarrow, Marian R., Campbell, John D., and Burton, Roger V. "Reliability of Maternal Retrospection: A Preliminary Report," *Family Process* 13 (1964), 207–18.

338. Yashki, Michele A. "Relationship Problems in Inter-racial Casework," *Smith College Studies in Social Work* 41 (1970), 8.

339. Young, Leontine. *Wednesday's Children*, New York, McGraw-Hill Book Co., 1964.

340. Zelan, Joseph. "Interviewing the Aged," *Public Opinion Quarterly* 33 (1969), 420–24.

341. Zeligs, M. A. "The Role of Silence in Transference, Countertransference, and the Psychoanalytic Process," *International Journal of Psychoanalysis* 41 (1960), 407–12.

342. Zimmerman, Don. "Tasks and Troubles: The Practical Basis of Work Activities in a Public Assistance Organization," in *Explorations in Sociology and Counseling*, Donald Hansen, ed., Boston, Houghton Mifflin Co., 1969.

343. Zurcher, Louis. *Poverty Warriors*, Austin, Tex., University of Texas Press, 1970.

Index